Buying a property
CROATIA

CADOGANguides

Contents

Letting Your Property 173

References 189

Appendix 211

About the Authors

Felicity Aston is a freelance writer based in east Kent. Originally emerging from university with a physics degree and an MSc in applied meteorology, Felicity has spent the last 10 years living and working in some of the world's wildest places, including, most notably, Antarctica. Finally settling in the UK, she has worked as a travel writer for various publications including *Geographical* and Rough Guides. Her work has prompted many extended forays across Europe, travelling as far as Eastern Europe and Northern Siberia.

Carol Southgate resides in Croatia with her husband and their young children. Until she moved to Croatia, Carol was a fund manager working for investment banks and investment management companies in the City. However after the birth of their second child in 2004, Carol and her husband decided on a complete change of direction and left the UK for Croatia. Together they own and run the British-Croatian estate agency A Place in Dalmatia, and an investment advisory business. Bridging the culture gap on a personal and professional level has been perhaps their single biggest challenge. Their British buyers expect good information flow and to be guided step by step through the property-buying process. Carol finds herself often replicating some of the work and advice normally provided by a lawyer in Britain, and it this experience which she has brought to bear in this book.

Cadogan Guides is an imprint of
New Holland Publishers (UK) Ltd
London • Cape Town • Sydney • Auckland

New Holland Publishers (UK) Ltd   80 McKenzie Street   Unit 1, 66 Gibbes Street   218 Lake Road
Garfield House,   Cape Town 8001   Chatswood, NSW 2067   Northcote
86–88 Edgware Road   South Africa   Australia   Auckland
London W2 2EA   New Zealand

Cadogan@nhpub.co.uk
www.cadoganguides.com
t 44 (0)20 7724 7773

Distributed in the United States by Globe Pequot, Connecticut

Cover photograph: © Joseph Birkas
Photo essay photographs © Croatian National Tourist Board (for details *see* end of essay)
Maps © Cadogan Guides, drawn by Maidenhead Cartographic Services Ltd
Cover design: Sarah Rianhard-Gardner
Editing: Susannah Wight and Linda McQueen
Proofreading: Elspeth Anderson
Indexing: Isobel McLean

Produced by **Navigator Guides**
www.navigatorguides.com

Printed in Finland by WS Bookwell
A catalogue record for this book is available from the British Library

ISBN: 978-1-86011-374-1

Introduction

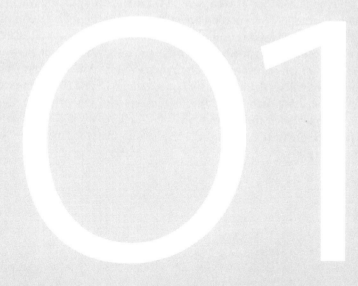

'The Mediterranean as it once was' is how the Croatian National Tourist Board sums up the old-world charm and irresistible natural beauty of the glittering Adriatic country of Croatia. With a sumptuous coastline that is long enough to wrap twice around Portugal, it's not difficult to see why the country has such an enduring allure. As well as clean beaches, impressive mountain ranges, bucolic islands and ancient cities studded with historic architecture, it is the natural warmth and hospitality of the Croatians themselves that has made Croatia one of the most desirable destinations in the world. Little physical evidence of the devastating war of the 1990s remains, and the country is once again blooming, both socially and economically.

If you are reading this book, the likelihood is that you have already been swayed by Croatia's numerous charms and need no further convincing. This book aims to help you navigate the eventful road ahead, whether you are looking for a sound investment, a second home, a new life or a mixture of all three. From big legal questions to trivial practicalities, you will find answers to a host of questions within these pages – even those you hadn't yet thought to ask. Succinct profiles of each region, backed up with market information and property trends, will kick-start your property search and enable you to make economically shrewd as well as aesthetic decisions. Once you have found your ideal property, be it a new beachside development in Istria or a restoration project in the rural hills of the Zagorje, our legal chapters will guide you through the intricacies of the purchasing process so that you are well prepared.

Whether you intend to stay in your new property for two weeks or two decades, this book will then also be your first step to settling in. You will find plenty of indispensable information about the nitty-gritty of life in Croatia, from getting visas and residence permits, to applying for benefits and health care, to utility connections and banking arrangements. Want to know if you can drive your British-registered car on Croatian roads? Whether your electrical appliances will work in your new home? Where to find DIY materials? Look no further. Vital addresses, useful contacts and essential Croatian vocabulary are included throughout, as well as advice in the form of case studies from the greatest experts of all – those who have stood in your shoes and gone on to purchase their own property in Croatia.

First Steps and Reasons for Buying

Buying property in any country and at any time of life represents a large commitment of time, energy and money. The aim of this book is to make sure that your commitment is finally rewarded with hassle-free ownership of your very own property in Croatia.

The first step in this process is to establish exactly why you have chosen Croatia and why you have decided to buy. Whether it is an objective decision or a more emotive calling, stopping to think about your core motivations now may help later on when you are pressed to make crucial and sometimes difficult choices. You probably already have a good idea of the answers to these questions, but just in case you are a little fuzzy we offer some suggestions in the first half of this chapter to make things a little clearer.

Once the soul-searching is over and you are certain about 'why', we can begin on 'how'. The second half of this chapter contains everything you need to know about visas, work permits, residence and citizenship – the foundation of your new venture in Croatia.

Why Croatia?

There are hundreds of reasons why you might have decided on Croatia as the focus of your property ambitions, and each one of them will be very personal to you. However, all these different motives are likely to boil down to one simple desire – a wish for a better quality of life. You may be seeking a new business enterprise, a cultural getaway or a quiet spot in the sun in which to idle away your days. Croatia is certainly not the only country in the world in which these ambitions can come true, but there are plenty of reasons why it is a good choice.

The Lifestyle

Croatia's scenery maybe reminiscent of the Mediterranean, but the affinity between the two regions runs deeper than the landscape of olive groves and sage-spotted hillsides that they both enjoy. Like their Greek and Italian neighbours, Croatians have a pleasantly relaxed attitude towards daily routine, in which time spent with family and friends is of paramount importance. Shops and offices often close for three or four hours in the afternoon to allow for prolonged family lunches, and no town or village, however small, is complete without at least one café where friends can be seen lingering over coffee at any time of the day. This philosophy is most potent on Croatia's 47 inhabited islands, where any attempt at frantic activity seems unnaturally perverse. People routinely choose to walk rather than take a car, much of the agricultural work is still done by hand, food is bought fresh and from half a dozen shops rather than from one big convenience store, and there always seems to be time simply to sit in the sun or enjoy a coffee by the harbour. Islanders appear to work to a slower rhythm than the rest of the world, and yet the neatly walled vineyards and heaps of stones that have been cleared from the fields are testament to the productivity of these hard-working people. The same can be said of Croatia's other rural regions, such as the Zagorje in the northwest and the more central Lika region.

However, this slower pace of life doesn't commit you to a back-to-basics existence. Croatians enjoy the highest standard of living of all the Balkan countries and arguably in eastern Europe. Everyone carries a mobile phone and coverage is good; most families own at least one car; the high streets of the larger towns feature western designer fashion labels; and flushing toilets come as standard. Although not ridiculously cheap, the cost of living in Croatia is noticeably below that of western European countries. Apart from cheaper housing, you will also find utility bills, petrol and healthcare costing a lot less than in the UK.

In many ways Croatia can provide the best of both worlds: the modern comforts of the West mixed with a more traditional approach to life; it is a place to forget the pressures of home for a few weeks a year, or somewhere to achieve the work-life balance you always dreamed of.

Natural Beauty

Mention Croatia and most people will immediately visualise the Dalmatian coast – an enticing mix of secluded bays, azure-blue water and shady, forest-covered islands burnished by a spotless indigo sky. It was this image that first drew people to Croatia in the 1960s, making it one of Europe's foremost holiday destinations, and it is this image that continues to captivate people today.

Croatia's coastline snakes alongside the sparkling Adriatic for more than 2,000km, seeming to crumble into the sea in a jumble of over 1,000 islands of various sizes. The character of these islands changes dramatically as you travel along the coast. Some are lush with vegetation, bristling with spruce forest, while others are almost bald, still starkly beautiful in their rocky barrenness. Only a tiny fraction of these islands is inhabited, and the allure of a secluded refuge among the endless unpeopled coves and bays attracts thousands of mariners each year. Leaving the crowds on the more accessible islands, yachts and pleasure boats head for the further-flung and more isolated clusters of rock to find their own personal haven in the sun. Some strike out on their own, while others join organised flotillas. There are plenty of high-quality marinas and facilities all the way along the coast to accommodate any seafaring ambition you may have.

What surprises many people is that Croatia is also a mountainous country. The Dinaric Alps rise dramatically out of the sea along much of the coast, providing a stunning backdrop to the offshore islands. During the day the sun bounces off the snowcapped peaks, while in the evening their rock-faces glow red in the dying light. The mountain ranges provide an endless playground for the outdoor enthusiast, with possibilities for caving, hiking, mountain-biking, climbing and hang-gliding among other activities. Beyond the mountains, inland Croatia is unjustly ignored by many visitors. True, the vast plains of Slavonia are mainly flat and featureless, but to the east the pudding-bowl hills of the Zagorje, topped with fortresses and surrounded by fertile valleys, have an engaging charm and offer a rural retreat away from the heat and bustle of the coast, while the wetlands of the Lonjsko Polje teem with fascinating wildlife and provide a lush setting for picture-box riverside villages. Those who take the time to explore Croatia's interior will not be disappointed.

The Croatians are acutely aware of the value of their country's natural beauty. They have paid close attention to the lessons learned by Mediterranean countries, particularly Spain, whose overdeveloped coastlines have lost much of their original charm. The country is extremely proud of its eight well-established national parks and 11 smaller nature parks, created to protect Croatia's most beautiful environments. Most famous of these is Plitvice Lakes National Park, in the high Lika region, which has been designated a UNESCO World Heritage site and is Croatia's single biggest tourist attraction. Within the park, water tumbles between a series of lakes, taking a multitude of routes through the intervening forest and creating a magnificent display of waterfalls and rivulets along the way.

Every country has its own beauty spots, but what sets Croatia apart is the clarity of its waters and the purity of its air. The locals claim that Croatia's lack of pollution is the result of the cleansing effect of the *bura* wind that scours the country each winter. Perhaps it is the limpid air that makes the views seem more vivid and the colours more intense in Croatia than anywhere else on the Adriatic.

The People

For many people the Croatians themselves are the country's greatest asset. Talk to any expatriate about why they decided to live in Croatia and it won't be long before the warm nature and welcoming character of the populace is mentioned. Croatians are overwhelmingly friendly, and the fact that you have taken the time to visit their country, never mind invest in it, is taken as a personal compliment. Stories of small acts of kindness are common, such as the bus driver who made a long detour on an out-of-service bus to take a couple home, the shopkeeper who returned a wallet full of euros that had been accidentally left behind, and the neighbour who left a bountiful supply of fresh produce outside a holiday home to welcome the owners' seasonal return. People are very trusting of each other, particularly in the smaller villages and rural areas, where it is perfectly safe to leave your bike unchained and your doors unlocked. It is rare to come across the suspicion towards newcomers that has frequently been encountered by foreigners in areas of France; second-home-owners in all parts of Croatia, particularly on the islands, have found themselves welcomed and rapidly integrated into the local community. If immersion in another culture is one of your objectives, Croatia is an enjoyable place to achieve it. Even so, wherever you decide to settle, there are likely to be other English-speaking people in the area if you find that you require that safety net.

The Culture

Successive civilisations have left their mark on Croatia, and the effect is simply unforgettable. The country has a rich architectural heritage that ranks among the most outstanding in the world. No fewer than five towns and cities along Croatia's coast alone have been given the prestigious title of UNESCO World Heritage site. Among them is Split, a historic city grafted onto the ruins of an ancient Roman emperor's palace, and Trogir, an almost completely preserved 13th-century medieval town. In fact, the UNESCO selection committee must have been spoilt for choice. Croatia is littered with medieval towns bursting with sculpted portals and brooding cathedrals, Renaissance fortresses crammed with religious art, and Baroque castles plastered in rococo frescoes. Away from the main centres there is ample hidden cultural treasure to be discovered – small stone chapels on remote hilltops, mountain fortresses on knife-edged ridges almost lost in the encroaching undergrowth, and miniature castles stranded on tiny islets in clear lakes. Out of season you are guaranteed to have these jewels of antiquity completely to yourself.

The Croatians are naturally a creative and artistic people who have soaked up influences from Greece, Rome, Turkey, Austria, Italy, France and Hungary to produce many prolific and celebrated sculptors and artists. Today, all over the country there is a palpable enthusiasm towards all things artistic. Most towns will hold some kind of summer cultural event, and with such an unbeatable backdrop of historic architecture at their disposal, be it an open-air concert in Pula's Roman amphitheatre or a traditional folk performance above a stonewalled island harbour, these are usually worth attending. Croatians are equally enthusiastic about local traditions and customs. The annual jousting tournament at Sinj near Split, known as the Alka, has been held in the city since 1715 and others have been held on and off since the Middle Ages (see box, over-leaf). Even several centuries after their inception, the riders compete as fiercely and the crowds cheer as passionately as ever. Elsewhere, the Dalmatian Kaštela towns and hilltop towns of Istria all have their own quirky celebrations that generally involve the entire local population and draw all other business to an inevitable halt. These celebrations are a great opportunity to sample the myriad variations of regional gastronomy, from truffles to cheese, that differ from town to town. You will soon develop your own favourites. If you crave culture, Croatia can satisfy you for several lifetimes and still have some treasures to spare.

Tilting at the Ring

During the Middle Ages, equestrian contests were all the rage in towns throughout the Adriatic. Croatia is the only country in the world in which these have survived. Chronicles as far back as 1696 mention an annual Tilting at the Ring contest, known as 'Trka na prstenac', taking place in Barbar near Pula – a tradition that was successfully revived in 1976. Competing riders attempt to spear a small target hung from a rope while at full gallop to cries of '*Sridu!*' (Bullseye!) from the crowd. The target, just a few inches wide, is formed of two concentric rings, and riders score points depending on what part of it they hit.

The Trka na prstenac is extremely popular, but the largest and most famous contest is easily the Sinjska Alka, which is held in the southern city of Sinj some 35km inland from Split. The tradition started when, in 1715, a small band of 700 local militia successfully defended the strategically important fortress of Sinj from 60,000 invading Ottoman Turks. To commemorate their great victory the local people decided to hold a Tilting at the Ring contest using a Turkish stirrup as the target. Stirrup is '*halka*' in Turkish, so the tournament became known as the Alka and, barring one or two interruptions, has been held in Sinj every year since. Competitors, called Alkari, are all members of the prestigious Alkarsko Društvo association of riders whose membership is limited to men born in Sinj and the surrounding area. Taking part in the Alka carries great kudos locally, and the three-day festival, usually held during the first weekend of August, has become the focus of much regional pride. The Alkari wear elaborate uniforms of fur and brocade and the weekend is filled with a great deal of procession and ceremony. Proceedings reach a climax after the final contest on the Sunday afternoon when the overall winner is announced. The victor wins a substantial amount of money, but is obliged by tradition to spend it all on his victory party that night, ensuring plenty of eating, drinking and revelry.

Why Buy?

By now, the reasons why you have selected Croatia as the focus of your attention should be clearly outlined in your mind, but why should you decide to buy? There are many other options, ranging from short-term lets to house-swaps, which will allow you flexible access to the country's delights without requiring such a consuming year-round obligation as owning property. Perhaps you are resolved on a new life in Croatia, in which case buying a house or apartment may be an initial stage in putting down permanent roots in the country. Otherwise your motives are likely to fall broadly into one of two categories: the desire for the holiday home of your dreams, or the desire for a profitable investment. For most people, the primary incentive for buying is a balance of both.

Whatever your reasons, in deciding to buy, you won't be alone. Barclays Bank recently estimated that the number of people from the UK owning property overseas will rise to 4.4 million in the next four years (other estimates place this figure even higher). 'The impact of growing prosperity, cheaper flights and the low cost of borrowing – even lower in the Eurozone than in the UK – means the trend for buying property abroad is expected to accelerate,' explains the managing director of HIFX, a leading foreign exchange company. 'There has been a shift from a second home being regarded as a luxury to it being something aspirational that is attainable by most people.'

A Second Home

A recent government survey in the UK revealed that escaping to a warmer climate, avoiding long working hours and leaving behind stressful lifestyles were a greater priority for Britons buying a second home overseas than the potential for long-term profit. For many people, the knowledge that they are just a short flight from being mesmerised by Italianate views from their hilltop villa in Istria, soothed by the scented breeze on the balcony of their stone house by the sea on Hvar or refreshed by the pure water surrounding their lakeside cottage in Lika is a great comfort in their otherwise hectic lives. If you really crave complete isolation and have at least £1 million to burn, you could even buy your very own uninhabited Croatian island – there are still hundreds available for purchase.

Escaping to a second home for holidays and hot summer weekends is common practice for Croatians. Many families, particularly those based in Zagreb and inland Croatia, own a second property on the coast. As soon as the warm weather appears, the roads are quickly filled with coastbound families bolting from the cities to enjoy their seaside refuge. Property in Croatia has traditionally been passed down through families rather than bought and sold, so many of these second homes have been inherited from parents and grandparents. It was the unwanted, inherited real estate that was first snapped up by foreign investors and which alerted European buyers to the bargains to be had in Croatia. But, as the country has become more prosperous, Croatians have become increasingly reluctant to let go of their second homes and many are joining the foreign rush to snap up a dream holiday retreat. The coastal regions are as popular with Croatians as they are with foreigners, but many of the affluent from Zagreb are also looking for country property in the regions closer to the city such as around Samobor, Žumberak, the Zagorje and Medimurje.

There are many reasons why owning a property is preferable to renting. Instead of paying out money on a short-term let, you are paying into a longer-term investment. Then there are the more practical and aesthetic reasons: you can adjust the house to suit your needs, furnish the rooms the way you want them and have everything in place for your visit rather than completely decamping every year. Returning to the same town or village allows you time to get to know a place, to explore a bit deeper and really make a connection with the local people and way of life.

Depending on how long you intend to spend in your second home, many people expect to offset some of the cost of ownership by letting their property for part of the year. This can work out tremendously well. In Croatia the demand for holiday accommodation consistently outstrips supply – and it is a demand that is likely to get bigger with the introduction of direct budget flights from the UK to several regional airports and Croatia's increasing popularity with holidaymakers from all over Europe. The temperatures stay balmy from May through to October and rarely fall below 7°C, even in the depths of winter, ensuring a long, and therefore profitable, rental window. However, letting your second home comes with its own risks and drawbacks. Rental income is never guaranteed, no matter how good your agent, and your property is likely to be full of holidaymakers at precisely the times you want to be there yourself.

Investment

The demand for property in Croatia is not a new trend. The country has long been a chic tourism hotspot with its pure waters and sleepy islands, counting among its smitten devotees icons such as Elizabeth Taylor and Richard Burton, Edward VII and Wallis Simpson. Holidaymakers dazzled by Croatia clamoured to buy a permanent second home on its shores, but, until the country's independence in 1991, the law prohibited foreign ownership of real estate. Then came the horrendous troubles of the 1990s and Croatia became more famous as a war zone than as a place of cultural and natural beauty.

As the country recovered, the tourists returned and were now free under the new independent government to invest in property. Germans and Austrians were the first to capitalise on the opportunity, snapping up neglected villas and old stone houses right along the coast from Istria to Dubrovnik and on the most accessible islands, such as Brač and Hvar.

British interest in the country started in 2002 but was slow to catch up. People were put off by the 18-month wait for obligatory purchase approval from the Croatian government, during which time they were prohibited from letting their new property. Within the last year this wait has been reduced to less than six months and the government has made moves to ensure Croatia's long-term economic stability; see pp.95–7. Meanwhile tourism continues to grow at a rate of 6.9 per cent annually, creating an ever-increasing market for holiday property. This has been enough to sway many potential investors, and the property market is attracting a lot of attention. Many investors and agents are reporting a consistent 15–20 per cent annual increase in property values over the last five years – and yet this is still lower than the increase experienced in other countries, suggesting there is room for further appreciation.

There are two highly anticipated events on the horizon that promise to bring the much-heralded Croatian property boom. The first is the introduction of more favourable mortgages for foreign investors wishing to buy property; the

Case Study: The Best Laid Plans

In the spring of 2006, Lucy Dalton decided it was time she invested in an overseas property. She considered several countries. 'I did a lot of research and eventually settled on Croatia because I'd heard a lot of good things. I was buying purely as an investment, so I got advice on what part of the country gave the best rental yields.' Lucy decided to focus on the area around Split, and flew out for a weekend to look at 15 different potential investment properties. She decided on a one-bedroomed apartment in Čiovo within striking distance of Split airport. It was part of a newly built development due to be completed a couple of months later. 'The apartment was 100m from the sea, with great views and plenty of attractions nearby, including Split with its shops, restaurants and harbour. There was one bedroom but a sofabed in the living area so that the apartment could sleep up to four people.' Lucy paid a deposit and felt pleased with her buy. 'It was in a good area and was good value for money.'

By December the apartment was finished and fully paid for. It was then that Lucy hit her first hitch. 'There are two ways to buy property in Croatia: privately or as a company. As a private buyer I discovered that I needed approval from the Ministry of Justice before I could acquire a rental licence and start letting my apartment. At the time, getting this approval and licence could take up to two years.' Searching for a solution, Lucy came across several property management agencies in Split who were willing to take on her apartment without the necessary licence. This is illegal and something that the government is clamping down on. Lucy decided not to risk it. 'It was clear that I needed to set up a Croatian company, so I found a property management agency that could guide me through the process. It took €3,000 capital to start the company, but I can use that money to pay for things in the flat. The application will cost another €500 but it means I should be able to start letting my apartment from June.'

Lucy is now looking forward to a projected five per cent return on her investment through rental income as well as capital appreciation. 'I've been quite nervous at times,' she admits, 'as it's a big investment, but throughout the process it has been really reassuring to be dealing with an agent that has a physical office in the UK. It's worth a lot to speak to someone in your own language – especially when things don't go to plan.'

second is Croatia's accession into the EU, expected in 2010. Until very recently mortgages were only available to Croatians or Croatian companies. It is standard for private Croatian mortgages to be heavily cross-guaranteed by family members and friends, while company mortgages tend to be unattractive, with high interest rates and subject to unfavourable conditions. Another drawback is that Croatian banks refuse to lend against off-plan property or property still under construction. But one Austrian-owned bank and one other have recently started offering mortgages to foreigners in Croatia, and many other banks are waiting attentively in the wings to see the outcome of this; see pp.91–2.

Croatia's bid for EU membership has already resulted in large-scale invest-ment in the country's infrastructure. The EU donated €62 million in 2003 and a further €76 million in 2004 to help improve economic and social development in Croatia in preparation for membership. Already there have been dramatic improvements in the country's road network and transport links as a result of this investment, which can only be good news for foreign property investors.

As buying property in Croatia has become an easier, less risky business, so the type and number of properties available have changed. In Dubrovnik and parts of southern Dalmatia prices have risen dramatically so that now, although they are still cheaper than equivalent European resorts such as those in Spain, they don't represent the dream bargain many foreign buyers are looking for. Similarly, restoration projects along the coast and in central Istria are rare nowadays and surprisingly pricey when they do appear. Some people have diverted their attention away from the coast towards inland Croatia, where the property market has yet to be exploited by foreign buyers and there are still plenty of bargains to be had. However, the market in general seems to be driven increasingly towards new developments. Mindful of the fate of much of the Mediterranean coast, the Croatian government has introduced new regulations restricting the number and type of new developments along the Adriatic. This is bad news for developers but good news for investors, ensuring the aesthetic quality of developments (no high-level, tower block developments are allowed) and ensuring that coastal property will always be in demand.

When drawing up your initial budget, remember to take into account the cost of upkeep of your property, the cost of finding it and the costs associated with the purchase. An agent will typically charge 1–4 per cent of the property's value, an independent lawyer will expect a further 1–3 per cent, and there is a tax payable on all real estate purchases that is fixed at 5 per cent.

It is unlikely that the slow-burning Croatian property market will make you a fortune overnight, but if you are attracted by high rental yields and the poten-tial for good long-term returns on your capital investment, then Croatia could be the right move for you.

Living in Croatia

As well as holidaymakers and property investors there is a small number of foreign buyers looking for a permanent home in Croatia. If you fall into this cat-egory there is often a strong impetus driving your decision. Perhaps you are moving to be with a loved one or family member, to raise your family surrounded by a different culture or to spend your retirement in a sunny corner of a beautiful part of the world. Whatever your rationale, starting a new life in a new country – especially a non-English-speaking one – can be a daunting prospect. Later in the book we discuss many of the practical details you will need to consider if you intend to spend the majority of the year in your Croatian home; here we give a brief overview of the main issues surrounding living permanently in the country.

Starting a Business

Croatia has been described as a 'nation of smallholders' and the proof is evident. All over the country the markets are full of people making extra money on the side by selling their surplus produce – from olive oil and cheese to citrus fruit and truffles. Similarly, almost everyone, particularly those living in the coastal regions, benefits from the tourist industry. Some let spare rooms or second properties, while others take on seasonal work, or provide services to tourists directly. So if you are intending to set up your own business you can be sure of an enthusiastic welcome but also a great deal of competition.

Croatia may be a nation of enthusiastic entrepreneurs but over 40 per cent of the country's business is still controlled by the state, and the bureaucracy of Croatia's Communist years casts a long shadow. The government is eager to encourage new businesses, but assistance tends to apply to either very small ventures or large-scale foreign investment. Despite this, it has never been easier to start up your own business. Originally, founding a limited liability company in Croatia involved registering with several different government agencies and involved 10 different procedures. Now, a Croatian Financial Agency (*Financijska agencija*), FINA, has been set up to simplify the process. FINA can be accessed through the government website **www.hitro.hr**, where there is surprisingly helpful and complete guidance on the entire procedure (*see* pp.111–14). All you need is a passport, around €3,000 start-up capital and €500 to cover registration costs and your new Croatian company could be established within three to four weeks. The company must have an open bank account and employ a Croatian accountant for a stipulated number of days a year.

Once your Croatian company is set up, you have a number of additional rights that can be extremely useful. You can apply for a business permit and your family is entitled to apply for a residence permit; you can buy, sell and let real estate without restriction; and, most importantly, you can claim a rebate of the 22 per cent PDV tax (equivalent to VAT) charged on purchases such as vehicles, property and office equipment. If your business generates new employment, introduces new technologies, focuses on services to business or produces goods or offers services for the international market, you can also expect additional tax breaks and other incentives from the government, which is keen to develop the economy in these areas.

One big advantage Croatia has over many other European countries is that companies owned by foreign investors operate on a level playing field with locally owned companies. As such, you can enter any market, including consulting, retail and tourism, without suffering any penalties.

Case Study: The Paper Trail

Four years ago Sue Ramsden and Nigel Simpson packed up their lives into a specially fitted-out bus and set off to find a new home. They had no particular country in mind and expected to be travelling for two years or more, but after just three months they arrived in Istria. 'We arrived at a great campsite,' said Nigel, 'and were welcomed as if we'd been there a hundred times. Within three hours we were sitting together on a fabulous beach looking out over the islands. We just looked at each other and thought, "Oh dear – end of our travels."'

Almost immediately they found an ideal property with enough land to start a campsite business of their own, but after five months of wrangling the owner pulled the plug. By this stage the couple needed to apply for a permit to stay. They wanted to apply for a business permit that would allow them to stay *and* work in the country, but first they needed to own a property so they could start a tourism company. They searched for the cheapest properties they could find in the area and found a perfect farmhouse in Glavani, 20 minutes from Pula. 'We turned up in our big bus in this tiny farming community and wondered what the locals would make of us,' says Sue. 'They were nothing but welcoming. They are just the friendliest people and really rallied round.' Nigel dealt with the admin. 'It seems like a lot of paperwork but it is no more than you would deal with in the UK. The only difference is that, rather than the solicitor taking care of it, the individual or their estate agent has to do all the legwork, and the Croatian notary then just checks and stamps it.'

The effort was worth it. After spotting the property at 5pm on a Friday evening, the couple were its new owners by 8pm the following Monday. 'The house was a complete ruin,' admits Nigel. 'It was still plastered and still had windows, but by the time I'd finished the plaster had gone and the builders took the roof off.' In a little over a year after the first blow of the sledgehammer, Nigel and Sue were putting the finishing touches to their new property. It took them the same amount of time to receive their first business permit. 'We were the first people to apply for one with the police force in Pula as far as we could tell,' says Sue; 'they seemed to be learning as much as we were. It's a lot better now. Now that we know exactly what they need, it takes less than six weeks to renew our permits each year.' Three years on, the couple run a successful tourist agency but have yet to spend a night in their new house. 'The house is for guests,' explains Nigel; 'the bus is our home.'

Self-employment

For many it's the ultimate dream: working for yourself from a home office in a quiet corner of a restored villa overlooking the sea. With excellent mobile phone coverage, broadband capability and usually only a one-hour time difference with the UK, there is no reason why a successful freelance career working from home in the UK couldn't be transferred to fit a life in Croatia. Unfortunately, those of us lucky enough to have such flexible working lives are few and far between. Frequent flights between Croatia and the UK for face-to-face meetings could become impractical, and many clients become nervous if their employee or consultant is no longer based in the same country as them.

If you intend to find a new client base in Croatia it is worth bearing in mind that unemployment in Croatia is high, with a well-educated and skilled workforce that asks lower wages than their UK counterparts. Make sure that you have done your research before you take the plunge, and are confident that you can offer a skill that is in demand. The English language is a common exportable skill, but in order to capitalise on it you often also need a certain degree of proficiency in Croatian. *See* **Settling In**, pp.142–43.

Educating and Raising Children

Children are extremely important in Croatian culture, and Croats simply adore them. The family is seen as the hub around which life rotates and, as in many other Mediterranean countries, blood-bonds take on a special significance. Weekends are seen as time to be spent exclusively with the family, and with the children in particular. Sundays usually involve some kind of extended family get-together, be it a sit-down lunch or a picnic at a local beauty spot. Grandparents play a major role in the life of most Croatian children, often living together with the family and naturally taking on the role of babysitter while the parents are at work. For this reason, professional childcare provision is not a well-developed facility in most parts of the country, but there are several nanny agencies, particularly around Zagreb.

Croatia is a wonderful place to raise children. As well as the nurturing tendency of many Croatians, the diet is healthier (obesity is rare) and the beautiful surroundings encourage an outdoors-based, active lifestyle in an environment that is safe and secure. Children are free to roam and explore, particularly on the islands, and can leave their bikes in the street without having them stolen.

Most towns and islands have their own school, which is nearly always run by the state. Before 1991, private education was not permitted, and even now there are only a handful of private schools across the country, including one in Varaždin and another in Šibenik. International schools are also relatively rare, and confined to Zagreb, where the American International School of Zagreb, the Deutsche International School and the French School are all based. Except for these few international institutions, all schools use Croatian in the classroom, and using the state education system will involve a certain level of grappling with the language. However, many schools are sensitive to the needs of non-Croatian speakers (thanks to the influx of refugees during the 1990s) and provide extra help for foreign students. Most teachers speak good English and

Croatian pupils learn English in primary school so that they are fluent by the time they reach secondary school.

As in any country, the quality of education varies from institution to institution. Schools lack modern facilities but are generally well run throughout the state system. Teachers must train for at least four years before they are assigned to a school and, although methods can be antiquated, the standard of teaching is excellent. *See* **Settling In**, 'Education', pp.167–8.

Retirement

If you are considering spending your retirement in Croatia, you are following in prestigious footsteps. The Roman emperor Diocletian chose Split as his retirement home in the 4th century AD, building a luxurious palace in which to enjoy his release from office. You may not have such grandiose plans, but an increasing number of developments along the coast, particularly in Istria, are being designed with retirees in mind.

The stunning scenery, the promise of a quieter life and the year-round amenable climate combine to make Croatia a desirable place to live, but there are reasons why it is attractive specifically as a retirement destination. Sitting at

Dental Tourism

It is hard to think of two words less likely to be put together, but dental tourism has become a significant medical trend in Croatia. As the shortage of NHS dentists becomes critical in the UK and the price of private treatment soars, many people are looking abroad for treatment and to Croatia in particular. Private dental surgeries in Croatia are modern and well equipped with professional staff who have the same level of expertise as their British counterparts. Many speak English and all are regulated by the Croatian Dental Chamber. Best of all, waiting lists are non-existent and patients can undergo expensive procedures at a fraction of the price it would cost in the UK.

With budget flights to Croatia costing less than £30, it's easy to see why the idea is catching on. The savings are so substantial that an increasing number of people are deciding to combine their trip to the dentist with a family holiday. Croatian dentists have been quick to capitalise on the idea; just a few foreign clients each month can make a substantial impact on the fortune of their practice. As a result, many are actively promoting themselves to foreign clients and some are even relocating to the coast so that they are more accessible to tourists and holidaymakers looking for quick treatment. From root canals and crowns to straightening and whitening, a Croatian dentist could save you money – not to mention your smile. However, be aware that most dentists will require payment in cash and won't accept credit cards. The British Embassy website provides a full list of English-speaking dentists across Croatia.

Diocletian – The First Retiree

Some say that the greatest achievement of the Roman emperor Diocletian was to retire. Rome's top job came with a short life-expectancy, and by retiring he was the first emperor to survive his time in office without being assassinated, killed in battle or forcibly removed. Instead he spent the last seven years of his life living by the sea and growing cabbages.

Like any successful retirement, it was well planned. Diocletian built himself a colossal palace by the sea at a small settlement destined to become the modern city of Split. Complete with luxurious apartments, temples, servants' quarters, 2m-thick fortified walls and a small garrison, the building took 10 years, by which time, aged just 60, he was ready to step down from power. In an impressive display of forethought, the palace also featured its own mausoleum to house his body when he died – he clearly intended to end his days there.

Diocletian most likely chose Split because he grew up just a few miles inland at the Roman centre of Salona (near modern-day Solin). He was born to freed slaves but entered the Roman military and swiftly rose through the ranks, becoming emperor in AD 284 at the age of 39. He was a complex character, bringing stability to the empire but at the price of complete autocratic rule, dispensing with any last remnants of republicanism. Many of his policies were contradictory. Although his wife and daughter were Christians, during Diocletian's reign there was one of the first large-scale purges of the religion, producing a rash of martyrs including Pope Marcellinus, St Sebastian, St George and, ironically, the patron saints of Split, Domnius and Anastasius.

Diocletian presented himself as a demigod associated with Jupiter, removing himself completely from public view to become a distant and mysterious figure, and yet he founded the Tetrarchy, an experiment in power-sharing. Splitting the empire in two, he decided each half should have its own senior and junior emperor – a scheme that failed disastrously shortly after Diocletian's retirement. Even in death, which finally came in AD 312, he remains an enigma. His body, which lay in the palace mausoleum for 170 years, eventually disappeared without explanation and was lost.

the 'crossroads of Europe', Croatia is an ideal base if you intend to travel. Italy, Greece, Austria and Hungary are all a few hours away by boat, car or train, and the whole of Europe lies within realistic reach. Cruise liners ply the Adriatic and, if you have access to a yacht, the Mediterranean awaits your further attention. Yet just two hours on a plane can return you to the UK to meet with friends and family, ensuring that you are never too far away from home.

If you are eligible for a UK pension, it can be paid directly to you wherever you are, and Croatian law allows any pension payments received from abroad to be tax-free. This is great news for British pensioners intending to settle in Croatia, especially as the strong pound and the low cost of living will make your money stretch a lot further than it would do at home. Although not yet part of the EU, Croatia has opened up free use of its state health system to all EU citizens. A European Health Insurance Card (EHIC) – forms available from the post office or apply online – and a European passport allow you free consultation and emergency care. However the Croatian public health system, although staffed with well-trained professionals, is heavily stretched and short of cash. The standard of facilities and availability of important drugs is not always guaranteed. Most expatriates choose to make use of the large number of private medical and dental facilities that are available. This is less costly than it sounds, as private treatment in Croatia is a fraction of the price of private healthcare in the UK. Facilities may not be plush, but the quality of private healthcare in Croatia is highly regarded throughout Europe, so much so that there is even an increasing trend of western Europeans, Americans and Canadians travelling to Croatia for medical and dental treatment to avoid the long wait and high cost of treatment in their home countries. *See* **Settling In**, pp.163–4 and 158–9.

Visa and Permits

Croatia is one of the easiest countries in the world in which to live and work as a foreign national. Very few Europeans need a visa to visit the country, and there are only three main types of residence permit that you need to be aware of (far fewer than in bureaucratic hotspots such as Italy and the USA, for example). Owning a property, or even a yacht, in Croatia is considered a valid reason for you to be allowed to stay in the country. The only common gripe about the system is that it seems to be in a constant state of flux. There are frequent changes in the regulations and requirements for various applications and it is sometimes difficult to obtain reliable up-to-date information. The details provided in this chapter are correct at the time of publication but it is worth using the contacts and resources provided in the text to get the most current information you can before starting an application.

Many of the work and residence permits can only be obtained once you are in Croatia, where the local **police station** should be your first port of call for queries and information. Officials, although universally helpful, sometimes appear to be at as much of a loss as the applicant, particularly in rural areas where these kinds of procedures may not be regularly implemented. In any case, getting hold of permits in a hurry can be a provoking and ultimately fruitless experience, so make sure you leave plenty of time for your applications to be processed. The good news is that, once you have successfully completed your first application, subsequent applications get a lot easier. With EU accession on the horizon in a few years' time, it is likely that application procedures will become much more consistent and simplified even further.

Entry Visas

Citizens of the United Kingdom of Great Britain and Northern Ireland do not require a visa to enter Croatia. With just a valid British **passport** you can enter and leave Croatia as often as you wish and stay for up to 90 days in any six-month period. The same applies if you hold a passport from any member country of the EU, Andorra, Argentina, Australia, Bolivia, Bosnia-Herzegovina, Brazil, Brunei, Canada, Chile, China, Costa Rica, Guatemala, Honduras, Hong Kong, Iceland, Israel, Japan, Korea, Liechtenstein, Macao, Macedonia, Malaysia, Mexico, Monaco, Nicaragua, New Zealand, Norway, Panama, Paraguay, El Salvador, San Marino, Singapore, Switzerland, Turkey, Uruguay, the USA, Vatican City or Venezuela. Nationals of countries that share a border with Croatia (including Italy) need only an identity card. If you intend to stay for longer than 90 days, you must apply for a **temporary stay permit**. If you are a citizen of a country not on this list, you must obtain a **visa** *before* you arrive in Croatia. Visas can be issued by the Croatian Diplomatic Mission or Consular Office in your home country. Further details on exactly who needs a visa can be found on the website of the Croatian Ministry of Foreign Affairs and European Integration (**www.mvpei.hr**) or the Croatian Embassy in London (**http://uk.mfa.hr**).

Whether or not you require a visa, once you arrive in Croatia, you are obliged to report to a police station within 24 hours. If you are staying in tourist accommodation (including campsites and self-catered lodgings) this will be done for you, but if you are staying with friends or family or in privately arranged accommodation, your hosts will need to register you. In practice, police attitudes towards registration are fairly relaxed, and it is not uncommon for tourists and visitors to go unregistered. However, if you intend to stay in Croatia for a long period of time and remain unregistered, you risk being deported.

Applying for a Visa

If you need a visa (e.g. if you live in the UK but are not a citizen of a country in the list above), the first place to begin your visa application is on the website of the Croatian Embassy in London to understand the requirements. Even if you already have this information, it is worth checking the website, as procedures can change without notice. You can print out many of the forms necessary for the application process. Visa applications cannot be sent by post, they must be made in person, so the next step is to make an appointment with the Croatian Consular Office in London by telephone, e-mail or in person during the Consular Section office hours (*Mon–Thurs 11–2, Fri 10–12*).

Embassy of the Republic of Croatia in the UK
21 Conway St, London W1T 6BN
t (020) 7387 2022, **f** (020) 7387 0310
http://uk.mfa.hr
croemb.london@mvp.hr

In exceptional circumstances you may be able to send your visa application without travelling to London, but you will be obliged to appear at the Consular Office once the visa is issued. The process can takes two days to six weeks, so it is prudent to leave plenty of time between your appointment and your departure date. The embassy cannot process visas on the same day as your appointment. Once your visa has been approved, there will be a small fee. The size of the fee depends on the type of visa you are applying for and the rate of exchange but it is rarely more than £30.

Types of Visa

Valid for one year, **travel visas** allow an unlimited number of visits to Croatia as long as the total time spent in the country is no more than 90 days in any six-month period. Depending on your reasons for visiting Croatia you will need to apply for one of two types of travel visa: a tourism travel visa or a business travel visa.

Tourism Travel Visa

To apply for this visa you will need:

- **your passport or travel document, which must be valid for three months beyond the duration of the visa applied for and your entire stay in Croatia.**

- **a completed and signed visa application form, which can be downloaded from the Consular Office (http://uk.mfa.hr).**

- **a colour photo 30mm by 35 mm.**

- **two copies of a document proving your reasons for visiting Croatia.**

- **if you are travelling to Croatia for a private visit, a letter of invitation from a Croatian citizen or someone giving official permission to stay in Croatia; the content of the letter is strictly regulated and a template can be downloaded from the Consular Office website (http://uk.mfa.hr); the person inviting you to Croatia must sign the letter and have their signature verified by a public notary or be with you when you apply for the visa; you will need two copies of the letter – one remains with your visa application and the other must be kept with you in case it is required at the border when you arrive in Croatia; the website of the Notaries Society (www. thenotaries society.org.uk) contains an extensive list of affiliated notaries in England and Wales.**

- **a document confirming you have accommodation for your stay in Croatia.**

- **evidence that you have sufficient funds in your bank account to cover the cost of your stay in Croatia; this is fixed at a rate of €100 per day; if you have a letter of invitation or confirmation of pre-booked accommodation, this rate is reduced to €50 per day; a bank or credit card statement showing sufficient funds is usually all that is required.**

- a document to prove your intention and ability to return to your home-land or to a third country; if you do not have a return or onward travel ticket, you must demonstrate that you have enough funds to pay for your return to the UK or travel onward to a third country; again, a bank or credit card statement showing sufficient funds should cover this.

- a document that states your method of travel; this can be an airline ticket, a car hire voucher or something similar.

Business Travel Visa

To apply for this visa you will need:

- your passport or travel document, which must be valid for three months beyond your entire stay in Croatia and the duration of the visa.

- a completed and signed visa application form, which can be downloaded from the Consular Office website (**http://uk.mfa.hr**).

- a colour photo 30mm by 35 mm.

- two copies of a document proving your reasons for visiting Croatia.

- a letter of invitation signed by an authorised representative of the company you are visiting and validated with an official stamp; a template for this letter can be downloaded from the Consular Office website (**http://uk.mfa.hr**).

- a document that confirms you have accommodation and means for your stay in Croatia.

- proof that you have sufficient funds in your bank account to cover the cost of staying in Croatia, fixed at a rate of €100 per day; if you have a letter of invitation or confirmation of pre-booked accommodation, this rate is reduced to €50 per day; a bank or credit card statement showing sufficient funds is usually all that is required.

- a document to prove your intention and ability to return to your home-land or to a third country; if you do not have a return or onward travel ticket, you must demonstrate that you have enough funds to pay for your return to the UK or travel onwards to a third country; a bank or credit card state-ment showing sufficient funds should cover this.

- a document that states your method of travel, e.g. an airline ticket, a car hire voucher or something similar.

Transit Visa

A foreign citizen wanting to cross Croatian territory will need a transit visa. It is valid for six months and permits a stay of up to five days in Croatia. In order to apply for a transit visa you must have the relevant visa or permit to enter the country you are travelling to.

Airport Transit Visa

If you are a citizen of Afghanistan, Bangladesh, Congo, Eritrea, Ethiopia, Ghana, Iran, Iraq, Nigeria, Pakistan, Somalia or Sri Lanka, then you will require an airport transit visa if you plan to land in a Croatian airport – even if you will not leave the aeroplane or international transit area. It is issued for a specified number of transits through the airport international transit area over a maximum of 24 hours. However, if you hold a residence permit issued by the UK, any EU member state or the United States, the requirement for an airport transit visa is waived.

Group Visa

Groups of between five and 50 people can apply for a group visa. This is much cheaper than applying for individual travel or transit visas. It is valid for a single entry or transit across Croatia of up to 30 days. If you are travelling as part of an organised tourist group, this visa can be organised for you by your operator and can be issued for groups larger than 50.

Permits

Temporary Stay Permits

No matter what your nationality, if you wish to stay in Croatia longer than 90 days in any six-month period, you must apply for a temporary stay permit. Your first temporary stay permit is valid for up to one year and will enable you to stay continuously in the country for as long as you like within that year. It does not automatically allow you to work in Croatia; for that you will need a work or business permit.

To make an application you will need proof that you have a valid reason to stay in the country. There is no exhaustive list of justified grounds accepted by the Croatian government, but if you are at all unsure of your justification for staying you should consult the Consular Office at the Croatian Embassy in London or your home country to get official advice. Some of the most commonly cited reasons for requiring a temporary stay permit are:

- **owning or renting property in Croatia.**
- **owning a yacht moored in a Croatian marina.**
- **marriage to a Croatian national or someone with official permission to stay in Croatia.**
- **to study.**
- **because applicant is staying with family members.**
- **for work.**

If you did not require a visa to enter Croatia, you can apply for a temporary stay permit once you are in the country, at the **police station** closest to the area in which you intend to stay. For people who do need a visa, the application has to be submitted in person to the Consular Office of the Croatian Embassy in your home country before you travel. Make sure you have with you:

- a completed and signed temporary stay permit application form 1a, which can be downloaded from the administration page of the Ministry of Interior website (**www.mup.hr**).

- proof of your reason to stay – depending on the grounds for your temporary residence, this could be proof of Croatian property ownership or lease, a marriage certificate to a Croatian national or a letter of acceptance on a course in a Croatian university.

- passport and travel documents (your passport must be valid for three months beyond the expiry date of the temporary stay permit you are applying for.

- proof of means of subsistence.

- proof of accommodation.

- health insurance documentation.

- two 30mm by 35mm photographs.

- a police clearance certificate from your local police service stating that you have no criminal record; it must be less than six months old. You can apply for this using a Police National Computer Form (Ref 3019B); for the Metropolitan Police area (most of London) this form is available at **www.met.police.uk/dataprotection**. It can take up to 40 days to process the request, so make your application in good time. You will only need this for your first temporary stay permit application, not for extensions.

Once your application has been processed, the temporary stay permit is entered into your passport. If the permit was processed in a Consular Office outside Croatia you must register your permanent address with the local police station within three days of your arrival in the country. Throughout your stay you are also obliged to report any change of address. This rule applies, as well, if you were already living in Croatia at the time you applied for your permit. In both cases you should notify the police that you are leaving the country when your permit expires if you do not intend to renew it. This may sound officious but in reality the local police are very reasonable about registration and notification, so, although it is something you need to keep track of, it shouldn't cause you sleepless nights. Once you have your permit there are no penalties for leaving the country; the permit will remain valid for a year regardless of how much time you spend outside Croatia. As long as you return to the same address (or notify the police if you change your address or decide not to return) you are free to enter and leave the country as often as you like and to stay for as long as you want.

At least 30 days before your permit expires you can apply for an extension of up to a year at your local police station. Once you have been issued with your first temporary stay permit, obtaining subsequent permits becomes a lot easier. For a start you will be familiar with the routine and more confident about exactly what paperwork is required from you. There is also no need to provide a police clearance certificate. Several people have found that local notaries are willing to photocopy forms before they are dated so that all you have to do when re-applying the following year is fill in new dates. This can save a lot of time if you are applying year after year. Once you have applied, and been granted, a temporary stay permit for five continuous years, you are eligible to apply for permanent residence. If your stated reason for staying in Croatia was to study, your temporary stay permit can be extended for a further two years beyond the end of your studies.

Work Permits

Working in Croatia requires a work permit, even if you have already been granted a temporary stay permit. Working without one is illegal and is treated very seriously, resulting in deportation for many offenders. However, obtaining a work permit is the responsibility of your employer and should require minimum effort on your part. Work permits are issued for a limited period of time and are generally only valid for the length of your contract – up to a maximum of two years. Beyond that, you must apply for an extension. If you work for yourself, freelance or starting a business, this is not the appropriate permit for you – you will need to apply for a business permit (*see pp.30–31*).

At the beginning of each year the Croatian government decides on the number of work permits to be issued over the subsequent 12 months. The number fluctuates but is usually around 2,000. Half of these are reserved for the renewal of already authorised permits, leaving around 1,000 new work permits available each year. This quota is shrunk further by allocating a certain number of permits to particular industries and professions. For example, in 2006, 516 work permits were put aside for jobs in the tourism industry while only 16 work permits were available that year for healthcare workers and just 10 for those wanting to work in science and education.

There are a handful of professions and exceptional cases that are not included in this quota system, including:

- **professional athletes with a contract in Croatia.**
- **schoolteachers teaching minorities the national language and script.**
- **staff on secondment or an exchange programme.**

Whether or not work permits for your profession are controlled by the quota system, the application procedure is the same. Once you have been offered a contract of employment by a Croatian company, your employer can apply for your work permit by submitting an application at the police station closest to the company headquarters. They must supply:

- a completed and signed work permit application form – form 9a, which can be downloaded from the administration page on the Ministry of Interior website (**www.mup.hr**).
- information on you, the employee.
- information on the job to be undertaken by you.
- information on working conditions.
- a certificate of company registration in Croatia.
- your tax certificate.
- an official company letter justifying your employment.

Within 15 days of filing the application, your work permit will be issued at the police station where the application was made. Once the work permit has been issued, your employer has a further 15 days to sign a contract with you before you are able to start work. It is worth noting that the whole process could take up to a month before you are able to do your first day's work. This doesn't take into account the time your employer will need to gather the documents necessary to file your application in the first place.

If your employment contract runs for more than two years, or is renewed beyond the expiry date of your work permit, your employer must apply for an extension of your permit. The application has to be submitted at least 45 days before the expiry of your original permit and is once again made at the police station closest to the company headquarters. As well as all the information supplied for your first work permit, your employer must also supply:

- a copy of your previously issued work permit.
- a copy of your current and/or new contract.
- a copy of your employment record.

There are a small number of foreign employees who do not need a work permit. If you think you may meet any of the criteria listed below and may not need a work permit, it is a good idea to talk to someone at the Consular Office of the Croatian Embassy in the UK just to make sure.

People who do not need a work permit include:

- company founders and board members who spend less than three months of the year in Croatia.
- indispensable personnel of certain companies.
- professors invited as lecturers by Croatian universities.
- scientists taking part in further studies or in research important for Croatia or representing international organisations.
- foreign correspondents reporting on Croatia.
- representatives of religious communities carrying out work related to religious service.

- authors, artists, performers, organisational and technical staff taking part in opera, theatre, concert and other cultural events, meetings and workshops who do not stay in Croatia for more than 30 days.
- those providing professional training to Croatian nationals and who are spending less than three months in the country.
- employees undergoing professional training of not more than three continuous months.
- competitors in sporting and chess events.
- administrative personnel, experts, teachers and lecturers from educational and cultural institutions taking part in reciprocal cultural and educational programmes.
- contractors of the government of Croatia relating to national security or defence.
- those involved in the delivery, assembly or servicing of machinery and equipment as long as they are in Croatia for less than 30 days continuously or less than three months of the year discontinuously.
- students in full-time education undertaking temporary work through authorised agents.
- cultural heritage, archive and library conservators spending less than 30 days in Croatia.

The above list is not exhaustive. A complete list of exemptions can be found on the website of the Ministry of the Interior (**www.mup.hr**). If you do not need a work permit but intend to stay and work for more than 30 days, then you will still need to apply for a temporary stay permit.

Business Permits

If you are freelance, self-employed, own a majority share of a registered business or plan to start your own business in Croatia, you will need a business permit rather than the standard work permit. It enables you to both stay and work in the country, so you do not need to apply for a separate temporary stay permit. Applications are submitted in Croatia at a police station near where you intend to work. In some cases an application can be made at the Consular Office of the Croatian Embassy in London or your home country before departure, but only if you are intending to provide a service on behalf of a foreign employer.

As this permit allows you to stay and work in Croatia, the application for a business permit requires all the documentation demanded for a temporary stay permit plus some additional credentials. You are asked to supply:

- a completed and signed business permit application form 1a, which is available to download from the administration page of the Ministry of Interior website (**www.mup.hr**).

- proof of your reason to stay; this must take the form of a contract with a Croatian national or Croatian-registered company, evidence of your free-lance status or registration documents for your company or small business. Registration is made with the Croatian Financial Agency, FINA, and can be done through the government website, **www.hitro.hr**.

- your passport and travel documents; your passport must be valid for three months beyond the expiry date of the business permit you are applying for.

- proof of means of subsistence.

- proof of accommodation.

- health insurance documentation.

- two 30mm by 35mm photographs.

- a police clearance certificate from your local police service stating that you have no criminal record; it must be less than six months old. You can apply for this using a Police National Computer Form (Ref 3019B); for the Metropolitan Police area (most of London) this form is available at **www.met.police.uk/dataprotection**. It can take up to 40 days to process the request, so make your application in good time. You will only need this for your first business permit application, not for extensions.

Once approved, it is vital to be fully aware of the conditions of your business permit, as any irregularities could have disastrous consequences for your work and business. If you have been granted a business permit for starting a business, you must do so within four months of the permit being issued, otherwise it is annulled. If you start trading with an annulled permit, you are risking the same penalties as those who are found doing business with no permit at all. In the worst case this can lead to deportation, but it can also result in future applications for a business or work permit being turned down. The nature of the business for which the permit is issued is quite specific. If the nature of your work or business changes, you must inform the authorities of the change within eight days or risk your permit being withdrawn. If you breach employment, social and labour insurance or business regulations, or become bankrupt, your business permit is automatically void and it is unlikely that you will be granted another.

You are also subject to the same conditions as the temporary stay permit. If you have obtained your business permit before departing for Croatia, you are obliged to report your arrival and permanent address to the local police station within three days. After that, you must report any change of address. Similarly, if you are already living in Croatia when you are granted your business permit, you must let the authorities know if you move.

Administrative Departments in Croatia

Ministry of Foreign Affairs and European Integration
(*Ministarstvo Vanjskih Poslova I Europskih Intergracija*)

The Ministry of Foreign Affairs and European Integration is in charge of shaping and implementing Croatia's foreign policy and international relations. It is also the ministry in charge of the country's diplomatic missions and consular offices around the world. On the ministry's website you can find a list of all the Croatian embassies and consulates outside Croatia and contact information for each one.

Within Croatia, the **Directorate for Consular Affairs** (*Uprava za konzularne poslove*), one branch of the Ministry of Foreign Affairs, has several separate departments that deal with individual issues including the Department for Visas, the Department for Foreigners, the Department for Property Relations and the Department for Citizenship and Travel Documents.

The Ministry of Foreign Affairs is also responsible for the registration of foreign correspondents, foreign freelance journalists and their staff. Further details on accreditation can be found on the website.

Until 25 July 2006, anyone wishing to own property in Croatia had to seek the permission of the Ministry of Foreign Affairs. This function has now been moved to the Ministry of Justice, and any applications that had not been processed by 25 July 2006 are now being handled by the Ministry of Justice.

Ministry of Foreign Affairs and European Integration
Trg N. Š. Zrinskog 7–8
10000 Zagreb
t + 385 (0)1 4569 964
mvpei@mvpei.hr
www.mvpei.hr

Directorate for Consular Affairs
Medulićeva 34–36
10000 Zagreb
t + 385 (0)1 4598 014
tkonzularni.poslove@mvpei.hr

Ministry of the Interior
(*Ministarstvo Unutarnjih Poslova Republike Hrvatske*)

The MUP is in charge of Croatia's police (*Policija*) but it is also the administrative department that deals with the movement and staying of foreign nationals within the country. During all but the shortest of visits to Croatia you will find it necessary to visit the local administration office of the Ministry of the Interior or MUP (usually the police station) at least once. This is where you are obliged to register your visit to Croatia, apply for residence and work permits and notify the authorities about any changes in your situation once you have been given permission to stay, including any change of address. The final decision on all admission and nationality affairs rests with the MUP. The MUP website is a first stop for further information about residence and work permits and has all the relevant application forms for download.

Ministry of the Interior
Ulica grada Vukovara 33
10000 Zagreb
t + 385 (0)1 6122 111
www.mup.hr

Ministry of Justice (*Ministarstvo Pravosuđa*)

Anyone from the UK (or a country that has a reciprocity agreement with Croatia allowing their nationals to buy property) must seek official approval from the Croatian government before they can go ahead with a property purchase. Until recently these applications for permission to purchase were made with the Ministry of Foreign Affairs and European Integration and involved a wait of 18–24 months. In July 2006 this function was passed on to the Ministry of Justice, a much bigger and better-resourced ministry. As a result, waiting times for purchase approval have been slashed to as little as five months, although seven to eight months is more common. Applications for purchase approval are usually made through lawyers, so it is unlikely that you will need to have direct contact with the Ministry of Justice yourself.

Ministry of Justice
Trg Republike Austrije
1410000 Zagreb
www.pravosudje.hr (Croatian language only)

Croatian Residence

If you plan to live in Croatia for years rather than months, applying to renew your temporary stay permit and work permit or business permit every year will become an annual chore that you might prefer to do without. Once you have been granted a temporary stay permit or business permit for five years or more you are automatically eligible to apply for permanent residence in Croatia. If your application is successful, you are granted a Croatian identity card with a national identification number. This will leave you free to live and work in Croatia for an indefinite period of time without the need to apply for any additional permits or extensions. It also releases you from any visa requirements you may have had to enter and leave the country. Once you have been granted permanent residence you are obliged to report any change of address to the police within eight days of your move.

You are eligible for permanent residence if you:

- **have had a temporary stay permit for the last five continuous years.**
- **have been married to a Croatian national or someone with permanent residence for three years and have been issued a temporary stay permit.**
- **are staying for humanitarian reasons or your stay is in the interests of Croatia.**

The latter qualification is extremely unusual and you should check with the Consular Office of the Croatian Embassy in your home country if you intend to use this as your grounds for permanent residence. You are automatically excluded from permanent residence if you have been convicted of a crime with a non-suspended prison sentence or if you are deemed to present a threat to national security and public health. Your application can also be turned down if you have no means of subsistence, no guaranteed accommodation or if you do not have health insurance.

If you are applying for permanent residence on the grounds that you have been granted temporary stay for the last five years continuously, you will need copies of the permits that cover that entire time period. If you are applying on other grounds, you will only need a copy of your current temporary stay permit or business permit. Remember, you must have made an application for an extension of your temporary stay permit or filed an application for permanent residence at least 30 days before your permit expires. If not, you risk being forced to leave the country and starting the process all over again. You will need:

- **proof of sufficient means of subsistence.**
- **proof of accommodation.**
- **health insurance documents.**
- **a marriage certificate, plus proof of spouse's Croatian nationality if your grounds for permanent residence is that you have been married for at least three years to a Croatian national, or spouse's residence permit if your grounds is that you have been married for at least three years to someone with permanent residence; the marriage certificate must have an official stamp and cannot be more than six months old.**

The application for permanent residence is made at a police station in Croatia. You need to have with you:

- **a completed and signed permanent residence application form 1a, which is available to download from the administration page of the Ministry of Interior website (www.mup.hr).**
- **two 30mm by 35mm photographs.**
- **a valid passport or travel document.**
- **a birth certificate; any copy must be less than three months old and have an apostille or legalisation certificate attached to it, *see* below.**

A minor (anyone under the age of 18) is eligible for permanent residence if they have been issued a temporary stay permit and at least one parent has been granted permanent residence. If their second parent is not a permanent resident also, they will need to give their written consent to the minor's application.

Obtaining Birth Certificates and Apostilles

The apostille is a certification that serves to ensure that documents issued in one country are recognised for use in another country (*see* **www.apostille.org.uk**). In the UK, an apostille can only be issued by the Legalisation Office in London at a cost of £19 per document. Further details are available at **www.fco.gov.uk**. You can send a document for an apostille by post or take it in person to the public counter at:

The Legalisation Office
Foreign and Commonwealth Office, Old Admiralty Building, The Mall
London SW1A 2LG
t (020) 7008 1111
LegalisationOffice@fco.gov.uk
Open Mon–Fri 10–12 and 2–3

Copies of your birth certificate are available from local register offices or your national General Register Office. If you were born in England or Wales you can obtain a copy of your birth certificate from the General Register Office in Southport. Copies can be ordered online at **www.gro.gov.uk** and are dispatched within four working days at a cost of £7 per copy. All queries should be addressed to:

General Register Office
Certificate Services Section, PO Box 2
Southport PR8 2JD
t 0845 603 7788
certificate.services@ons.gsi.gov.uk
Open Mon–Fri 8–8, Sat 9–4

If you were born in Scotland you must apply to the General Register Office for Scotland (**www.gro-scotland.gov.uk**) in Edinburgh. You can order copies of your birth certificate in writing or on the phone (Certificate Ordering Service **t** (0131) 314 4411), but the quickest method is to apply in person at:

General Register Office for Scotland
New Register House, 3 West Register Street
Edinburgh EH1 3YT

Orders made in person before 1pm are available by 4pm, otherwise copies can take up to 14 days to be dispatched. Further details (including fees) can be found on the website.

National Identification Number (JMBG)

Every Croatian citizen or permanent resident is issued with an identity card displaying their unique master citizen number, known as a **JMBG** (*Jedinstveni matični broj građana*). Rather like a National Insurance or social security number, the JMBG is used as a form of identification in official correspondence with government and administration departments.

Made up of 13 digits, the JMBG number contains information about an individual's date of birth, their gender and their region of origin. The JMBG system was first introduced in 1976 by the old Yugoslav state and has been inherited by Slovenia, Macedonia and Serbia as well as Croatia. The Croatian government has in the past put forward plans to replace the JMBG with Croatian Citizen ID numbers, but the idea wasn't popular and plans seem to have been shelved for the time being.

Birth certificates for those born in Northern Ireland can be found at the General Register Office (Northern Ireland) in Belfast. On the website (**www.groni.gov.uk**) you can apply for a copy of your birth certificate online or download an application form that can be posted or taken in person to:

General Register Office (Northern Ireland)
Oxford House
49–55 Chichester Street
Belfast BT1 4HL
t (028) 9025 2000
gro.nisra@dfpni.gov.uk

Police Clearance Certificate

A police clearance certificate is a letter from the UK police stating that you have no criminal record. It is issued by your local police service and applied for using a Police National Computer Form (Ref 3019B). It can take up to 40 days before you receive the necessary letter, so make your application in good time.

For the Metropolitan Police area (most of London) this form is available at **www.met.police.uk/dataprotection**.

Croatian Citizenship

Becoming the citizen of a country is a complex personal decision often made for emotional as well as practical reasons. A foreign national is perfectly able to live indefinitely in Croatia with a permanent residence permit and Croatian ID card, but sometimes becoming a full-blown citizen can be the one remaining piece that is still missing from a larger jigsaw. Citizenship brings security, and for many it acts as a recognition of their commitment to the country and the new life they have built there. Once you are a Croatian citizen there is no piece of paper, form or permit that can be found to be out of order and force your expulsion or bring the dream life you have worked so hard for crashing to the ground. However, becoming a citizen also brings its share of responsibilities. There may be tax consequences. In addition, young men between the ages of 18 and 27 should be aware that, as Croatian citizens, they will automatically be eligible for compulsory military service (although the government is currently debating legislation to phase out conscription from 2008).

Croatian law doesn't recognise dual citizenship. This means that in the process of becoming a Croatian citizen you agree to renounce all other citizenship, including that of your home country. In practice this law isn't enforced and dual citizenship seems to be tolerated, but it is worth seeking advice on the implications this may have for you.

There are three ways you can acquire Croatian citizenship: by origin (you were born in Croatia); by birth (you were born to Croatian parents); or by naturalisation (you have come to consider Croatia as your home country or consider yourself to be Croatian).

Croatian citizenship **by origin** or **by birth** is automatically given to:

- a child of Croatian parents.
- a child who was born in Croatia with either a Croatian mother or a Croatian father.
- a child who was born outside Croatia with one Croatian parent and one unknown or stateless parent.
- a child born in Croatia with unknown or stateless parents.
- anyone born abroad with one Croatian parent who has registered as a Croatian citizen by the age of 18.
- anyone abroad with one Croatian parent who has established residence in Croatia by the age of 18.
- those who have one Croatian parent and would be left stateless without Croatian citizenship.
- those whose Croatian citizenship was terminated when they were still a minor and who have resided continuously in Croatia for the last 12 months.
- those who were born in Croatia and have lived in Croatia continuously for the five years before their application for citizenship.

If none of the above criteria applies to you, you can be granted citizenship **by naturalisation**. This is a slightly more complicated process and can take some time. You are eligible to apply for citizenship by naturalisation if:

- **you have been granted legal residence in Croatia for the last five years continuously.**

- you are married to a Croatian national and have been granted permanent residence.
- you live outside Croatia but consider yourself to be Croatian.
- both your parents are Croatian citizens by naturalisation.
- you are a minor who lives in Croatia with at least one parent who has been granted citizenship by naturalisation.
- you are a minor who lives outside Croatia with one parent who has Croatian citizenship by naturalisation and a second parent who is of unknown citizenship or stateless.
- your spouse or either parent emigrated from Croatia.

Before you can begin an application for citizenship by naturalisation you must fulfil several prerequisites. If your grounds for naturalisation are that you have been legally resident in Croatia for some time, you will probably have to satisfy all of the conditions listed below. If you fall under one of the other categories for naturalisation you may be eligible for one of several exemptions and exceptions which are listed in detail on the Ministry of Interior website. You can also seek advice and the latest information at the Croatian Embassy in London.

The prerequisites are that:

- you are over 18.
- you are prepared to relinquish citizenship of all other countries.
- you have been granted legal residence in Croatia for the last five years continuously.
- you are proficient in the Croatian language and Latin script.
- you show evidence of accepting the Croatian legal system and laws.
- you have embraced Croatian culture.

Profiles of the Regions

03

Perhaps your decision to buy a property in Croatia sprang from a love of a particular region or a magical holiday that you would like to repeat. In which case you probably have a very good idea of where you would like to start the search for your ideal property. However, it is more than likely that you have only a vague notion of where to buy property, or would like to explore alternative options before limiting your search to a particular geographical area. This chapter is designed to give you an overview of each region in Croatia so that you can begin to narrow down your target area. Regional character, history, geography and climate are introduced, as well as the more practical matters of transport links and property trends.

Croatia has a complex history and a chequered heritage. For centuries it was not a unified country at all but was fragmented into regions occupied by different European powers. The Greeks, Turks, Hungarians, Venetians, Austrians, Italians and even the British have all occupied parts of Croatia at various periods throughout the centuries, and have left their unmistakable footprint in different parts of the country. Today, Croatia is divided into 21 counties that are grouped into loosely defined, often historic regions. Each region has its own distinct flavour, with marked differences in culture, customs, architecture and heritage.

The most obvious divide is between coastal Croatia, which has a very Mediterranean feel and a fairly developed tourist industry, and inland Croatia, which has historically been more central European in attitude.

Inland Croatia

Surrounded by Slovenia, Hungary, Serbia and Montenegro, inland Croatia is the northern part of the country, which is almost cut off from the coast by the triangular wedge of Bosnia-Herzegovina that protrudes from the east. Its physical and metaphorical isolation from the coast is reinforced by a distinctly continental climate and a history largely independent of the rest of the country. Since the Middle Ages, coastal Croatia has been dominated by Mediterranean powers, while inland Croatia was occupied alternately by the Hungarian, Habsburg (Austrian) and Ottoman Turk empires. Northern Croatians tend to be more central European in outlook and style.

Inland Croatia's continental climate brings hot summers, which are mostly dry, with most rainfall occurring in late spring. In contrast, the winters are cold, with occasional but bitter winds. In the mountainous areas, temperatures are low enough to keep snow on the ground well into the year.

Stretching from the hilly regions of the Zagorje in the west to the flat, fertile, flood plains of Slavonia in the east, inland Croatia is an essentially rural landscape of vineyards, pastures and tumbledown, timber-framed farmhouses. The bucolic peace is punctuated by several thriving commercial centres that at first glance appear disappointingly industrial and of little interest. Persevere through the unattractive shell of Communist-style housing, however, and you will often find a charming city centre drenched in historic buildings and regional character that is well worth exploring. Zagreb is the pivotal focus of the region, from which all the main roads spread like tentacles across the rest of the country. There is unrivalled access to the rest of Europe, with major overland routes into Slovenia, Austria, Hungary and beyond.

Zagreb

A region as well as a city, Zagreb is the political, cultural and economic heart of Croatia. The pace of change since the 1990s has been more rapid here than elsewhere in the country, and signs of Croatia's emergence as a modern European nation are more visible here.

Surrounded by sprawling suburbs and satellite commuter towns, Zagreb is squeezed between the River Sava in the south and the rambling flanks of Mount Medvednica in the north. It was originally two cities, occupying adjacent hilltops and separated by a river. **Kaptol** was dominated by the Archbishop's Palace; on the opposite side of the river, **Gradec** huddled around a military garrison. Over the centuries these two districts combined; they now form the heart of old Zagreb and are the most artistically appealing part of the city, where narrow streets wind between pastel-coloured buildings and pass beneath ancient stone archways to spill out onto quiet squares.

Today the real hub of the city lies below in **Donji grad** (lower town). From the central square, Trg bana Jelačića, spread busy streets lined with shops and modern office blocks. The pedestrianised squares are full of pavement cafés, whatever the time of year, but, for all the espressos and gridlocked traffic, Zagreb still has a provincial air. Men with accordions spark impromptu sing-songs, and, in the central Dolac food market, headscarfed matriarchs sell olive oil in reused cordial bottles, and pungent home-made cheeses.

Zagreb is often touted as the new mini-break hotspot, following in the wake of central European cities like Prague and Budapest. These claims should be taken with a large dose of realism. Despite the city's burgeoning nightlife, Zagreb remains a long way off the tourist radar, and the city itself seems heavily preoccupied with its development as a centre of commerce rather than tourism. Sitting at 'the crossroads of Europe', Zagreb is well placed for both the central European and emerging eastern European markets, encouraging an increasing number of multinationals like Philips, Bosch, Ericsson and Nestlé to set up headquarters in the city. This is producing a swell of affluent Croatian professionals as well as international staff looking for property.

The demand is good news for investors, but has made Zagreb one of the more expensive capitals in southeastern Europe. Apartments in the most desirable part of the city around the central square are promptly snapped up for

€3,000–5,000 per square metre when they occasionally come on the market, falling to between €1,800 and €2,000 per square metre in the streets just a few tram stops further away. Moving into the suburbs and the region's commuter towns, such as **Samobor** and **Velika Gorica**, apartments become less common than houses and prices average at €1,600–1,800 per square metre. These towns offer a quieter and more rural lifestyle but are within easy reach of Zagreb and well connected to the centre. Velika Gorica in the Turopolje to the south is surrounded by fields and vineyards and is popular with families moving out of the suburbs, while Samobor to the west is full of heritage and close to wooded hills that are a favourite of hikers wishing to escape the city on sunny weekends.

The Zagorje

Occupying the far northern corner of the country, the Zagorje stretches from Zagreb to wash up against the Slovenian and Hungarian borders. Looking like a rumpled blanket, the closely packed hills and valleys are the final foothills of the far-off Alps, petering out in the flatlands of the Međimurje beyond the River Drava. As if to strengthen the alpine connection, the red-brick houses that dot the hillsides have wide A-frame roofs and top-floor verandas that are vaguely reminiscent of alpine chalets.

Zagorje is one of the prettiest parts of inland Croatia, with small, rocky streams running between grassy hills, and valleys splashed with neatly cultivated fields. It has an instant rustic appeal. Every house seems to have its own barn or orchard, chickens and turkeys peck contentedly at the grass, and haystacks litter the fields. Small villages form the centre of tightly knit communities, and even the most remote will have at least a well-stocked shop and a café.

Inland Croatia hasn't yet attracted the intense property speculation experienced by the Adriatic coast, and there are still plenty of old houses in fabulous

Krapina Man

In 1899 Dr Dragutin Gorjanović led an archaeological excavation in a small cave on Hušnjak Hill near Krapina. What he found provided a vital clue in piecing together the evolution of modern man. Over the next six years he unearthed over 900 bones belonging to *Homo sapiens neanderthalensis*, who roamed the hills of the Zagorje over 130,000 years ago. These weren't the remains of just one individual but of dozens of men and women aged between two and 40 years old. None of the skeletons was complete, but there was enough to show that Krapina Neanderthals had dramatic sloping brows, no chin, large teeth and barrel chests with powerful arms. Not the most flattering description we could hope for of our earliest ancestors but subsequent research has proved that these were indeed distant relations. Perhaps more disturbingly, many of the remains showed evidence of cannibalism.

Case Study: Beware Magnolia

André Wilding first visited Croatia more than 30 years ago while he was serving in the army. 'It was an extremely poor country back then. I took my family on a camping holiday along the coast and, although facilities were primitive, the country was lovely and still very much unexplored by Brits.' So, four years ago, when offered a chance to part-own a second home in Croatia, André jumped. 'My partner's brother-in-law was born in the Zagorje and wanted to buy a property there so he could spend more time with his mother. He'd found a traditional wooden house in a hidden valley that needed restoring and asked if we wanted to share it.' The house was only just habitable, with no electricity, no water and no sanitation, but it boasted four acres of land including a vineyard and a small wood. 'It was like *Jurassic Park*. We called the house "End of the World", and it almost was, but we loved it.'

André bought a half-share of the house and employed Bosnian builders to carry out the restoration work. Six months later he returned expecting to be able to move in, but instead found himself booking into a hotel. 'Most of the heavy work had been done, but everything decorative was dreadful. There were no taps and all the windows had been painted shut.' However, there was one silver lining to the experience. He'd left instructions for the house to be painted magnolia which, unknown to him, means 'pink' to the Croatians. Luckily the builders hadn't got around to painting anything yet.

André finished off the work himself and now spends six to eight months of the year in the Zagorje. 'I love the sense of freedom. Fences are positively frowned upon out here. You can go walking wherever you want and you are more likely to be invited in for a glass of wine than threatened with a 12 bore for trespassing.'

While out on a walk, barely a year after buying his first house, André spotted another property in the same village that needed restoring and bought that one too. This time he organised the work himself, using local builders, and found them reliable and efficient. Now managing and facilitating his fourth restoration project in the Zagorje for a British client, André admits he has been bitten by the bug, 'When faced with a run-down house, not everyone has the imagination to visualise what it could be like. Some people say they want a place to renovate when actually they want somewhere to do a bit of DIY. But I love it. I've found my heaven.'

locations at very low prices. Many of the properties are unwanted inheritances that have lain empty for years, with the result that the cheapest need pulling down, while others need major restoration. Even so, the figures are tempting, with desirable plots of land starting at as little as €5,000–10,000 and a fully restored family holiday home commonly priced from €50,000 to €60,000. Those looking for a relaxing place to retire and families tired of the bustle of the coast have been quick to look inland, but there is a rising trend among the affluent of Zagreb to secure themselves a country retreat here. Particularly popular are the spa towns of **Stubičke Toplice** and **Krapinske Toplice** and the pilgrimage centre of **Marija Bistrica**, which is set among some of the most spectacular scenery in the region. Others are opting for the forested hills along the Slovenian border, which are often topped with medieval fortresses and castles such as the famous **Veliki Tabor**.

Varaždin is the main city of the region, located on the banks of the River Drava within striking distance of both the Slovenian and Hungarian borders. For many years in the mid-18th century Varaždin was the seat of Croatia's government and the most prominent city in the country. But the city was almost destroyed by fire in 1776, and Zagreb took its place as the national capital. Heavily influenced by its powerful neighbours, Varaždin was rebuilt in the Baroque style of Austro-Hungarian architecture, which has left the city with a wonderful legacy. Today the wide stone-flagged streets of the centre are lined with colonnaded buildings painted in pastel shades and adorned with fanciful swirling details and elaborate wrought-iron balconies. Students amble past the numerous street cafés, and the decorative churches are almost constant venues for an endless stream of concerts and recitals. Property within the centre is so desirable that it only rarely appears on the market and is expensive when it does. A one-bedroom apartment sells for around €100,000.

Slavonia

Spread across the relentlessly flat flood plains of the Pannonian Basin, Slavonia is a region hemmed in on all sides by water. To the north the Drava forms the border with Hungary; to the south the Sava separates Croatia from Bosnia-Herzegovina; and to the east the Danube wiggles, more or less, along the border with Serbia. It was this corner of the country that was among the worst affected by the war and one of the few places in Croatia where you can still see the scars. The siege of **Vukovar** was one of the most significant actions during the early stages of the war, leaving thousands of Croats dead and many more missing in the mass graves that surround the outskirts of the city.

Vukovar was returned to Croatia in 1998 but the city was nothing more than ruins. Even today, more than 15 years after the end of the siege, a walk around the city centre is a shocking experience. **Osijek** to the north suffered a similar fate. Originally a thriving university city with Baroque buildings and manicured parks spilling onto the banks of the Danube, it endured a nine-month bombardment by Yugoslav and Serb forces in 1992. Escaping the level of devastation seen in Vukovar, the old town is still full of elegant charm, and the centre once again bustling with students and businessmen, but war damage is obvious on almost every building. It will be a few more years before Osijek is ready to get back on its feet.

The rest of Slavonia is dominated by flat fields of corn and linear settlements lining the main roads that criss-cross the region. There is little to attract the attention of foreign buyers, and if anything prices are a little higher in this region because the land has a high agricultural value.

Central Croatia

'Central Croatia' is a term generally used to describe several small but distinct regions that cover the territory between Zagreb and the coast. It's a jumbled blend of landscapes that is often ignored in the stampede to the coast. Yet it contains some of Croatia's most lovely natural wonders, including its single greatest tourist attraction, **Plitvice Lakes National Park**. The winding, single carriageway road that runs straight across the region (and past Plitvice) used to be the only route from Zagreb to the coast, causing endless jams throughout the summer season. It's at last been replaced by a high-speed motorway further west, which extends from the north to both Rijeka and Split, but still many people prefer to take the old road. Perhaps this is out of appreciation for the superior scenery, but more likely it is to avoid the costly motorway tolls. As a result there is a string of B&Bs, restaurants and cafés along its length, a growing number of them run by foreign nationals. On either side of the road there are sweeping vistas over densely forested hills cut in places by deep rocky gorges. In one of these gorges sits irresistible **Slunj**, perched on an island surrounded by cascading water, while in another nestle the famous Plitvice Lakes.

This whole upland area is encompassed by the **Lika region**, which flattens out into rolling grassland surrounded by mountain scenery as it nears the coast. Here, the sleepy villages that span the road have been all but abandoned. Rambling wooden houses sit in acres of land in the shadow of razor-backed mountains, and the only people you are likely to see are the shepherds tending their grazing sheep.

Property prices here are extremely low. A 15-year-old one-bedroomed holiday home is likely to cost as little as €12,000, but the region is close to the Bosnian border and many of the villages were badly affected by the war. Some locals have not been able to afford to repair their property, while other owners never returned when the war ended, leaving empty and badly damaged property. If you are planning to venture to some of the more remote and mountainous villages, a car is the only option, although public transport is surprisingly good in the valleys.

A car is similarly essential to access the **Lonjsko Polje**, a long, thin region north of Lika where a string of pretty villages with decorative wooden houses hug the banks of the Sava. The region has been made a national park and, despite the lack of tourism at the moment, this will undoubtedly be a popular destination in the years to come.

Also of potential interest in the future is **Žumberak**, just south of Zagreb, which snuggles against the Slovenian border. Often described as a 'wild Zagorje', its wooded valleys, fast-flowing rivers and vineyard-clad hills are dotted with villages of rustic, half-timbered buildings. Just a short drive from Zagreb, it is already gaining popularity with active weekenders from the city.

Coastal Croatia

Seen from above, the coastal regions take on the shape of a giant seahorse. The triangular Istrian peninsula in the north forms a downcast head, the Kvarner basin a rounded belly, and the narrow strip of Dalmatia, tapering to a point at Dubrovnik, an uncurled tail. Altogether, the coast is undoubtedly Croatia's greatest attraction. As well as clear aquamarine seas, a dramatic shoreline indented with sandy bays and sleepy sun-bleached villages full of historic character, the coastal regions can offer a near-perfect climate. Never too cold and never unbearably hot, temperatures rise to a maximum of 30°C in the summer and rarely fall below 5°C in the winter. The winters bring the cold *bura* wind that blows for days at a time across Kvarner and northern Dalmatia and dramatic downpours of rain, particularly in the south, but the summers are hot and dry, boasting an average of 2,700 hours of sunshine a year to warm the crystal waters to an inviting 26°C.

The climate and scenery are heavily reminiscent of the Mediterranean, similarities that are reinforced by cultural and historical ties. The coastal regions

Glagolitic Script

In the 9th century two monks, St Cyril and St Methodius, were sent by the Byzantine emperor to proselytise the Adriatic coast. In order to translate the bible into the local Slavic language they created the 38-symbol Glagolitic alphabet. Glagolitic means literally 'the marks that speak', and the alphabet borrows letters from Greek, Armenian, Georgian and Hebrew as well as introducing many of its own. The result is a highly intricate and ornamental set of symbols that wouldn't look out of place in a science-fiction movie.

Throughout the Middle Ages the script grew in popularity, forming the basis of the Cyrillic alphabet that is still in use today across Russia, Ukraine, Bulgaria and Serbia. Within Croatia, Glagolitic script was used for all government and religious documents and the symbols were even used as numbers, with a value dependent on their alphabetic order. Glagolitic became an emblem of Croatian national identity, but that was an association that damned its survival. Successive regimes, from the Ottoman Turks to the Habsburgs, forcibly eradicated the use of Glagolitic to suppress Croatian nationalism. Even so, it survived in pockets until the late 19th century, particularly along the Adriatic on the Kvarner Islands and in central Istria.

have belonged to one Mediterranean nation or another since they were first colonised by the Greeks in the 4th century BC. As a result the locals have a laid-back approach to life and a love of family that is more commonly associated with southern Mediterranean cultures, and the coast is littered with a wealth of cultural heritage, including some of the best-preserved Greek, Roman and medieval architecture in the world.

There used to be only one route along the coast, a scenic but slow single carriageway that twists its cumbersome way along the length of the littoral. In recent years, long-awaited motorways have been built all the way from Pula at the tip of Istria to Split in the south. The new roads may not have the same stunning sea views but they have cut travel times radically, making the southern parts of Dalmatia infinitely more accessible. There are plans in the near future to extend the motorway beyond the Makarska Riviera as far as Ploče. However, this still leaves the last tortuous stretch to Dubrovnik. Clinging to the steep shoreline, teetering above the sea, this is one of the worst roads in Croatia, but with so little room along the coast it is hard to see how it can be improved.

Istria

The largest peninsula in the Adriatic, Istria protrudes into the sea from the northernmost point of Croatia's coast like an arrowhead. Along the top lies the Slovenian border (separating Croatia and Italy by a mere 20km in places) and the **Učka mountains**, which bunch together to block the narrow strip of land connecting Istria to the rest of the country. Since the 1960s the peninsula's 537km of sun-drenched coastline has drawn large numbers of holidaymakers to the region from all over Europe, particularly Germany, Austria, Italy and the UK.

Quiet fishing villages and ancient Mediterranean fortress towns, like **Rovinj**, **Poreč** and **Novigrad** along the western shore, have grown into well-developed seaside resorts that continue to expand, sprouting campsites, water parks and private villas. Inland, the tourist clutter of the coast is replaced by pastoral scenes of forested valleys and pudding-bowl hills topped with the tiled roofs of medieval towns. Wandering through the cobbled streets of **Motovun** or **Buzet**, gazing out at a sweeping view of fields, vineyards and far-off mountains, surrounded by the lure of truffles and crisp white wine in every café and restaurant, it is forgivable to feel that you are in the heart of Tuscany.

Perhaps this is no surprise given the region's history. Istria was under Venetian control for more than 350 years and was ceded to Italy after the First World War, resulting in a programme of Italianisation of the populace, often by force. When Istria was returned to Croatia in 1945, those of Italian descent felt they had no option but to leave, and there followed a mass exodus on a huge scale. In less than a year, 28,000 of **Pula**'s 32,000 inhabitants had left, a story repeated all over the region. Houses were stripped of belongings, entire villages were abandoned and even dead relatives were exhumed to be taken back to Italy. The region was gradually repopulated by Croats, but some of the villages never recovered and were abandoned permanently. Fifty years later it was these abandoned stone houses and villas that were first bought up and renovated by foreign property investors.

Sadly, today, such idyllic renovation projects are thin on the ground and tend to be expensive now that local owners have been alerted to their potential worth. Instead, there is an increasing demand for new developments that provide traditional-look villas set in delicious rural scenery but with a high level of modern comforts.

Istria is not cheap. A brand new four-bedroom villa in central Istria is worth around €360,000, but people seem increasingly prepared to pay over the odds, with this sort of property regularly appearing on the market priced at €500,000 or more. A two-bedroom apartment in a coastal development will sell at around €180,000, working out at an average of €2,500 per square metre. Istria may be one of Croatia's most expensive regions, but property there still represents an investment with good potential returns. Owners are reporting at least 10 per cent capital growth annually in their investment over the last five years, and with tourism gaining pace in the region the opportunity for rental income in this area is among the best in the country.

Kvarner

Squeezed between Istria in the north and Dalmatia in the south, Kvarner is the awkwardly shaped region which surrounds the Kvarner Gulf. The biggest city in Kvarner is easily **Rijeka**, Croatia's leading commercial port and a transport hub for the entire Adriatic. The city centre gleams with pedestrianised streets and glittering fashion emporiums, but the suburbs are a mass of unattractive high-rise housing and heavy industry, which stretches along the coast in either direction. Further south the clean air and sparkling coastal views return as the **Velebit**, Croatia's greatest mountain range, rises out of the sea to a height of nearly 2,000m. The old coastal road clutches the shore as it creeps between the sea and the foot of the mountains.

There isn't much room for development along this part of the coast, but there are a few villages grasping onto the shore that offer dazzling views across the water to the cluster of islands lying in the Kvarner Gulf. Some of these islands are no more than large boulders barely peeping above the waves, but those of most interest are Krk, Cres, Lošinj, Rab and Pag. Of all Croatia's thousands of islands, the Kvarner Islands are the most accessible, with two, Krk and Pag, connected to the mainland by road bridge. **Krk** is the largest island in the Adriatic and is conveniently home to Rijeka airport. The northern part of the island is bleakly industrial but the south has retained its original charm and is popular with holidaymakers, as a result of its long sandy beaches.

Pag, closest to Dalmatia, has wonderful views of the Velebit mountains on one side and the outlying islands on the other. There are two main tourist resorts on the island, which cater for very different visitors. Pag town, a maze of narrow streets where women in doorways create traditional lace and home-made Pag cheese, is popular with families, while Novalja, at the northern end of the island, has been dubbed the Croatian Ibiza and is famous for its clubs and beach parties. Pag is a barren rock of an island where a stubby covering of sage bushes provide the only vegetation, but on neighbouring **Rab**, pine forests fringe the sandy beaches and shade its rambling medieval towns. **Lošinj** has a similarly verdant covering of Aleppo pine, producing a climate that was deemed so beneficial to health that it has been a popular tourist location since the 19th century. Today, it is connected to the larger island of **Cres**; although both islands experience a tourist explosion in the summer thanks to their accessibility, the villages have managed to retain much of their traditional character and are enchanting places to stay.

Prices on the Kvarner Islands are slightly cheaper than their southern counterparts. A one-bedroom apartment in a coastal development on Krk with sea views will cost between €150,000 and €180,000. Pag is even cheaper, as it is relatively far from any airports with a direct connection to the UK. This is set to change, with direct flights from London to Zadar on Ryanair having started in summer 2007. A new two-bedroom apartment in the beach resort of Novalja averages at €120,000.

Dalmatia

All beauty, all gold and our lives so dear
Cannot recompense thy beauty so clear.

So run the lines that open the Dubrovnik Summer Festival each year. They may as well be referring to the entire Dalmatian region. Stretching for 350km along the Adriatic from Zadar in the north to the Gulf of Kotor beyond Dubrovnik, Dalmatia encompasses some of the most spectacular coastal scenery in the Adriatic, if not in Europe. Beneath pale, sun-bleached mountains the tattered shore crumbles into an endless string of bays, inlets, coves and headlands, each concealing isolated sweeps of wheat-coloured sand or pools of vibrant blue water. Lush forests flood the valleys and sheltered bays, interrupted by the terracotta roofs of ancient stone villages where orange trees sprout between buildings like moss between roof tiles.

Since the Greeks first established colonies on the Dalmatian islands of Hvar and Vis in the 4th century BC, successive Mediterranean powers have claimed Dalmatia as their own. After the Romans came the Venetians, who ruled Dalmatia from the 15th to the 18th century, followed by the French, the Austrians and the Italians. It wasn't until 1918 that Dalmatia joined the rest of

Croatia as part of the Kingdom of Serbs, Croats and Slovenes, which later became Yugoslavia.

The legacy of this complex heritage are cities like Split and Dubrovnik. **Split** is the largest city in Dalmatia and is a historic town with an urban edge. Slick cafés, funky boutiques and contemporary restaurants are incorporated into the narrow medieval streets of the old town, itself cradled in the ruins of a Roman palace. **Dubrovnik** appears even less affected by the passage of time. Medieval monasteries, Baroque cathedrals and Venetian palaces encircled by thick city walls seem unchanged by the centuries except for the discreet cafés and boutiques hidden in its maze-like streets. Thankfully, after a remarkable programme of restoration there is little sign now of the damage caused by the six-month bombardment of the city by Yugoslav forces in 1991. Every year hundreds of thousands of visitors come to enjoy Dalmatia's natural wonders and cultural treasures, but it never seems difficult to leave the crowds behind. Away from the main centres there are hundreds of small villages, cultural curios and untrampled wilds to explore, particularly on the islands.

Dalmatia is often touted as the 'land of a thousand islands' by locals, and they mean it quite literally. So many islands crowd into the sea views that it is impossible to tell where one ends and another begins. **Brač** is the largest of the Dalmatian islands and home to Croatia's most famous beach, Zlatni rat, a perfectly horn-shaped beach that is ubiquitous in Croatian tourist literature. Close by is the lavender-clad island of **Hvar**, with its lofty central ridge, sleepy villages and bustling harbours. Tourism to the island has mushroomed in recent years, but its towns and villages, among the most ancient and well-preserved in Croatia, have been sympathetically developed without detracting from their traditional character. **Vis**, furthest from the mainland, has preserved many of its traditions and customs, entrancing the handful of visitors that reach its shores. Further north the **Zadar archipelago** and the **Kornati islands** provide a starkly

Klape

The word *klapa* (plural *klape*) means company, and traditionally referred to a small group of friends who met in the evenings to sing together for pleasure rather than performance. This was a common practice throughout the coastal fishing villages and islands of Dalmatia, and has become part of the regional heritage. Exclusively male, the *klapa* would sing complex harmonies, always by ear and rarely with any musical accompaniment. The songs are inevitably about love and have a slow, soothing rhythm reminiscent of Gregorian chant. Today there are an increasing number of mixed and female *klape* as well as the all-male variety, and the ensembles are often 10 or 11 members strong rather than five to eight, which were more common originally. Many *klape* perform at local summer festivals throughout Dalmatia, but there is also a popular festival of the Dalmatian *klape* held in Omiš each year, which brings together the very best *klape* from all over the region.

Case Study: The Impulse Buy

When Midge Story and her partner, John, went on a short autumn break to Dubrovnik, the last thing on their mind was buying property, although they had seen a feature on buying property in Croatia in the *Sunday Times*. By chance a buy-to-let opportunity in a village close to Dubrovnik caught their attention. The property was already sold but the idea stuck with them. As soon as the couple returned to the UK, John went on to the Internet. 'It was a complete whim,' Midge says; 'we had done no research, no planning, but there was a seminar in Sloane Square that week about buying property in Croatia, so we decided to go.

'We went back to Croatia to view properties four days later. We were picked up at the airport with five different properties to see. I was certain from the information we were given that the first one wasn't for us. It looked quite small, it was only partly furnished and it wasn't in our ideal location. But when we arrived I opened the door and that was it.'

Midge had fallen in love with a two-floor balconied apartment with its own pool in the quiet village of Marina, 14km up the coast from Trogir. Part of a block of three, the apartment had an enviable view across the marina that gave the village its name. Unfortunately, the apartment was more than the couple could afford and their first offer was refused. 'I just said, "I want it",' remembers Midge, 'so we arranged a meeting with the builder and sat around the table with his wife and his son until we had a deal. We were just 27 hours into our trip and had bought a property! We hadn't come out to Croatia with the intention of buying so we had no deposit with us, no money, but the builder was incredibly trusting. We shook hands on the deal, he gave us the keys to have another look around and allowed us to send the deposit from England.'

Six months later the couple have just finished paying for the apartment but, having bought as individuals rather than as a company, they are still waiting for the official paperwork to be finalised, which could take several more months. In the meantime they have already been back twice to put the finishing touches to the furnishings in their new holiday home and are planning a third trip in the next few weeks. During each visit they have had people knocking on the door to ask if the apartments are for sale. 'We did everything you shouldn't do,' admits Midge, 'but we are really happy with what we've got. It's fabulous.'

different kind of scenery and are much less visited than their southern sisters, while the **Elafiti islands** just north of Dubrovnik are widely considered to be the most unspoiled of all.

Dubrovnik is without a doubt the most expensive place in Croatia to buy property. You will pay between €4,500 and €5,000 per square metre for property within the old town and as much as €700,000 for a two-bedroom apartment in one of the most prestigious suburbs, which have perfect views of the old town.

Brač Stone

What do the Reichstag in Berlin, the White House in Washington and the high altar in Liverpool's Catholic cathedral have in common? The answer – they are all constructed from luminous white stone quarried on the same Dalmatian island of Brač. The stone has been quarried on the island since prehistoric times, but it wasn't until it was used to construct Roman emperor Diocletian's Palace in Split in the 4th century BC that it became a prized building material. Dignitaries throughout the Roman empire demanded the stone for their palaces, temples and sculptures.

As successive regimes took control of Croatia, the stone grew in popularity. Through the centuries, export of the stone became the rural islands' main source of income, and island life revolved around it. The natives of Brač were famed for the art of stonemasonry and provided Croatia with some of its finest stone master masons, who were in demand across Europe for their skills.

The stone is still quarried on the island just outside Škrip, beside the main road from Supetar to Bol. You can also see what the fuss is about at the cemetery in Supetar, which is packed with elaborate family tombs carved by Brač masons out of the distinctive milky-white material.

Prices drop considerably as you travel north along the Dalmatian coast, and areas around Split in particular are relatively cheap. A new two-bedroom apartment right on the seafront will cost less than €180,000. Of the islands Hvar is the most expensive, with prices in Hvar Town almost equivalent to those in Dubrovnik. Brač is cheaper: a small two-bedroom apartment can cost as little as €130,000.

Selecting a Property

Organising a trip to Croatia to search for your dream property is an exciting but often slightly daunting experience. Your head will more than likely be swimming with information before you leave, only for you to be swamped with even more details once you arrive and start looking at properties.

Just like searching for a new home in the UK, the secret is to get organised. Hopefully the previous chapters will have helped you focus on why you are buying in Croatia and what you want from your Croatian property as well as giving you a shortlist of regions to visit. This chapter will not only provide essential information for arranging your trip but will guide you through the process of choosing an agent and arm you with descriptions of typical Croatian properties and prices so that you will know what to expect. Not only are the sections useful in the preparation for your trip, but they will be handy as a reference in Croatia during your property search.

Travelling to Croatia

Flying is now more affordable than ever before, and with Croatia just a two-hour flight from the UK it is entirely plausible to travel there for the weekend. Buying property can sometimes be a nerve-racking experience, particularly when you live in an entirely different country, so it is comforting to know, when making a purchase, that you can quickly, easily and cheaply return to Croatia for a brief visit to check on renovation work or sign essential papers.

However, if you are worried about the carbon footprint of frequent flying there are other ways to travel. Europe's highly efficient motorway network and transport system is spreading ever further east year by year. It is now possible to travel by train from London to Zagreb in just over 24 hours. The coach is a less popular option, as it is expensive and takes over 30 hours. But if you have a lot of baggage with you, you may well decide to drive. The journey to Croatia is usually split into two days but, if you have the time, it can take the shape of a worthwhile road trip across Europe in its own right.

By Air

For a relatively small country, Croatia has an unusually large number of airports. Zagreb and Split are the country's main international gateways but Dubrovnik, Pula, Rijeka (on the island of Krk) and Zadar also provide connections with several European cities.

Zagreb Pleso is a busy modern airport offering easy access to the capital as well as to Croatia's continental heartland but it is a substantial trek from the Adriatic. More convenient portals for the Croatian coast are Split and the smaller regional airports such as Rijeka and Dubrovnik.

As Croatia has risen as a tourist destination, several European budget airlines have recently begun direct flights from the UK to a range of airports along the coast in answer to the growing demand. The introduction of flights from London to Pula at the southern tip of the Istrian peninsula by no-frills giant Ryanair has dramatically improved access to the region, and the Ryanair flights from London to Zadar in northern Dalmatia that began in summer 2007 are bound to have a similar affect on the surrounding region, which has, until now, been slightly inconvenient to reach and therefore less popular as a holiday destination.

The introduction of flights to Croatia by budget airlines has brought cheap air travel to Croatia. For much of the year it doesn't take more than a quick search on the Internet to find one-way flights for less than £20. The low season, and the best time to pick up bargains, runs from October through to April. Booking your flight well in advance of departure can also save you money. At other times the prices of no-frills flights vary wildly depending on demand. It's not uncommon for 'budget' fares to be as much as those offered by more luxurious airlines like Croatia Airlines and British Airways, so it's worth shopping around. Prices peak during July and August and at Christmas but Easter is also a very busy time to travel and seats are hard to find.

If the UK-based budget airlines are full, try their European competitors. TUIfly, German Wings and Sky Europe fly from various British airports to Croatia via other European cities. Although not as convenient (or as fast) as a direct flight, this can be a very economical option. They tend to fly from regional UK airports including Newcastle and Birmingham, which is handy if you live near one of these cities. Some of the national carriers such as Alitalia and Austrian Airlines offer similar flights to Croatia via another European city, but these tend to be expensive and are best avoided. If you are really stuck for a reasonably priced seat, consider flying to a nearby country and continuing your journey overland. Ljubljana in Slovenia is only 2½ hours on the train from Zagreb, while Trieste and Venice in Italy are just a short train journey, a 4hr drive or a bus ride along the coast from the Istrian peninsula.

The Main Airlines

- **British Airways (t** 0870 850 9 850; **www.ba.com)** flies direct three times a week from London Gatwick to Split and Dubrovnik and also from Manchester to Dubrovnik. One-way fares from London start at around £60 and £100 flying from Manchester.

- **Croatia Airlines (t** 020 8563 0022; **www.croatiaairlines.hr)** has daily direct flights from London Heathrow to Dubrovnik, Pula, Split, Zadar and Zagreb. Flights are charged in kunas and an economy return flight will set you back 1,042 kunas.

- **easyJet (t** 0905 821 0905 (65p/min); **www.easyjet.com)** has recently begun operating services to Croatia. There are three brand new routes flying from London Gatwick to Split four times weekly, and from London Luton and Bristol to Rijeka three times a week. Although it's not as cheap as Wizz Air, prices are generally low.

- **Flybe (t** 0871 522 6100 (10p/min); **www.flybe.com**) is a small budget carrier offering flights from Birmingham airport to Croatia from May through to October. It flies three times a week to Dubrovnik and operates a weekly flight to Split every Saturday. Tickets are around £50 return.

- **German Wings (t** 0870 252 1250; **www.germanwings.com**) flies from London Gatwick to Zagreb and Split via Hamburg; from Edinburgh and London Stansted to Zadar, Zagreb, Split and Dubrovnik via Cologne-Bonn; and from London Stansted to Zagreb, Zadar and Split via Stuttgart.

- **Norwegian (www.norwegian.no**) flies from Edinburgh, London Stansted and Manchester to Dubrovnik, Pula, Rijeka and Split via a Norwegian destination. There are too many combinations to list here, but full details can be found on the website.

- **Ryanair (t** 0870 156 9569; **www.ryanair.com**) operates budget flights from London Stansted and Dublin to Pula three times a week, and London Stansted to Zadar. Prices vary based on demand but can be as little as £9.99 plus taxes.

- **Sky Europe (t** 0905 7222 747 (25p/min); **www1.skyeurope.com**) operates flights from London Stansted, Manchester and Birmingham to Dubrovnik and Split for as little as £1.

- **TUIfly (www.TUIfly.com**) has flights from Newcastle and Manchester to Rijeka or Dubrovnik via Hanover, Cologne-Bonn or Stuttgart. It also flies from Birmingham via Cologne-Bonn to Rijeka.

- **Wizz Air (www.wizzair.com**) is an Eastern European-based airline that offers by far the cheapest direct flights from the UK to Croatia. It flies three times a week from London Luton to Split and Zagreb at bargain prices, which can be as low as a penny.

By Rail

Travelling by train may not be the quickest or most economical way to get to Croatia from the UK, but it is certainly the most romantic. Unlike the UK, rail travel through Europe can be an entirely pleasurable experience and a great way to avoid spending hours behind the wheel of a car or squashed into a seat on a coach. The Eurostar service between London and Paris has made rail travel to Croatia a plausible and efficient option. You can now leave London at 5pm one day and arrive in Zagreb at 8pm the next.

The quickest route is to take a late afternoon **Eurostar** to Paris, arriving at Gare du Nord and transferring to the Gare de l'Est, which is a short taxi ride or

10-minute walk away. From here, travel on the new sleeper train to Munich, choosing from several accommodation options on board. The most basic option is a berth in a four- or six-bunk couchette, but for a little more you can buy a berth in a standard compartment with a washbasin, and a shared shower and toilet at the end of the corridor. If you want to splash out for some extra comfort, deluxe compartments are available with their own private shower and toilet. After a good night's sleep you arrive in Munich and catch a modern EuroCity train (the Mimara) to Zagreb, via Ljubljana in Slovenia.

Deutsche Bahn (German Rail) offer a special return fare of £159 that covers the entire journey from London to Munich, including the Eurostar to Paris, and a basic couchette on the Paris–Munich sleeper train. Fares for a standard compartment include breakfast. The additional return fare from Munich to Zagreb can be as little as £75 depending on your class of travel. Both tickets can be bought online at **www.bahn.de**, where you can also find timetables and sleeper accommodation information. You can also buy tickets through Deutsche Bahn's UK office (**t** 0870 243 5363) and UK ticket agencies. Timetables for Eurostar are available at **www.eurostar.com**.

For more information and other possible routes, the independent website **www.seat61.com** is full of suggestions, timetables and fares.

By Coach

International coach services connect Croatia with most European countries including the UK.

National Express Eurolines (**t** 08705 80 80 80; **www.nationalexpress.com**) has daily departures from London to Zagreb, which take 33 hours plus an extra seven hours if you continue on to Split. However, the cost of tickets (which can be booked online) makes it cheaper to fly.

By Road

Depending on your start and end point, the drive from the UK to Croatia can be anywhere between 1,500km and 2,500km in distance. This may seem like a daunting journey, but if you intend to move bulky items of furniture or simply the personal belongings that turn a second house into a second home, it is often the only practical option. Many holidaymakers also decide to drive, because they consider the journey an integral part of their vacation. It is certainly a fabulous chance to see and experience more of Europe, especially if you take the time to make one or two detours.

There are any number of possible routes across Europe to Croatia, and your decision is likely to be based on how quickly you want to get there, how much you are willing to spend on tolls to use the faster motorways and whether you'd like to see some scenery on the way. The best way to decide on a route is to use a free online route planner. The better ones, like **www.viamichelin.com** and **www.rac.co.uk**, calculate not just the time and distance of your journey but the cost of tolls and likely fuel usage, and they even flag up roadworks.

Using the fastest (and most toll-heavy) route, the drive can take as little as 16 hours without breaking the legal speed limit. However, most people split the journey into two or even three days and take the opportunity to spend a night in one of the cities or places of interest along the way. Below are just three of the possibilities:

- **The fastest route** (using only motorways and toll roads): cross the Channel to arrive in Calais, then head north to Dunkerque and the Belgian border. Pass close to Bruges (Brugge) and Brussels (Bruxelles) to cross into the Netherlands briefly before entering Germany near Aachen. Head for Cologne (Köln) before crossing Austria via Graz, and traversing Slovenia via Maribor. Enter Croatia on the E59 heading straight for Zagreb.

- **The cheapest route** (avoiding the most expensive toll roads): cross the Channel to arrive in Calais, then head south to Lille before crossing into Belgium. Head straight for Luxembourg and then to the German border. Cross Germany via Stuttgart, entering Austria briefly on the way to Ljubljana in Slovenia. Cross the border into Croatia via the E70.

- **The scenic route** (especially convenient for Istria): from any Channel port in the north of France, head south to Lyon and Geneva across the Alps. Cross the Italian border via the Mont Blanc Tunnel and head straight for Milan. Pass close to Venice on the way to Trieste and briefly enter Slovenia before arriving in Istria.

If you are visiting one of the Dalmatian resorts during the summer, it may be worth considering driving to Italy and taking a short car ferry ride across the Adriatic to Croatia (see 'By Sea', pp.59–60).

Points to Bear in Mind when Driving to Croatia

- Your UK driving licence is recognised in most EU countries but must be carried with you. If you wish to apply for an international driving permit (IDP) you can do this online through the RAC, AA or Greenflag website. The IDP is valid for one year.

- Before departure, check with your car insurance company that you are covered for all the countries you intend to drive through. They should be able to issue you with an insurance green card, which is proof that you have at least third-party insurance (a minimum requirement in all EU countries). Insurance companies don't usually charge for issuing a green card, but some might claim an administration fee. If you decide to travel without a green card, then you must take a copy of your certificate of insurance with you.

- Fuel tends to be particularly pricey in the Netherlands and cheaper in Switzerland and Austria.

- If you are planning to use any of the Alpine tunnels, check that they are open before you leave – particularly in winter. It costs €32 to pass through the Mont Blanc Tunnel, with a discount for a return trip.

- Be aware that if you plan to drive through Switzerland you will be required to pay a one-off motorway tax called the motorway *vignette*. It is valid for multiple entries over one year and can be bought in advance online from **www.swisstravelsystems.co.uk** at a cost of £18.

- Once at the Croatian border, you will need a UK driving licence (the international driving permit is not valid in Croatia), vehicle registration documents and vehicle insurance documents, complete with a green card, in order to enter the country. If your green card doesn't cover Croatia, it is possible to buy third-party insurance at most major border posts, but this really is a last resort.

By Sea

There are no direct ferries from the UK to Croatia, but it is possible to drive to Italy and catch a car ferry across the Adriatic. This may well save you time, particularly if you are travelling to the southern parts of Dalmatia.

A number of companies operate services from Ancona, Bari, Pescara and Venice in Italy to Croatia, but only a few accommodate cars and even fewer are operational all year round. Most crossings are an overnight affair taking anything up to nine hours, but the faster passenger-only ferries can make the trip in just three or four hours.

Main Ferry Companies

- **Azzurra Line (t +385 (0)20 313 178; www.azzurraline.com)** operates weekly sailings between June and September from Bari in Italy to Dubrovnik. Passenger fares start at €61 and to take a car is another €66.

- **Jadrolinija (t (020) 7431 4560; www.jadrolinija.hr)** provides a regular year-round service from Ancona in Italy to Zadar, Split and Stari Grad (on the island of Hvar), from Pescara in Italy to Split and Stari Grad, and from Bari in Italy to Dubrovnik. Passenger fares vary from €45 to €82 one-way depending on the season and are anything from €55 to €119 for a car. There is a 20 per cent discount available on return tickets.

- **SNAV (t +39 0712 076 116; www.snav.it)** sails from Ancona and Pescara in Italy to Split and Dubrovnik, respectively, between June and September. The most basic passenger fare is €83 and €91 for a car but the company regularly runs promotions in which the car can sail for just €1. The crossing on their super-fast ferry takes just 4½ hours.

- **Blue Line (t +385 (0)21 352 533; www.splittours.hr)** departs from Ancona for Split on Monday, Wednesday and Friday evenings, returning the next day. Passenger fares start at €83 and €98 for a car but every seventh trip is free. See the website for more details.

• **Venezia Lines (t +39 041 2424 000; www.venezialines.com)** runs passenger-only ferries from April to October. The company offers regular (but not daily) sailings from Venice to Poreč, Rovinj, Pula and Rabac in Istria and to the island of Mali Lošinj. Fares range from €97 to €125.

• **Mia Tours (t +385 (0)23 254 300; www.miatours.hr)** is another passenger-only service. It sails between Ancona and Zadar in just three hours from June until the end of August on Mondays, Tuesdays, Fridays and Saturdays. Passenger fares are €130.

Travelling around Croatia

Selecting a property inevitably involves a lot of travelling around to meet agents, view potential properties and sound out the local area. You may be concentrating your search in one region or sampling what is on offer in various parts of the country but, either way, you probably won't want to be relying entirely on public transport. Having the use of a car gives you the freedom to get around, which is especially important if you only have a limited amount of time to spend searching for your ideal property. With Croatia's new and vastly improved motorway system it is possible to travel from one region to the next in a matter of hours and cover a large amount of ground in a relatively short space of time. However, the motorways end at Split, leaving the slow and congested coastal road (*Jadranska magistrala*) along the Adriatic as the only access to Dubrovnik and the south Dalmatian coast. Although this road provides a great opportunity to peek at the numerous villages and resorts that hide in the numerous bays and inlets along the Adriatic, you might want to consider flying into and out of Dubrovnik if you are short of time.

By Air

Until the recent development of modern high-speed motorways through much of the country, road travel in Croatia was a time-consuming and frustrating affair. For this reason many Croatians used air travel as a regular way of getting around the country, and still do. The price and frequency of domestic flights make flying an expedient way to get from region to region and can drastically reduce travel times. What would be a 12-hour journey by bus from Zagreb to Dubrovnik takes just 55 minutes by plane, cutting a whole day of travel down to just a few hours. Similarly, flights from Zagreb to Pula, Zadar, Split and most other airports around the country take only 45 minutes, so you can easily access any region in the country within a couple of hours. Air travel may be generally more expensive than bus tickets, but you can often get cheap deals by booking early, and the savings in terms of time and convenience are considerable.

The only airline that provides domestic flights within Croatia is the national carrier, **Croatia Airlines**. It has scheduled flights between all the country's airports, including Osijek airport in the far east of Croatia and tiny Brač airport on the island of the same name, near the popular beach resort of Bol. From Zagreb there are daily flights to Pula and Zadar, two flights a day to Dubrovnik and three flights a day to Split, with an extra flight a day to all locations during the summer peak season. There are also weekly flights from Zagreb to Osijek, Rijeka (on Wednesdays) and Brač (weekends only).

Further information on scheduled flights between airports can be found on the Croatia Airlines website where you can also book tickets online. Otherwise, all airports and most major towns will have a Croatia Airlines office where you can book and pay for tickets on internal flights.

Croatia Airlines
Head Office
Savska cesta 41
10 000 Zagreb
t + 385 (0)1 616 0236
www.croatiaairlines.com

One-way fares on the major scheduled routes tend to be very reasonable, but booking early makes a big difference to the price of a ticket. A one-way fare from Zagreb to Dubrovnik that costs 300 kunas when booked three or four months in advance can be as much as 700 kunas when bought at the last minute. It is worth remembering that there is a 25 per cent discount on domestic flights for passengers aged between 12 and 25.

Croatian airports are usually well connected to their nearest city by Croatia Airlines shuttle buses. Dubrovnik airport is perhaps the furthest out of town, but the bus ride to the centre is just 25 minutes. The only exceptions are Pula and Rijeka, where there is no public transport link between the city and its airport. Pula airport, situated 6km from the city centre, is just a few minutes' taxi ride, but Rijeka airport is 25km south of town and the taxi journey will cost around 200 kunas.

By Road

In preparation for its accession into the EU, Croatia has ploughed vast amounts of money into its road network, and the investment has paid off. Major transport arteries now spread in all directions from Zagreb. They traverse Slavonia to the Serbian border in the east, dart north across Zagorje to Hungary, cross the Slovenian border to connect with Ljubljana and Maribor, travel west via Karlovac to pass through Rijeka and on to Istria, cover the Istrian peninsula from north to south in a big 'Y' shape, and finally slither south along the Adriatic coast as far as Split. In all there is well over 700km of motorway, and there are plans to extend the network still further in the next five years. The long-awaited extension from Split to Ploče is due to open late in 2007, and there are plans to begin the final stretch along the coast to Dubrovnik as soon as 2008.

Tolls are charged on all Croatian motorways, but are not extortionate. The charge depends on the type of vehicle you are driving and how far you travel but, as a guide, driving a standard family car from Zagreb to Split will cost 157 kunas. Drivers are issued a ticket from automatic tollbooths as they drive onto a motorway, and pay the relevant charge as they exit. The tollbooths accept cash, credit cards, cheques and even euros. There are additional charges for using longer tunnels and bridges. For example the Učka Tunnel, which connects Rijeka and Istria, costs an additional 28 kunas one way. All the way along the new motorways there are large rest areas with amenities, and you will pass 24-hour petrol stations at no more than 45km intervals. **Petrol stations** offer a choice of lead-free 95, lead-free 98 and diesel, with prices noticeably below those in the UK. Croatian Motorways (Hrvatske Autoceste), the state-owned company that operates, constructs and maintains all of Croatia's motorways, has a website (**www.hac.hr**) with information on road conditions including updates on maintenance roadworks and webcams that monitor congestion at busy tolls.

Beyond the motorways, Croatian roads are generally in a good state of repair, although they get rougher the further you travel from the main towns and urban areas. The *Jadranska magistrala*, which currently extends beyond the end of the motorway at Split all the way along the Adriatic to Dubrovnik, is

The Croatian Automobile Club

If you are planning to drive to or around Croatia, the website of the Hrvatski Autoklub (HAK; **www.hak.hr**) is an invaluable resource. It provides **information** on the latest road and traffic conditions across Croatia, including congestion at border crossings and disruptions to ferry services. You can also compare the latest fuel prices in all European countries including Croatia, read weather forecasts, and find rates for motorway tolls across the country. If you don't have access to the Internet, this information is available from anywhere in Croatia or abroad on the HAK 24hr phone line (t +385 (0)1 464 0800 and press 0 after the answering machine for English).

If you have mechanical trouble, the HAK provides a nationwide **breakdown recovery service** that can be accessed by ringing **t 987** from any phone, anywhere in the country. They send out local contractors at a flat-rate charge of 160 kunas for up to 30 minutes' work and will tow your vehicle, if necessary, to anywhere within a 20km radius. Thereafter, it is 60 kunas for each additional 30 minutes of assistance and 5 kunas per kilometre towed. The charges increase by 30 per cent on Sundays and public holidays, but if you are a member of a foreign automobile club you may be eligible for a 10 per cent discount on all services.

simultaneously one of the worst and best roads in the country. It twists and turns along the coast, with fantastic views of the Adriatic islands on one side and the highland mountains on the other, making it a pure delight if you have the time to take in the scenery. Otherwise it can be a torturous journey, prone to slow-moving traffic. During the busy summer weekends it is hell on earth, despite the pretty views.

Finding your way around is not usually a problem, as both motorways and secondary roads are well **signposted**. In fact, if anything, the problem is too many signs. You will often find roadsides littered with placards pointing the way to everything from the nearest airport to the local pizzeria. Sometimes this is incredibly helpful – such as the municipal signs in all major towns that show the way to a selection of local hotels – but more often they are simply distracting, and one thing you will soon realise about driving on Croatian roads is that you need all your wits about you. This is a country where tailgating seems to be a national sport and overtaking (usually on blind bends into oncoming traffic) is an art form. Croatians are aggressive drivers, and the roads take some getting used to for the uninitiated. **Speeding** is common, despite the possibility of on-the-spot fines ranging from 300 kunas to 1,000 kunas and immediate driving bans of up to three months. Police use roadside speed traps and tend to lurk in places along busy main roads where they can see you, long before you notice them. Don't assume that being a tourist or foreign national will excuse you. Most police speak excellent English and dole out the same penalties to tourists and locals alike.

Speed limits are clearly signed on most roads and are given in kilometres per hour. Unless stated otherwise, national speed limits throughout Croatia are:

- **50 km/h in built-up areas.**
- **90 km/h outside built-up areas.**
- **110 km/h on main roads.**
- **130 km/h on motorways.**
- **80 km/h for any vehicle towing a caravan or trailer.**

Police issue on-the-spot fines for minor traffic offences such as overtaking on a solid white line, and these can be more expensive than speeding fines. There are several other **rules of the road** that it is wise to be aware of.

- **Wearing seatbelts in the front and back seats of a vehicle is obligatory.**
- **Headlights must be switched on whenever you are driving, day or night.**
- **Children must be at least 12 years old to sit in the front seat.**
- **It is illegal to use a mobile phone while driving.**
- **The blood-alcohol limit in Croatia is zero. Drivers are not permitted to have any alcohol in their blood at all when driving, and random breath tests are commonplace. Refusing a breath test is regarded as an automatic admission of guilt.**

- **You are required to carry a fluorescent vest in the car (rather than the boot) at all times and to wear it in the event of a breakdown.**

Whether you are driving a hire car or your own British-registered vehicle, you are obliged by law to have both the vehicle registration and insurance documents with you at all times. You should also carry your UK driving licence, which is valid for up to six months after first entering the country. If you are driving your own British-registered car, make sure that your vehicle registration documents have a green card that covers Croatia. You will also need coverage for Bosnia-Herzegovina if you intend to cross the Neum corridor – which is unavoidable if you want to drive to or from Dubrovnik.

Beware that many Croatian cities, towns and villages, particularly along the Adriatic, have narrow streets and old medieval centres that are completely pedestrianised. This gives rise to complex one-way systems and impossible parking. The only option in many cases is to park outside the old town either on the street or in haphazard parking lots. In both cases you will be expected to find a staffed parking booth, where you pay in advance for the hours you require. You are then given a separate ticket for each hour, which you display in your car. Parking is not expensive but is limited in many towns.

Car Hire

Hiring a car is an easy and convenient way to ensure that you have your own set of wheels, and you will be supplied with a left-hand-drive vehicle with all the necessary insurance and registration papers. Hiring a car in Croatia is much the same as hiring a car anywhere else in the world. All the big multinational car hire companies, such as Avis (**www.avis.com**), National (**www.nationalcar.com**) and Europcar (**www.europcar.com**), have outlets in Croatia's main airports and cities, but better deals can be found with smaller Internet-based companies such as **www.economycarhire.com** and **www.economycarrentals.com** as well as through price comparison sites like **www.carrentals.co.uk**.

The cost of car hire in Croatia is generally reasonable if you arrange it as far in advance of your visit as possible. Watch out for mileage limits, which can prove costly, and for additional insurance, which is often unnecessary. If you pay by credit card, check to see what insurance cover this affords you automatically. Some companies have a minimum age restriction of 21 or 25 years for drivers, and others insist that drivers must have held a licence for at least a year. Otherwise, all you need to hire a car is a credit card and a valid UK driving licence. All registration and insurance documents for the car should be supplied when you pick up the car in Croatia. Traffic drives on the right in Croatia, so take extra care to remember this for the first couple of days if you are used to doing the opposite, as it can be confusing, particularly at busy or complex junctions.

If you need a car for months rather than weeks it is worth investigating the possibility of leasing rather than hiring a car. This may work out significantly

Profiles
of the Regions

Inland Croatia

Bordered by Slovenia, Hungary, Serbia and Montenegro, inland Croatia is very Central European in style, cuisine and attitude. Stretching from the hilly regions of the Zagorje in the west to the flat, fertile, flood plains of Slavonia in the east, the region is a rural landscape of vineyards, pastures and tumbledown, timber-framed farmhouses. Almost every house has its own barn or orchard, haystacks litter the fields, and there is a strong sense of community within the tiny villages.

As well as rustic appeal, inland Croatia can boast a wealth of cultural attractions. Croatian as well as foreign tourists come to the region to see the medieval fortresses and castles that crown the forested hills along the Slovenian border, request heavenly favours at the many magnificent Marian pilgrimage sites, or attend the frequent music festivals held in the Austro-Hungarian centres of Varaždin and Osijek.

At the heart of the region is Zagreb, the political, cultural and economic focus of the country. It is here that the pace of change since the 1990s has been most rapid and where the signs of Croatia's emergence as a modern European nation are most visible. The narrow streets of the old city wind between pastel-coloured buildings to spill out onto pedestrian squares packed with pavement cafés and slick-fronted shops. However, despite the espressos and gridlocked traffic, Zagreb still has something comfortably provincial about it. Men with accordions spark

impromptu sing-songs on the street and, in the central Dolac food market, matriarchs wearing headscarves sell pungent home-made cheeses and freshly pressed olive oil in cordial bottles.

1 *Mirogoj cemetery, Zagreb*
2 *Waterfall, Lonjsko Polje National Park*

3

4

5

3 Osijek, Slavonia
4 Trakošćan Castle, Zagorje
5 Art Pavilion, Donji grad, Zagreb
6 Veliki Tabor, Zagorje

Central Croatia

Central Croatia is a term generally used to describe several small but distinct regions that cover the territory between the coast and Zagreb. It's a jumbled blend of landscapes that is often ignored in the stampede to the coast, and yet it contains some of Croatia's most lovely natural wonders. Plitvice Lakes National Park, the country's single greatest tourist attraction, is nestled within the central upland Lika region. Covered by forest and criss-crossed by yawning canyons, the scenery is wild and largely unspoilt. Moving towards the coast, the region flattens out into rolling grassland, fenced in by the glittering snow-capped peaks of the Velebit mountains. Despite being only a few hours' drive from some of Croatia's largest cities, this part of

central Croatia can feel very remote. The sleepy villages that span the lonely roads have been all but abandoned, rambling wooden houses sit in acres of land, and the only people you are likely to see are the shepherds tending their grazing sheep.

Opposite page (Inland Croatia)
7 *Village church*
8 *Fishing on the river Drava*
Above
1 *Plitvice Lakes National Park*
2 *Paklenica National Park*

Coastal Croatia

Istria

Since the 1960s, Istria's endless sun-drenched coastline has drawn large numbers of holidaymakers from all over Europe, particularly Germany, Austria, Italy and the UK. The region's near-perfect climate can boast 2,700 hours of sunshine a year, which warms the crystal waters of the Adriatic to an inviting 26°C. Never too cold and never unbearably hot, temperatures rise to a maximum of 30°C in the summer and rarely fall below 5°C in the winter.

Quiet fishing villages and ancient Mediterranean fortress towns, like Rovinj, Poreč and Novigrad, have grown into well-developed seaside resorts that continue to expand. Large campsites with modern amenities, family-friendly water parks and new villa developments line the western shore of the peninsula, ready to welcome the summer tourists. Inland, the clutter of the coast is replaced by pastoral scenes of forested valleys and pudding-bowl hills topped with the tiled roofs of historic medieval towns. Wandering through the cobbled streets of Motovun or Buzet, gazing at a sweeping view of fields, vineyards and far off-mountains, it is forgivable to feel that you are in the heart of Italian Tuscany. The lure of crisp white wine and

locally sourced truffles beckons from every café and restaurant, with each village hawking its very own gastronomic speciality.

Istria is for many the perfect mix of old and new. Luxury villas complete with modern comforts are built in a traditional style, villages set in remote hills are actually only a few hours' drive from the nearest airport, and even the busiest tourist towns have managed to keep a strong sense of their historic character.

1 Mosaic floor, Basilica of Euphrasius, Poreč
2 Rovinj
3 Venetian-Gothic architecture, Poreč
4 Sailing boats

5 Roman amphitheatre, Pula
6 Catch of the day
7 Brijuni National Park

Kvarner

Kvarner is the coastal region that surrounds the Kvarner Gulf, a sheltered stretch of the Adriatic scattered with islands. Some of these islands are no more than large boulders barely peeping above the waves; those of most interest are Krk, Cres, Lošinj, Rab and Pag. Pag is a barren rock of an island where a stubby covering of sage bushes provides the only vegetation, but, on neighbouring Rab, pine forests fringe the sandy beaches and shade its rambling medieval towns. Lošinj has a similarly verdant covering of Aleppo pine and is connected to the larger island of Cres. Although both islands experience a tourist explosion in the summer, thanks to their accessibility, their villages have managed to retain much of their traditional character and are enchanting places to stay.

Back on the mainland, Rijeka gleams with polished pedestrian streets and glittering fashion emporiums, while further south the coastal road clings to the foot of the Velebit mountains, which rise dramatically out of the sea along the shore.

1 Crikvenica
2 Coastline, Pag island

3 Seafront apartments, Opatija, near Rijeka
4 Krk island
5 Trsat, Rijeka
6 Rab town, Rab island

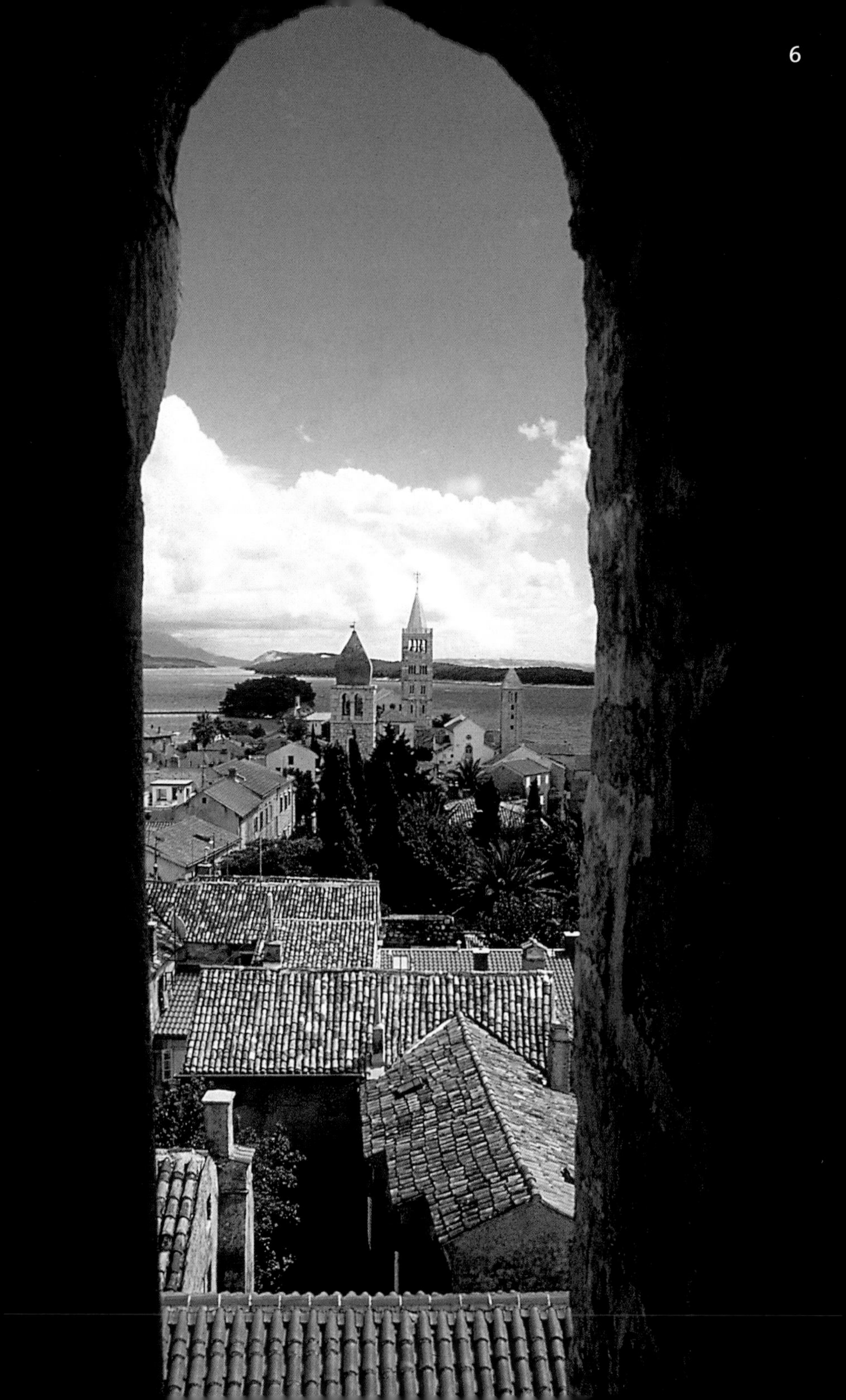

Dalmatia

Dalmatia is often touted by locals as the 'land of a thousand islands', and they mean it quite literally. So many islands crowd into the 350km stretch of Adriatic coastline that it is impossible to tell where one island ends and another begins. Beneath pale, sun-bleached mountains the tattered shore crumbles into an endless string of bays, inlets, coves and headlands. Each fold in the mountains conceals isolated sweeps of wheat-coloured sand, pools of vibrantly blue water, lush forests that flood the sheltered bays and ancient stone villages with terracotta roofs. The climate and scenery are heavily reminiscent of the Mediterranean, a similarity that is reinforced by the laid-back approach to life and strong family bonds displayed by the locals.

Dalmatia is littered with an abundance of cultural heritage, including some of the best-preserved Greek, Roman and medieval architecture in the world. Split, the largest city in Dalmatia, incorporates slick cafés, funky boutiques and contemporary restaurants into the narrow medieval streets of the old town, which is itself cradled in the ruins of a Roman palace. Dubrovnik appears even less affected by the passage of time. Medieval monasteries, Baroque cathedrals and Venetian palaces encircled by thick city walls seem unchanged by the centuries, except for the discreet cafés and boutiques hidden in the city's maze-like streets.

1 *Cathedral of St Lawrence, Trogir*
2 *Pleasure boats, Hvar*
3 *Cathedral of St Domnius, Split*
4 *Ochre-washed coastal houses*
5 *Murter island*

6 Church, Posedarje
7 Church of St Donatus, Zadar

7

6

cheaper in the long term. You can find more information at the website of Raiffeisen Leasing Croatia (**www.rl-hr.hr**).

By Bus and Coach

Public bus and coach transport in Croatia is well regarded by locals and visitors alike. Large inter-city coaches ply all the main routes between major towns and cities, while the smaller towns and islands are serviced by a dense network of local buses.

Coach travel has traditionally been the cheapest and most popular form of long-distance transport in Croatia, but, now that recent government policies have focused on the maintenance and improvement of the country's road system, it is also a convenient and efficient way to move around. New and better roads continue to cut travel times, so Zagreb is approximately 11 hours from Dubrovnik, 10 hours from Pula and four hours from Osijek by coach. Inter-city coaches are modern, comfortable and frequent, with hourly departures on popular routes and overnight travel over longer distances.

At first glance the system may seem slightly overwhelming. Each inter-city route is run by several private coach companies, so it is hard to get an overview of services, but **coach stations** (*autobusna stanica*), found in almost every town, are easy places to navigate and to find information. There you can check the timetables and buy tickets in advance. Coach stations in major cities are generally centrally located. Zagreb bus station (**t** 060 313 333 within Croatia for 24-hour information on departures and arrivals, or use the search engine at **www.akz.hr**) is 20 minutes' walk from the very centre of the city; in Dubrovnik the bus station is located in a port suburb 3km west of town; and Split bus station is next to the city's railway station.

The cost of coach travel is extremely reasonable and is charged by kilometre. There is an extra charge for luggage (around 6 kunas per item), which is loaded into the hold underneath the bus and must be collected when you get off. If the coach route involves a section by ferry the fare will usually be included in the price of the coach ticket.

Local buses on the islands and in rural areas are less comfortable than the inter-city coaches. They tend to be older machines that can get unbearably hot and stuffy during the summer but are only used for shorter trips. Coverage is generally good in the valleys, but services become less frequent in the more remote or mountainous areas. There is also likely to be a reduced service at the weekends. Nevertheless, even the smallest village will have some kind of regular bus connection to the nearest large town. Tickets can be bought in advance from kiosks and are cancelled during each journey by a punching machine on the bus. You can buy tickets from the driver when you board, but they are likely to be marginally more expensive and you must always have the correct change.

By Rail

The state-owned company **Croatian Railways** (Hrvatske Željeznice) manages and maintains all domestic and international passenger rail services throughout Croatia. The handy website **www.hznet.hr** provides information in English about timetables, train connections and ticket prices across the country.

Travel by train in Croatia is about 15 per cent cheaper than by bus or coach, but the rail network is not as extensive. There are rail links between major towns and cities, but local services are sparse, with coverage in coastal regions being particularly meagre. The bigger Adriatic towns like Pula, Rijeka and Split are connected directly to Zagreb but not to each other and, as with the motorways, there are no rail services at all beyond Split.

Croatian Railways operates two types of train. **Intercity (IC)** trains are modern, comfortable and reliable. They are fast express trains and so are correspondingly more expensive than other services but are more or less guaranteed to leave and arrive on time. Tickets are usually the same price whether you buy a single or a return and seat reservations are often obligatory. You are typically given the choice of first or second class as well as smoking or non-smoking carriages. There is a daily overnight IC service from Zagreb to Split which leaves around 11pm and arrives before 7am the next morning. Passengers are offered various sleeping options ranging from single to three-berth compartments. **Local trains** (*putnički*) tend to be older and less comfortable than the ICs. They make multiple stops at the smaller stations in between the larger towns and so tend to be very slow but are usually punctual and dependable.

Railway stations in rural areas are little more than a small building at the side of the tracks but in the cities they are nearly always centrally located or close to the ferry port for convenience. Arrivals and departures are clearly displayed, and you can ask for further information at the ticket counter, where you can also buy tickets in advance. If the ticket office is closed, you can buy tickets from the conductor once you are on the train.

By Sea

Croatia relies heavily on ferries. Local ferries provide the only access to all but two of the inhabited Adriatic islands and, in the absence of any coastal rail link or motorway beyond Split, coastal ferries provide a vital link between north and south Dalmatia. For Croatians living in the littoral regions, journeys by ferry are as commonplace as catching a bus, but for visitors it is often a highlight of their trip. The vessels weave through the offshore islands, providing matchless views that it is impossible to get from the mainland as well as wonderful maritime scenery. On the daily coastal ferry that travels between Rijeka to Dubrovnik there is nothing to do but relax and soak up the coastal panorama which, for many, is a far more appealing prospect than sitting behind the wheel of a car.

Jadrolinija is the state-run ferry company that operates all the major local and coastal routes in Croatia; there is a reduced service throughout the winter. There are Jadrolinija offices in almost every town along the coast but the main ferry ports are: Rijeka for the coastal ferry to Dubrovnik; Zadar for local ferries to the Zadar archipelago including Ugljan and Dugi otok; Split for local ferries to most of the Dalmatian islands including Brač, Hvar and Vis; and Dubrovnik for local ferries to the Elafiti Islands and the coastal ferry to Rijeka. In the Jadrolinija offices you can find information on prices and sailings, but you need a diploma in order to decipher the complex schedule information without help. The Jadrolinija website (**www.jadrolinija.hr**) is a lot more useful, with clear fare advice and sailing timetables, in English, for all local and coastal routes.

Passenger fares for local ferry routes are rarely more than 50 kunas per person one-way. There is no reduction for buying a return, but there is a 50 per cent discount for children under 12. Tickets for sailings must be bought in advance from Jadrolinija offices and kiosks on the harbour but cannot be reserved in advance, so there is often a long wait for busy crossings during the summer. Coastal ferries are more expensive. A passenger fare from Rijeka to Split in a four-berth couchette is just under 300 kunas, while the fare from Rijeka to Dubrovnik in a deluxe cabin with a private bathroom is nearly 1,000 kunas. Tickets for coastal ferries have a 20 per cent discount if you buy a return and can be reserved in advance by calling the Jadrolinija office in the relevant ferry port or a Jadrolinija agent. The main **Jadrolinija offices** are in Dubrovnik (**t** +385 (0)20 41 80 00/83 80); Rijeka (**t** +385 (0)51 21 14 44/66 61 00); Split (**t** +385 (0)21 33 83 33/04/05), and Zadar (**t** +385 (0)23 25 05 55/48 00). The addresses and contact numbers of all Jadrolinija offices and agents can be found on the Jadrolinija website (**www.jadrolinija.hr**).

On both coastal and local ferry routes, the cost of **taking a car** depends on its length and size. Taking a regular family saloon can cost as much as 670 kunas on the longest coastal routes and as little as 80 kunas on the shortest local journeys. In low season (mid-September to mid-June) both car and passenger fares fall by about 30 per cent.

During the summer Jadrolinija is joined by numerous private ferry companies making the most of the seasonal trade. Some of these companies ply the same routes as Jadrolinija, while others offer new ones or offer slightly different itineraries. Most of these seasonal services are passenger-only and have their own ticket kiosks at the ferry ports down on the harbour front. **Split Tours** (**t** +385 (0)21 352 533; **www.splittours.hr**) operates passenger catamarans that sail between Split and the islands of Brač, Šolta and Vis as well as a car ferry that runs between Split and Brač. Further north, **Mia Tours** (**t** +385 (0)23 254 300; **www.miatours.hr**) provides a passenger service by hydrofoil between Zadar and the local islands. Despite all the extra sailings, ferry crossings to the islands become extremely busy during high season, and if you are taking a car you will need to turn up several hours in advance.

Climate and Geography

Geography

Croatia has an awkward, wonky horseshoe shape rather like a wishbone. Istria in the far west forms the central bulge of the bone, while two pincer-like arms protrude southward, draped either side of Bosnia-Herzegovina. If you put all this linear territory together, the total area of Croatia is a little over 56,500 square kilometres, which is approximately a quarter of the size of England or a touch bigger than Switzerland. It may not be the largest of European countries, but with a population of less than five million it is certainly one of the most spacious. As a result of its unusually spread-out shape, Croatia shares borders with Slovenia, Hungary and Serbia as well as Bosnia-Herzegovina. In fact the country's most southerly arm, which stretches out along the Dalmatian coast, is completely severed by a 20km wide tract of Bosnia-Herzegovina territory at Neum. Officially the Neum Corridor completely isolates the region around Dubrovnik from the rest of Croatia, but in reality, despite the flags and border posts, the political oddity causes little disruption.

Geographically, Croatia can be split into three distinct regions: Pannonian, mountainous and coastal. The Pannonian Basin covers most of inland Croatia and is part of a vast swath of rich, fertile land that stretches across a substantial

Earthquakes

Beneath the waves of the Adriatic Sea the Adriatic platform slowly pushes east, colliding with the Dinarides, which range along the Croatian coastline. The geology leaves Croatia prone to low-level seismic activity. Earthquakes aren't common, but every few years a moderate tremor will surprise everybody and add a few cracks to old, crumbling houses. A thick strip of Dalmatia along the Bosnia-Herzegovina border from Dinara mountain near the city of Knin stretching southward to Imotski and Metković, is the most susceptible. Every few years the region will experience an earthquake around 4.0 on the Richter Scale, which is large enough to shake the ground but isn't likely to do any serious damage. Surprisingly, the other region of Croatia that is particularly susceptible is around Zagreb and the northern part of inland Croatia. Every few years the city experiences a mild tremor, but the strongest quakes are reported in the area around the Kalnik mountains and Bednja river valley to the north. However, the last earthquake in Croatia to cause any significant damage was back in 1996. Centred on the southern Dalmatian towns of Ston and Slano near Dubrovnik, the earthquake, which measured 6.0 on the Richter Scale, damaged or destroyed 90 per cent of properties and left over 1,500 people living in temporary accommodation throughout the following winter. Thankfully, earthquakes of this magnitude are a rare occurrence.

part of central Europe. It was once the floor of an immense inland sea that spread from the Alps in the east to the Balkan mountains in the west and from the Dinaric Alps in the south to the Carpathian Mountains in the north. The result is an expanse of flat, agricultural flood plain crossed by wide, snaking rivers. In places there are pockets of low, rolling hills, never higher than 500m, interspersed with lush, humid valleys.

Croatia's mountainous region forms a long strip right the way across the country from Istria to the very southern tip of Dalmatia. The highest mountains are arranged along the Bosnia-Herzegovina border in southern Dalmatia, with the 1,831m peak of Dinara edging above the rest to claim the highest summit in Croatia. Further north, above the Makarska Riviera, the Biokovo rise to a height of 1,762m, forming a spectacular elevated plateau. The plateau, like many of Croatia's mountains, has a strange eroded geology known as karst. The soft limestone rock is gradually carved by water into gorges, caves and mesmerising rock formations. Water sinks into underground river systems, leaving the rock above to be baked by the summer heat and scoured by the dry winter wind. With little moisture, the soil dries to dust, turning the mountains into a barren wilderness devoid of animal life, and of flora save for hardy grasses and lichen. This stark wall of rock acts as a divide between the fertile Pannonian Basin of inland Croatia and the country's third geographical region, the narrow coastal strip squeezed between the mountains and the sea.

Croatia has the most indented coastline in Europe, mustering an incredible 1,777 kilometres of rocky headland and sheltered inlet. If you add the islands, Croatia has a shoreline that is nearly 6,000 kilometres long. The islands, all 1,185 of them, are surprisingly mountainous. This is because they are actually the peaks of underwater mountains belonging to the Dinaric chain. Unlike their mainland cousins, the island peaks tend to be more verdant, covered with forests that thrive in the temperate Mediterranean climate. Approximately half of Croatia is covered in woodland, the majority state-owned to ensure its protection and conservation.

One reason for the country's fertility is that Croatia is an extremely water-abundant country. Inland Croatia is home to the Sava, Drava and Dunav (Danube) that together weave for over 1,000km across Croatian soil while their flood plains give rise to hundreds of hectares of precious wetland, some of the most unique and valuable in Europe. On the coast, rivers like the Krka, Zrmanja and Cetina tend to be shorter and faster as they cut through the mountains on their way to the sea, frothing in a series of spectacular rapids and waterfalls. Croatia's lakes are not vast (the largest is Vrana near Biograd, covering just 30 square kilometres) but what they lack in size they makes up for in splendour, with several of the country's lakes famed for their beauty including Plitvice, Prukljan near Šibenik, and Vrana on the island of Cres.

Climate

The band of mountainous uplands that cuts Croatia in half also creates a distinct dichotomy in climate. Inland Croatia is shielded from the mild and humid air of the coast and instead has a climate more in keeping with central Europe. Winters are cold, while summers are warm and wet. Zagreb enjoys an annual maximum of nine hours of sunshine per day in July and August, while the wettest months are May, June, October and November. In contrast, on the other side of the mountains Split receives heavy winter rainfall in November and December, and hot, dry summers, basking in an annual maximum of 11 hours of sunshine per day in June, July and August. For more detailed temperature and rainfall charts, *see* **References**, 'Climate Charts', p.210.

Winters along the coast are mild, with warm Adriatic currents, and sea temperatures never falling below 10°C; the mountains act as a shelter from the cold continental winds. In summer the heat, which can be oppressive, is pleasantly tempered by cooling sea breezes. The *maestral* starts around noon and blows from the sea onto the shore, while the *tramontana* from the north cools the evenings on clear days. Less welcome is the *jugo*, a wind from the southwest that blows onshore along the entire coast in spring and autumn, bringing with it rain, humidity and the occasional thunderstorm. However, the most bothersome wind of all is the infamous *bura*, sometimes announced by cloudcaps forming over the Velebit. Cold, dry air rushes down the mountains in blasts lasting several hours, reaching moderate speeds of 11 metres a second. At the water's edge the gusts lift sea-spray into the air, causing what locals call 'sea dust', coating the scrub in sea salt. The *bura* is unpredictable but tends to start in the morning and occurs more frequently during the winter. The advantage is that the *bura* always leaves behind clear, sunny weather, as if in apology for its rude but brief intrusion.

When to Go

Croatia's clement climate invites house-hunting at pretty much any time of year. If you plan to pack a lot into your visit you might want to avoid the summer heat, particularly if your search is concentrated on the coastal regions. In high season the coastal roads become congested and the ferries to the islands rapidly fill up, making travelling from one place to another quickly nigh on impossible. If you travel out of season you escape the most exhausting weather and there are fewer people around. Winter is low season, but your trip might be blighted by bad weather and it can be difficult to see the true potential of a place in the pouring rain or concealed by sea mists. The optimum compromise is to plan your viewing trip in spring when the days are warming up, late summer when the worst of the crowds have gone home, or autumn when the forests are at their most glorious.

Croatian property agents are keen for business and will usually accommodate weekend as well as weekday house-hunting visits at any time of the year as long as they are prearranged. Obvious exceptions are Christmas, New Year and Easter. From May through to the end of September many property agents in Croatia stay open over the weekends to oblige drop-in enquirers, but don't bank on finding a notary or lawyer willing to work on a Sunday.

Choosing a Location

The success of your property venture will be determined almost entirely by one single factor – its location. No matter how perfect the property, if it is located next to a cement works, can only be accessed on foot or is prone to flooding for a certain part of the year, what seemed like a dream come true can quickly reveal itself to be a nightmare. Your personal attraction to a location is only one of a whole raft of considerations and should often come lower on the list of priorities than it actually does. Those priorities are likely to be very different depending on your motivation for buying. The distance to the nearest airport and the wealth of local tourist attractions are important issues if you are looking for an investment or rental property, whereas the standard of local schools and healthcare facilities may be a greater concern if you are intending to move to the area permanently.

It is a good idea to make a list of your own personal priorities before you start visiting properties, and to use it as a checklist as you go. Viewing trips are often thrilling affairs, with a certain amount of pressure to make decisions. In these circumstances it is very easy to get swept up in the moment and carried away by the ideal without taking a close enough look at the reality. Having a physical checklist will help you to identify the pros and cons of all aspects of a potential property's location and ultimately make the right choices.

This section presents some practical issues that you might want to include on your list as well as some tips and advice on finding the right location that have been passed on from other house-hunters.

Country Life

When deciding whether a pastoral existence is for you, remember to strip away some of the gloss and look at the reality. Country life isolates you from the stress of the city but also from the nearest tradesman with the spare parts necessary to fix your immersion heater. You get closer to nature but will encounter all its forms, including pests, vermin and the neighbours' chickens sauntering over your lawn. If a full-on rural retreat is daunting, look for a place closer to town.

Shopping

Living in a place where meat is bought from a butcher's, bread from a bakery and eggs from the lady next door might be an important part of the experience you are craving. For others, a hair-raising 40-minute drive along mountain roads to buy a replacement light bulb might not be so alluring. Investigate what is stocked by the local shops and how far you would have to travel for those creature comforts you can't live without.

Healthcare

The standard and availability of both private and state-run healthcare centres such as hospitals and dental surgeries varies from region to region. If you regularly need repeat prescriptions or require check-ups for an existing medical problem, find out how far you would have to travel for appointments. You may also want to consider the coverage of emergency services in the area.

Schools

If you wish to send your children to a private or international school, this is likely to determine the locality of your property, as there are very few of them in Croatia. Otherwise you will need to check whether there are places for your children in a local state-run school and how far they would have to travel each day.

Amenities

The selection and proximity of various amenities is likely to be a factor in your decision whether you are buying a holiday home for yourself or to let to others. Golf courses, marinas, swimming pools, cultural attractions, cinemas, restaurants, nightclubs, hiking areas and water sports are all factors buyers commonly bear in mind, but a good local beach is often the make-or-break issue.

Transport

Think about door-to-door travel times from the UK to the property you are viewing. If it is difficult to reach for a weekend stay, this might limit the amount of use you get out of it. Similarly, a property within easy reach of an airport served by direct flights from the UK will be a lot more successful as a holiday let. If you plan to live and work in Croatia, easy access to an airport may also be important, as might commuter links to the nearest city.

Budget

Everybody likes value for money, and location is key to getting the most out of your budget. For example, a ground-floor apartment in a desirable suburb of Dubrovnik will cost the same as a four-bedroom stone villa with its own pool in

Istria. It comes down to personal choice, but if you are struggling to find what you want at a price you are happy with in a particular location, widening your search to include neighbouring towns and villages could save you thousands of kunas.

Expatriate Communities

The British are relative newcomers on the Croatian scene, which has always been dominated by the Italians and Germans. Every June the Italians start to arrive along the coast, filling the semi-permanent campsites along Istria's western shore and making Croatia their summer home until the end of August. Meanwhile German holidaymakers and second-home-owners tend to congregate in the Makarska Riviera resorts and the string of Kaštela towns north of Split. In these areas, shop signs and hotel advertisements are commonly written in German as well as Croatian to make their guests feel at home.

The number of British expatriates in Croatia is still too small to have formed into distinct communities, and most people seeking a new life in the country seem to prefer it that way. British home-owners are enough of a rarity that locals will quickly alert you to any fellow countrymen living in the area, particularly if you spend time in your property out of season or live away from the main resorts. If there is any pattern at all, expatriates from the UK tend to gravitate more towards Dubrovnik, Istria and the island of Brač than any other region, but they are well integrated into the local community. Wherever you settle you will find other Brits if you go looking, but equally you will have no trouble going for months without hearing another British accent.

Useful Tips

Some advice from fellow house-hunters on choosing a location in Croatia:

- **Always get out of the car and take a good walk around the nearest town or village rather than simply driving through. You will get a much better feel for what type of community you would be joining and the sort of amenities that are available.**

- **Talk to locals and potential neighbours. They will be an invaluable source of knowledge about the surrounding area and are likely to be far more open about any local issues that may cause a problem than an estate agent or seller.**

- **Seek out other expatriates in the area and ask them about their experiences. This is often the only way to find out the reality of life in an area through foreign eyes.**

- **If possible, try to visit the property or area at different times of the day and at the weekend. You may discover that the wonderfully lethargic fishing village you love turns into a frenzied beach resort at the weekends,** or the market town that bustles during the day turns into a tumbleweed alley in the evenings.

• Often the hardest thing is to imagine what a property or location will be like at a different time of year. This is particularly important if you intend to spend a significant portion of the year in your new home. If you visit in summer, remember that a good number of businesses along the coast shut during the winter and that the weather in some regions of Croatia can get quite cold.

Choosing a Property

Croatian Homes

Thanks to the excellent preservation of its illustrious heritage, which extends back thousands of years, Croatia can boast a remarkable variety of architectural styles from Romanesque to Renaissance to Baroque. In terms of the property market there is an equally impressive array of options, ranging from traditional stone cottages to contemporary luxury apartments. With such a wide selection of properties, there is guaranteed to be something to suit all tastes.

The greatest range of traditional styles can be found across continental Croatia, where houses are more common than apartments. It is not unusual for houses to be arranged over three floors rather than two, and it is a typically Croatian design to have the main entrance to the house on the first floor rather than on the ground. The door is reached via an external stairwell covered by its own porch. Each region has its own characteristics, but, generally speaking, the further you travel from the urban centres, the more you notice wood replacing brick as the material of choice. The most famous wooden architecture is found in the Lonjsko Polje region, where the traditional dark-wood houses have distinctive pointed roofs and scalloped wooden roof tiles.

Along the coast and on the islands, traditional houses with their stone façades and terracotta roofs often sit cheek-by-jowl with modern apartment blocks and holiday homes. Many of the new buildings have been constructed by an enterprising local or a small co-operative, and consist of no more than two or three apartments in a single block. These sorts of properties tend to have a similar style, featuring shaded balconies and neutral tones.

At their heart, coastal and island towns often have a historic core dating back to the Middle Ages, presenting an opportunity to own a little slice of history – providing you are willing to take the property as it comes. The potential for even the slightest alteration is usually restricted both by Croatian law and the limited available space. Medieval buildings are tall and narrow, with small rooms branching off a steep central staircase that spirals up through the landings. Some have a roof terrace but most have no outside space whatsoever, and receive very little natural light thanks to the tightly packed streets. You will find similar properties in the ancient hilltop towns of inland Istria, but these have the added allure of dramatic views across the surrounding countryside from their lofty vantage points. Croatia is one of the few places in the world that has the ability, every once in a while, to throw up a historic property that is truly unique, such as the house built into the city walls of Dubrovnik or the two-floored apartment set into the ruins of Diocletian's Palace in Split. The cost will reflect the rarity of this sort of property, but the satisfaction of owning something so exceptional, if you can afford it, must be priceless.

Property Types

Off-Plan Properties

Buying 'off-plan' means that you are purchasing a property before it has been built. You are not able to see the finished product before you pay for it and you may have to wait months or even years before you can move into or let your new investment – but buying off-plan has important advantages. Prices are significantly lower than for equivalent properties that have already been completed, and during construction the capital invested continues to grow. You have a longer period over which to make payments, and you get to have a say in the fixtures and furnishings of the new building, from the kitchen and bathroom suites to the colour of the walls.

Plots of Land

Plots of land are readily available all over Croatia, but very little of it has planning permission. Some land includes outbuildings, which can then be knocked down and new buildings, using the same footprint, put in their place.

Modern Apartments

Modern apartments are usually part of a larger development where a single building has been split into a number of separate units. One-bedroom apartments are the most popular, but two- and three-bedroom apartments are also common. They are nearly always close to the sea, and some developments offer a number of communal facilities or services such as landscaped grounds, access to a private marina or a swimming pool.

Urban Apartments

In the centre of the old coastal cities, apartments are hard to find and are usually tiny. You are generally forced to search in modern areas that surround the historic districts. In Dubrovnik the apartments in suburbs with a view over the old city are the most desirable. You can occasionally find wonderful urban apartments in the Baroque centres of inland Croatia, like Zagreb and Varaždin.

Old Stone Houses

Old stone houses are part of what makes the fishing villages of the Dalmatian coast and associated islands so alluring. Many of the old properties have been renovated and are now highly sought after. Stone houses in well-known places like Hvar sell quickly, but there are plenty of other islands to explore.

Villas

These are big detached houses that often have spacious sun terraces and swimming pools. The most expensive, and sought-after, are the large, historic stone villas by the sea in southern Dalmatia, but modern villas are just as popular and come in every conceivable size and style.

Traditional-style Villas

This is a new building that has been constructed in the old style with heavy stone walls. The advantage over renovated properties is that they are completely fitted out with all modern comforts inside. Popular in central Istria, they usually include land, vineyards and private swimming pools.

Traditional Wooden Houses

The traditional wooden house of inland Croatia typically has a living room, kitchen, bedroom and a storage room that can be converted into a bathroom. Unless the property has already been renovated, these traditional country houses are likely to need a lot of work.

Wine Houses

Concentrated in the Zagorje region of inland Croatia, wine houses are small buildings traditionally used as a shelter by locals tending the vineyards. They are characteristically small, no more than two or three rooms, and sometimes include a smaller outhouse. You couldn't live permanently in one, but they make great holiday homes and are often located in simply spectacular spots.

Guide Prices

In the rush to own the most desirable properties, particularly in the coastal regions, property agents operating in Croatia have noticed that foreign buyers are paying over the odds for their dream holiday homes. 'A four-bedroom stone villa in a village in central Istria is worth around €360,000,' says Andrea Marston, of established British estate agency Dream Property Croatia, 'but we regularly see identical properties advertised on the Internet for €500,000 or more. People are paying too much. Just because a property is advertised at a certain price, that doesn't mean that is what it is worth,' she warns.

Some sellers, excited by the recent swell of interest in Croatian properties, are inflating their prices for the foreign market, and equally enthused foreign buyers are paying what is being asked. A good agent will tell you if a property is overpriced, but it's a wise idea to spend time beforehand browsing property listings on the Internet to get a feel for the going rates. With property prices increasing by as much as 30 per cent per annum, the value of real estate is changing rapidly, and there are wide variations in cost depending on location, views and condition.

The website **www.globalpropertyguide.com** compares rental yields and cost to buy per square metre in a limited number of locations across Croatia. The list isn't extensive, but it is regularly updated and may give you a useful indicator. Real estate is a new industry in Croatia, so there is very little official guidance on property value but again, a good agent should be able to give you guide prices for the sort of property you are looking for. Here are some examples taken from listings in 2007 to get you started.

€10,000 or less
- traditional one-bedroom wine house in Zagorje needing restoration.

€10,000–50,000
- fully renovated two-bedroom family holiday home in a spa town, a one-hour drive from Zagreb.
- old stone ruin needing complete renovation with a large garden on the island of Hvar.

€50,000–100,000
- traditional farmhouse in a central Istrian village needing complete renovation.
- one-bedroom apartment in the Baroque centre of Varaždin.

€100,000–120,000
- two-bedroom off-plan apartment 15 minutes from Split and 200m from the sea.
- two-bedroom apartment, part of a new development in the Pag beach resort of Novalja.

€120,000–150,000
- new one-bedroom apartment in Hvar Old Town.
- small two-bedroom stone house in a coastal village on the island of Brač.

€150,000–200,000
- new two-bedroom apartment near the beach in an Istrian coastal resort.
- new one-bedroom apartment in a building of four on Krk with views of the Kvarner Islands.

€200,000–300,000
- two-bedroom apartment in a coastal resort close to Dubrovnik.
- newly renovated two-bedroom house within Dubrovnik city walls.

€300,000–400,000
- new four-bedroom traditional-style stone villa in a central Istrian location with swimming pool.
- two-bedroom, ground floor apartment in a Dubrovnik suburb with a view of the old town.

€400,000–600,000
- large, four-bedroom renovated house in Hvar Old Town.
- two-bedroom renovated apartment spread over two floors within the Roman palace walls at the centre of historic Split.

Over €1,000,000:
- restored Baroque seafront villa in the Istrian resort of Opatija.
- luxury three-bedroom beachfront villa on the island of Korčula.

Research and Information Sources

The first and most invaluable resource for finding general information on the Croatian property market is inevitably the **Internet**. There are hundreds of websites offering advice on how and what to buy as well as endless listings of Croatian properties for sale, from renovation projects and plots of land to off-plan villas and luxury apartments. The sheer bulk of information can be overwhelming, and as always with the Internet it is wise to be fussy about what you read. The existence of a website doesn't guarantee the quality of the property agent, the advice they are offering or the property they are advertising. Beware of online articles and features given to hyperbole and exaggeration about the investment opportunities in Croatia, and check the date they were written. Property laws and purchasing procedures have recently changed in Croatia, so old advice is likely to be redundant.

The vast majority of information is contained within individual **agency websites**. These sites allow you to browse tantalising pictures of a whole variety of properties and to compare prices. They also usually offer a certain amount of advice on searching for and buying your ideal second home as well as on financial and legal issues. The website **www.findcroatia.com** provides an extensive directory of Croatian property agents (follow the Real Estate/Property link) and is a good place to start. Most of the agency websites you'll come across will focus primarily on property in the coastal regions and many specialise even further, concentrating solely on one particular region or island. Dream Property Croatia (**www.dreamcroatia.com**) and A Place In Dalmatia (**www.aplacein dalmatia.com**) are among the best websites for a general overview of properties in locations right the way along the Adriatic.

Croatia Property Services (**www.croatiapropertyservices.com**) specialises in Istrian property, while Hvar Property Services (**www.croatianhouse.com**) and Milenka Real Estate (**www. milenkarealestate.com**) concentrate on the islands of Hvar and Brač respectively.

For inland Croatia, Croatia Select (**www.croatiaselect.co.uk**) has an excellent selection and an honest appraisal of each property it features. For a wider list of property agency websites, *see* **References**, 'Estate Agents', p.193.

Apart from the Internet, **magazines** are often a useful resource. Croatia Exclusive (**www.croatiaexclusive.com**) is a monthly UK publication with features on all aspects of buying a property in Croatia; it can be ordered online. You can also order recent back issues of the glossy magazine *Homes Overseas*, which contain large features on the Croatia market from the website **www. homesoverseas.co.uk**.

Features about Croatian property regularly appear in other similar magazines such as *A Place In The Sun* (**www.aplaceinthe sunmag.co.uk**) and *World of Property* (**www.worldofproperty.co.uk**), which also posts many of its features online, and in newspapers such as the *Sunday Times*. The biggest property classified magazine in Croatian is *Mali Oglasnik* (**www. malioglasnik.com** or **www.malavrata.com**).

Property Exhibitions

Croatia is increasingly well represented at overseas property shows, which are themselves becoming ever larger and more frequent. They provide an opportunity to see what is available and also to meet agents face-to-face. Many of the shows include free seminars on subjects like buying off-plan, retiring abroad, using the Web to let your property and raising finance. This is an ideal opportunity not only to get good general advice but to have those nagging questions answered by independent experts.

The exhibitions are usually held over a weekend in spring and autumn. Homes Overseas (**www.homesoverseas.co.uk**) present exhibitions twice a year in Birmingham, London and Manchester, while A Place In The Sun Live (**www. aplaceinthesunlive.com**) takes place annually in Birmingham.

The smaller International Property Show (**www.internationalpropertyshow. com**) is a free event that travels to various locations across the country.

Croatia is better represented at some shows than others, so it is worth checking the exhibitor list on the show's website before buying tickets.

Estate Agents

The complaints you occasionally hear from foreign nationals buying property in Croatia (gazumping, paperwork, ownership issues and so on) can all be circumvented by surrounding yourself with the right people. A good notary will explain the paperwork, a good lawyer will organise the necessary permissions and permits, and a good property management company will smooth the rental process.

Key to all of this is choosing the right estate agent. Once you have found a good agent, everything else will seem to fall into place. They will not only help you find the perfect property but they will advise you on the risks and pitfalls and put you in touch with reliable professionals to fill all the other necessary roles. In return, the estate agent will charge both buyer and seller a percentage of the sale price of the property, typically 4 per cent fo the buyer.

To avoid these fees there is the option of acting independently, but this is a decision fraught with difficulty. The main problem, of course, is the language barrier, followed by a lack of knowledge of Croatia's sometimes overly bureaucratic property and legal system. Add to this the fact that the concept of buying and selling property is a relatively new one in Croatia, so many sellers will be as new to – and confused by – the process as the buyer, and you begin to see why proceeding without an agent can cost you time, sanity and ultimately money.

Complaints about Croatian property agents are not common, but it is important to recognise that there until very recently no regulatory body governed Croatian estate agents. In order to trade, estate agents had simply to be an officially registered Croatian company, leaving customers with no clear comeback if they were unhappy with the service or wanted to make a complaint. The introduction of a compulsory registration scheme in summer 2007 is on the way to changing this situation.

Even with new regulation, it is essential to do your research before deciding on an agent. Word of mouth or personal recommendation is often the best assurance of quality, but always ask for a reference list of foreign investors who have recently bought property through the agency and contact them. A good estate agent will be more than happy for you to contact past clients to hear their opinions and experiences of the services provided.

Communication with your agent is important, so if you don't speak Croatian, make sure your agent has a good level of English and preferably more than one English-speaker in their office; it can be incredibly frustrating if the one English-speaker isn't available at the time you need to consult someone. Many potential buyers prefer estate agencies that have permanent staffed offices in the UK or that are owned and run by British nationals. Language aside, this can be immensely reassuring. However, if it is a Croatian registered company (as most of them are), this actually offers you no additional protection over those companies run by Croatians or based in Croatia.

Milenka Real Estate (**www.milenkarealestate.com**), an established property agency on the island of Brač, suggests some other pointers to bear in mind when choosing an estate agent:

- **How long has the company been in business?** Over the last few years there has been a swell in the number of estate agencies operating in Croatia to capitalise on the emerging market. The newer the agency, the less experience they are likely to have of the common pitfalls and problems affecting the Croatian market.

- **Has the agent dealt with foreign buyers and investors before?** The more experience the agent has of the issues surrounding foreign purchases of Croatian property, the more assured you are of a smooth road.

- **Do the registered company name of the agency and the names of the company owners appear on the website?** The lack of this information may indicate that the company has not been officially registered.

- **What is the company's track record and reputation in the marketplace?**

- **Is the agent able to answer all your queries?** As well as speaking to past clients, don't be afraid to ask questions of the agent. A good agent will be happy to explain all stages of the purchasing process and willingly answer any questions you may have.

- **Is the agent asking for money too early?** If an agent is asking for money up front, ask why. You should not be asked to pay an agent until the final purchase contract is written and signed.

Viewing Trips

As discussed earlier in this chapter, viewing trips are exciting but can result in information overload. Properties tend to blur into one if you are viewing several in quick succession, so you will thank yourself for getting organised beforehand. Take a digital camera with you (with a large memory card so that you are free to snap away) and a notebook. As you view each property, take pictures of every room as well as of the exterior, garden and views. Jot down notes about the property including any good and bad points that occur to you as you walk around. Work through any checklists you have prepared and take the time to imagine yourself using the property.

It is tempting to cram as many viewings into your trip as possible, particularly if you only have a short space of time but make sure you leave a break at the end of each day so that you can sit and look through your photos, read your notes and evaluate what you have seen.

What Questions to Ask

Never be afraid of asking too many questions either during the viewing trip or once you return home. In the **Appendix** (p.ooo) is a comprehensive checklist that you can use as a prompt when viewing properties. There are also the questions to ask yourself about location that were suggested earlier in the chapter, plus a few more to add to the list outlined below:

• **What is your budget, and can your finances support it?** As an approximation, it is not unusual for buyers to spend 1.5 to 2.5 times their annual income on a second home or investment property.

• **Do you need to secure a loan?** Loans in Croatia have high interest rates, so many buyers take the option of securing equity on their home in the UK. You may want to investigate ahead of time whether your bank is prepared to mortgage your home for a property abroad – some won't. *See* pp.91–2.

• **Do you plan to remodel or renovate?** If so, make sure to take this extra cost into account in your budget.

• **Should you spend money on a home inspection?** Yes! Arrange for a surveyor to inspect the property including plumbing, roofs and floors.

• **What is the water and utility situation?** If the property doesn't have adequate water and utilities, factor the cost of resolving this into your budget. If there are utilities, confirm that there are no unpaid bills.

• **Does the property have the relevant planning permission and building permits?** Properties that have been built without proper permission and permits can be demolished without warning by the Croatian government.

• **Have you checked the zoning?** If you are buying land to build on make sure it is within a designated residential (rather than agricultural or commercial) zone. If you are buying property with an empty plot of land nearby, check the land has been designated as a green zone that therefore can't be developed later and spoil your view. *See* p.104.

• **Are the titles 'clean'?** Having 'clean' titles means that when you purchase the property you are assured of being its sole official owner. This subject is dealt with in more detail in **Making the Purchase**, pp.102–103.

• **What taxes and fees do you face?** As well as agency fees, you should expect to pay 1–3 per cent of the purchase price in legal fees and 5 per cent of the purchase price in tax.

• **Are you dealing with a separate estate agent and independent lawyer?** If an estate agent offers to draft purchase contracts, insist on an independent lawyer. Similarly, if a lawyer offers you real estate services – refuse. Both practices are illegal.

Renting Before You Buy

While you are searching for your ideal second home in Croatia you will need somewhere comfortable to stay. As long as you travel outside the busy summer months of July and August, this shouldn't be a problem. Almost every town will have at least one hotel of a decent standard, and the nightly rates will become increasingly reasonable the further you base yourself from the major tourist centres and popular attractions.

However, even the cheapest of hotels can get expensive if you plan to stay for an extended period of time. Apartments (*apartmani*) are often a more cost-effective option with the additional benefit of allowing you your own space. A simple search on the Internet will reveal literally thousands of short-term lets, from coastal apartments to country retreats (*agroturizam*). These are clearly aimed at the holiday market, but prices fall by as much as 50 per cent outside the peak season and many offer reduced rates for longer-term lets of more than three weeks. If you are feeling adventurous, by far the cheapest option is a pitch on one of Croatia's many campsites. Some have mobile homes with their own bathrooms that you can move into, while others allow you to bring your own motor home.

If you intend to take your time over the search for a new property or would prefer to live in an area for a while before committing yourself permanently, you might consider a long-term lease. This will undoubtedly be cheaper in the long run than renting a holiday apartment, although you will be asked to pay up to three months' rent in advance as well as a deposit of at least a further month's rent. In Croatia, a typical long-term lease is agreed for one year, but in most instances you can terminate the rental agreement early after a prearranged notice period (normally 30 days). The widest choice of long-term-lease property can be found in the urban areas of Zagreb, Split and Dubrovnik, but your first step should be to find an estate agent who deals with residential leases.

Leasing agents are unregulated in Croatia and the only way of checking the integrity of the agent is through word of mouth and by asking to speak to past clients. Be aware that as a foreigner you will be expected to pay more for the lease than a local, and that the agent will charge you a commission either as a flat fee or as a percentage of the annual lease. Make sure you have explicitly agreed the rate of the commission with the agent before you view any properties.

Once you have found a place you like, the agent should produce a rental agreement that clearly states the responsibilities of both the landlord and the tenant. Make sure every detail of the lease is included in writing in the agreement, including liability for utility bills, notice period and inventories. It's a good idea to have an independent lawyer check the rental agreement before you sign it to make sure that all is in order.

Buying to Let

Most foreigners buying property in Croatia are confident in the knowledge that they will eventually make a profit on their investment through capital growth. In the meantime many people decide to let their second home on short-term lets to holidaymakers. The extra income can be used to cover mortgage payments on the second property and is a way of making a holiday home pay for itself. You may even plan to earn back your initial capital investment over a number of years.

Letting your property can be an easy business to run, which is what makes it such an attractive option. You can employ a property management agency to take care of everything for you or take on a certain proportion of the work yourself. After all, as a non-Croat in Croatia, you are extremely well placed to know exactly what foreigners wanting to spend time in the country are looking for. You can advertise your property in the UK, spread the word among friends and colleagues, distribute leaflets or even set up your own website. With Croatia's tourist industry blossoming and visitor numbers increasing year on year, it appears to be a sure bet. However, there are some issues to bear in mind and these are all presented in detail in a later chapter: *see* **Letting Your Property**, pp.173–88.

Building from Scratch or Renovation

'Renovation required' is a term that cuts a huge swath across the Croatian property market. It can be used to describe a place that simply needs a fresh coat of paint throughout, or one that is no more than a stack of stone bricks and shaky timbers. Do not underestimate the level of work, effort and commitment that even the most modest of renovation projects requires, and be realistic about your limitations. Estate agents can be very enthusiastic about the potential of a wreck, but at the end of the day it is you who will be spending your days plastering walls and laying floors or supervising builders and hunting for bathroom fittings.

However, there is huge satisfaction to be had from breathing new life into an old property, and for many it remains the ultimate dream. Despite renovation properties becoming rarer on the Croatian market over the last few years, a quick Internet search will reveal that there are still plenty of possibilities. Traditionally property in Croatia was passed down through the family, so many of the neglected and derelict properties are an inheritance that is unwanted or unused by the present generation. Empty properties in inland regions like the Zagorje are extremely cheap, but similar places along the coast and on the islands are significantly more expensive. Even properties that are essentially ruins can be surprisingly pricey along the Adriatic, thanks to their potential and popularity. Therefore you must do your homework carefully if you hope to make any money on your project. Experienced hands say that if you buy an old house you should expect to pay at least the same again in renovation costs. This is despite the fact that labour and materials cost around one-third less than in the UK.

Home improvement is as popular as a pastime in Croatia as it is in the UK, and as a result, DIY hypermarkets are widespread and well stocked, as are builders' yards and specialised hardware stores. Croatia is close to both Slovenia and Italy, countries with a good reputation for producing high-quality fittings and furniture, so there is no shortage of superior materials flooding across the border.

There is also no shortage of skilled tradesmen and builders. As in the UK, the best way to find a reliable builder is through word of mouth. A local builder is more likely to do a good job because his reputation in the area depends on it, so ask around locally. However, be prepared to wait, as the best builders are likely to be busy and you will have to book their time in advance. It is common practice for building work to stop around mid-June and recommence in September, thus avoiding both the midsummer heat and the tourist congestion in peak season. This needs to be factored into any time estimates you may have for completion.

The first and most time-consuming job when renovating is often connecting water and utilities to the property. The majority of old houses don't have sewage, electricity or mains water, having a rainwater tank on the roof instead or occasionally a well (in which case you need to have the water quality checked). Adding a septic tank and other utilities is a straightforward process in all but the most extreme cases (for example in a very remote or mountainous area), but it is a good idea to have someone with you who can speak the language to make sure that there is no breakdown in communication.

Complete absenteeism by the owner during any building or renovation work is generally a bad idea. There are a small number of British outfits in Croatia that offer various facilitation and project management services if you are unable to be in Croatia full time. They can provide regular progress reports, contacts with reliable tradesmen that they have worked with before and, of course, ensure everyone understands each other.

Looking at some of the rickety shells offered for sale on the Internet, you may wonder if it wouldn't be easier to start from scratch, and this is indeed another option that is open to you. Land isn't particularly cheap in Croatia. The average price on the most popular islands is €50 per square metre, while near Dubrovnik it can be as much as €200 per square metre. Despite this, there is money to be made, and property development is a booming business. If you are considering this route there are a number of things to consider.

Case Study: Busman's Holiday

Two years ago, after watching a TV programme about overseas property hotspots, British builder Tim Batson bought himself an apartment in Supetar on the island of Brač. Just five minutes from Supetar harbour, the apartment takes up the middle floor of a three-storey block, has three double bedrooms and a large garden overflowing with fruit trees. 'The apartment was 30 years old and was very dated inside,' says Tim, 'so we gutted it completely and started again.'

As he started work, Tim was surprised by the availability of materials on the island. 'Locally, you could get hold of most of the bits you needed including things like kitchens, furniture and double-glazing. They didn't have a lot of electrical supplies but I could order what I wanted from the mainland or go myself to the big hypermarkets in Split. There wasn't anything you couldn't find.' He was also impressed with the professionalism of local builders. 'They turn up on time, first thing in the morning, and do a good job.'

Encouraged by his experiences and having completed his apartment, Tim has been tempted to take on a larger project – building from scratch. He found an ideal plot of land on Brač's hilly interior with stunning 180° views and registered his own Croatian company so he could buy it.

'There was loads of paperwork but the process was pretty straightforward. A lawyer takes you to a notary, who records what business your company will do. Everyone spoke English and all the papers were translated to ensure you know exactly what is going on.' The local planning office was able to give Tim clear advice on the building possibilities for the land and he has now hired an architect to begin drawing up plans. The biggest trouble, says Tim, is getting his family to agree on what type of property they should build. 'We were up there the other week and sat with a few beers looking at the view. To be honest, I'd be happy with just a log cabin and a fridge.'

If you intend to buy **agricultural land or a vineyard** you will need to set up your own Croatian-registered company (*see* **Making the Purchase**, 'Deciding Whether to Buy as a Private Purchaser or as a Company', pp.95–7).

Before you buy a plot of land, check that it has been properly **registered** with the Croatian authorities. Before 1992 Croatia had no land registry system and a single property could be simultaneously owned by several members of the same family. This made ownership of a particular property or plot of land difficult to ascertain. Many properties are only now being registered for the first time, ensuring that the property has what is known as 'clean' title (*see* **Making the Purchase**, 'Clean Title', pp.102–103). This makes sure that you will not have to face the sickening prospect of someone coming forward after the sale to claim the land as theirs.

Verify the **zoning** of the land you are about to purchase with the local planning office (*ured za graditeljstvo i prostorno uredenje*). The Croatian government has recently cleaned up its planning protocol, announcing a moratorium on all coastal development and the introduction of a new zoning system. Plots of land fall into one of four zones. Green zones cannot be developed at all, while private houses are only allowed to be built on land designated as a residential zone.

Once you have purchased the land, you need to liaise closely with both an architect and the local planning office to establish exactly what you are allowed to build. The architect's plans are submitted to the planning office for provisional approval before being sent to Zagreb for final planning permission. The whole approval process can take around 7–8 months.

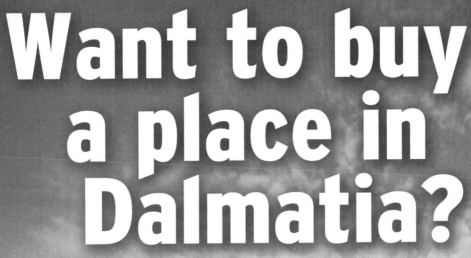

Making the Purchase

Just like everywhere else in the world, there is no substitute for research when buying a property in Croatia. Books such as these are excellent starting points and the Internet provides a rich source of information, too, though it can be a little unreliable or out of date. However, there is no way of avoiding a considerable amount of legwork before making such a major purchase as buying a property abroad.

Even though some properties can take years to sell, buyers can and do lose out on buying properties sometimes when another buyer is better positioned to make the transaction quickly. It is worth doing some research in advance, getting your finances in place, signing a pre-contract agreement and paying a deposit on a property you are interested in, and not dithering when the time comes to buy.

Once a deal is agreed it can take as little as a few days to buy a property – if the buyer already has the deposit money in Croatia, theoretically the purchase can be made on the same day. More usually, however, around a week is devoted to agreeing the pre-contract and checking the documentation. There is no rule about how long it takes to finalise the deal, but one month is quite common if there are no complications.

Understanding the System

Unsurprisingly, the system of buying and selling property in Croatia is very different from the system of buying property in England or Scotland. In many ways, buying a property can be less complicated in Croatia than in the UK; for example, 'property chains' are almost unheard of. However, there are some potential pitfalls and it is important to appoint a good lawyer.

The steps to buying a property in Croatia can be summarised as a follows:

- research the best method of financing the purchase.
- set a budget.
- transfer currency, at least for the deposit.
- find a lawyer and a public notary.
- decide whether to buy privately or as a company.
- find a professional estate agent.
- find a property.
- make an offer.
- assemble and check documentation.
- confirm the title and legality of the building.
- try to obtain a written survey.
- negotiate and sign a pre-contract.

- pay a deposit.
- sort out pre-emptive rights.
- apply to the foreign ministry department for permission to purchase or establish a Croatian limited company.
- sign the sales contract.
- complete the final paperwork.
- submit documentation to the land registrar.
- submit documentation to *katastar* office.
- pay real estate purchase tax within a 30-day deadline.

Raising Finance to Buy the Property

Many people take out a mortgage in order to buy property abroad. If the property is viewed simply as an investment, a mortgage allows you to increase your benefit from the capital growth of the property by 'leveraging' the investment. If you buy a house for €200,000 and it increases in value by €50,000, it has yielded a 25 per cent return on your investment. If you had only put in €50,000 of your own money and borrowed the other €150,000, then the increase in value represents a return of 100 per cent on your investment. If the rate of increase in the value of the property is more than the mortgage rate or costs, you have gained. In recent years, property in the most popular areas of Croatia has risen in value by much more than the mortgage rate. The key questions are whether that will continue.

Taking Out a Mortgage on Your UK Property

There is fierce competition to lend money and there are some excellent deals to be done, whether you choose to borrow at a variable rate, a fixed rate or in one of the hybrid schemes now on offer. Read the Sunday papers or the specialist mortgage press to see what is on offer, or consult a mortgage broker. Perhaps most useful are mortgage brokers who can discuss the possibilities in both the UK and Croatia.

It is outside the scope of this book to go into detail about the procedures for obtaining a UK mortgage.

Croatian Mortgages

At the time of writing, June 2007, the very first 'mortgage' products for foreigners to buy Croatian property are coming on the market. 'Mortgage' is written in inverted commas because the terms and conditions are very different from typical mortgage products in the UK. Things look as if they will start to change quickly from now on, but at the time of writing there are only two products available.

The first is available from **Hypo Alpe Adrie Bank** through its London office, and is specifically aimed at British and Irish people who wish to buy property in Croatia. It is essentially a leasing product, which has been financially engineered to turn it into a mortgage. It has high fees and redemption penalties compared with UK products, so ensure you read the small print and understand the obligations.

The second is offered by **OTP Banka** through its branch network in Croatia, but to date no mortgage has been successfully completed.

Other Loans

Sometimes, especially when you are intending to live in Croatia rather than buying a second home, it is not necessary to take out a mortgage as such. Suppose a buyer intends to move to Croatia permanently. They have already paid off their UK mortgage and their UK home is on sale. They have found the perfect place in Croatia and have, say, £80,000 of the £100,000 available from savings and pension lump sums. The balance will be paid from the sale of their UK home but they are not sure whether that will take place before they are committed to the purchase of the house in Croatia in a few weeks' time. It is probably unnecessarily complicated to mortgage the UK home for such a short period, and indeed, it could be difficult to do so if the bank knows you are selling and if you are, say, 65 years old and not working. In this case it is often simplest to approach your bank for a short-term loan or overdraft. This might be for the £20,000 shortfall or it could be that you don't really want to sell some of your investments at this stage and so you might ask for a facility of, say, £50,000.

Some people choose to make out formal two- or three-year UK loans for, say, £15,000 each while still resident in the UK, before leaving for Croatia, to cover a gap such as waiting to receive a pension lump sum. Despite the high interest rates on such loans, the overall cost can be a lot less than taking a short-term mortgage and paying all the fees relating to it.

The Cost of Buying a Property in Croatia

Apart from the price of the property, the major costs involved in buying a property abroad include estate agents' fees, legal costs and the real estate transfer tax. Additionally, there is the cost of establishing a Croatian company if you decide to take the company route versus the private route.

A good rule of thumb is to expect to add between 10–12 per cent to the purchase price to cover all these expenses.

Making Preparations

Finding a Lawyer

Finding a good lawyer (*odvjetnik*) can make all the difference to a stress-free property sale. The best way to find someone to represent you is through recommendation, but it is wise to avoid using any lawyer recommended by the estate agent selling the property or the developer, who has a vested interest in the sale. In the absence of friends who have already bought in Croatia, a practical route to finding a good lawyer is to ask several of the more reputable estate agents in the region in which you wish to buy. Chances are the same handful of lawyers' names will crop up repeatedly. Alternatively, the British Embassy (**www.britishembassy.gov.uk/croatia** then click on 'lawyer') has a list of English-speaking lawyers throughout the country.

The key to a successful relationship is to be specific from the very beginning about fees and the standards of service expected from the lawyer. If the lawyer's independence from the vendor is important, then this must be established at the first meeting. There are cultural differences between Croatia and the UK, and these can be especially wide on the Adriatic coast. Lawyers are often not accustomed to being required to giving regular briefings to their clients and some do not return phone calls or answer e-mails quickly. British buyers often expect their lawyer to guide them through the process of purchasing, which is understandable, but it is good advice to establish up front what work will be required of the lawyer and how much hand-holding is wanted. Ascertain whether they are happy to communicate via e-mail and whether they speak English themselves or whether they use a colleague to provide translations.

Finding a Public Notary

In Croatia, as in most of mainland Europe, the role taken by a solicitor in the UK divides into two separate jobs: lawyers and public notaries. Lawyers draw up contracts, attend court and provide legal advice, while notaries authenticate signatures and provide notarised copies of documents. They also often offer a chargeable service of holding money in escrow.

In Croatia, a contract is not valid if signed by a private person unless they sign it in the presence of a notary. This applies to a whole range of documents including loan agreements, receipts and property contracts.

When the person attends the notary's office to sign any document, the notary will check the person's identity by examining their ID card (if Croatian) or their passport (if not Croatian). Then the notary will stamp and sign the document, making it legally valid.

Case Study: Get Help

'It's all about having the right person in place to help you,' says Simon Champ, a lesson he learned from experience after his first attempts to buy property in southern Dalmatia ended in disappointment. 'I found the restoration project I was looking for, a villa right on the coast, and agreed a price with the seller. I didn't know what I was doing and in the six weeks it took me to organise surveys, lawyers and contracts the seller decided he wanted more money.' Simon returned to the UK thoroughly disillusioned.

Luckily a friend in Croatia was still scouting on his behalf and introduced him to Andreas Dussmann, a property developer based in Istria. Simon flew out to meet Andreas and was blown away not only by the Tuscanesque scenery but also by the professionalism of his Istrian contact. 'I was taken to see five or six plots of raw land and then to some of the other villas that Andreas had already built. I was impressed with the quality of the build and the ease of the process. Andreas spoke English, knew the rules and the regulations, recommended local lawyers and even sourced the Italian furniture. All I had to do was to sit down and pick the kitchen.' The week after Simon's visit the sale of the land was agreed and building started the following month. Simon visited the site a couple of times during the subsequent year and was once again impressed with the quality of the work that was being done.

Just a little over a year after his very first visit, Simon now has his own Tuscanesque villa 5km north of Motovun. Set in two acres of land on a valley hillside, the villa features five bedrooms, three bathrooms, a 50ft swimming pool, a (newly planted) mature olive grove and a working vineyard. 'It's nicer than I ever thought it would be,' enthuses Simon,' so I'm likely to use it a lot more than I expected.' The contrast between his two experiences couldn't be greater. 'Andreas made money on the villa,' reflects Simon, 'but I'm happy for him to have the profit to insulate myself from the risk. The rules, regulations and layers of bureaucracy can be daunting at first, but once somebody points you in the right direction they're not too bad.'

Buoyed by his good experience, Simon has already bought a second Istrian villa with a friend and has plans to start a small property business. 'Once you've done it the first time, you might as well do it again!'

Similarly, when copies of documents are required, the notary will photocopy the original and sign and stamp the copy with their official seal, creating notarised copies that are then regarded the same as the original document.

There are notaries in the UK, too, but they are not in the 'notary system' and their work will not be accepted in Croatia. Instead, when a British citizen wishes to sign a document that will be accepted in Croatia without having to travel abroad to do so, they need to sign in front of a solicitor who will sign and stamp the document to authenticate the signature and then get it apostilled. Apostilles are the British equivalent of the notary's certification as described above. They are issued by the Legalisation Department of the Foreign and Commonwealth Office (FCO) in London. There is a counter service and a postal service, and the cost is £27 per document. Full details are available on the FCO website, **www.fco.gov.uk/legalisation**; see also **www.apostille.org.uk**.

Deciding Whether to Buy as a Private Purchaser or as a Company

One of the first decisions to be made when buying a property in Croatia is the appropriate route to buy. Under the terms of the reciprocity agreement between the UK and Croatia, the citizens of each country may buy property in the other country. However, in Croatia, this right is not automatic, and British citizens, along with all other foreign nationals, are required to first gain permission from the Croatian Ministry of Justice to buy as a **private purchaser**. The permission is granted for an individual property and so cannot be gained in advance and applied to any property purchase: it is deal-specific.

However, the process of buying is complicated by the length of time the ministry takes to process these applications. The process is bureaucratic and there is a considerable backlog, which has grown steadily since buying property in Croatia became popular. There is little in the way of published official statistics to report the extent of the problem, but in 2003 buyers typically reported waiting for six months; by 2005, the delay was 18 months; and by 15 January 2007 the application backlog had reached approximately 5,600 buyers, with some buyers only receiving permission up to three years after the application was made. Under pressure from the EU, the Croatian government has made some moves to clear the backlog and as a result there have been cases recently where people have received their permission in a matter of weeks, but there are plenty of others at the time of writing (June 2007) who are still waiting today after a year or more.

The alternative is to establish a Croatian **limited liability company** (a 'd.o.o.', pronounced Day ooh ooh!). The Croatian company can then buy the property and does not require government permission, thus allowing the immediate lodging of the ownership documentation at the land registry.

Advantages and Disadvantages of Both Routes

Private Purchase: Disadvantages

As stated already, the greatest disadvantage is the long delay. Apart from requiring patience, the main disadvantage of not having permission to buy is that the new owner cannot record their ownership in the land registry. Until ownership is recorded, you cannot apply for planning permission or a licence to let the property. Another drawback to the delay in receiving government permission is that selling the property becomes difficult because, until your purchase contract has been successfully submitted to the land registry, you are not the recorded owner of the property and therefore you cannot sell it. People work around this problem using all sorts of complicated solutions which involve the participation and co-operation of the person who sold the property to you in the first place, but it can be messy from a tax perspective and you have to hope your seller remains on friendly terms with you and stays in good health!

The delayed permission also has implications for tax. Selling a personally owned property within three years of ownership attracts capital gains tax in Croatia of 25 per cent. If it takes one year to achieve ownership, then you can only be clear of a capital gains tax liability four years after actually buying the property. However, those people who sell before the permission has even arrived find themselves in a grey, mostly untested area for which there does not appear to be a consistently applied formula for calculating the tax liability.

Another disadvantage may be the fact that, under Croatian tax rules, if you own a property as a private purchaser, you will be considered tax resident in Croatia simply by having the property available for your use, even if you only visit the property for two weeks every year (*see* pp.120–21). This means if you let it for part of the year for income, you will need to fill in a tax return. *See* the **Financial Implications** chapter for more information.

Private Purchase: Advantages

Buying privately has the significant advantage of eventually reaching a position where you can sell the property and repatriate your money without incurring any Croatian tax liability after three years. Once the permission has been received, it is also the cleanest way to own a property.

The Company Route: Disadvantages

There are two main disadvantages to the company route:

- **the cost of setting up and running a company.**
- **the 20 per cent profit tax liability incurred if the company eventually sells the property.**

The cost of running a dormant company amounts to around £70 per year in taxes, such as Croatian Chamber of Commerce membership fees and the cost of an accountant's services for basic book-keeping. Book-keepers do not have a standard tariff, but one should expect to pay around £200 per year.

When a company makes a profit, it will incur a corporate tax liability, which in Croatia is charged at 20 per cent. Unlike capital gains tax, which is applicable for private purchases only, the corporate profit tax does not have a time limit. However, there currently does appear to be something of a legal loophole, as people who sell their company, rather than just the property owned by the company, are not taxed by the Croatian government on any profit made.

The Company Route: Advantages

Apart from the potential to sell the entire company and all its assets without incurring any tax liability at all, which is an advantage for the vendor, there is also a tax advantage for the buyer in buying a company that owns a property: the five per cent real estate transfer tax is not applicable.

However, the main reason people choose the company route is the time advantage over the private route, which becomes relevant if they wish to let their property or do some building work requiring planning permission. Unlike with the private route, ownership of the property can be recorded immediately at the land registry, although it takes a few weeks for the record to be updated.

The final big advantage relates to letting. Although it is possible to let a privately owned property, the activity of letting a property is viewed as a business activity and it is very difficult for foreigners who own a property privately rather than through a company to let their houses legally in Croatia without owning a Croatian company to receive the revenue.

The Role of Estate Agents

The role of Croatian estate agents is similar to that of their British counterparts in that their primary function is to introduce prospective buyers to properties that are available for sale, and to broker a deal. However, there are also some key differences.

In the UK, anyone can become an estate agent, but, under legislation which came into force in 2007, estate agents practising in Croatia must be registered with the Chamber of Commerce and within the agency there must be at least one person who has passed the professional real estate exam and therefore gained accredited status. It will take a while for agencies that have no training or expertise to be weeded out from the industry.

Training and experience matters because estate agents in Croatia do much more than just advertise a property and conduct viewings. A good estate agent will add value to his or her services by being able to review the legal documentation of each property, establishing whether there are any ownership issues, building permission issues and restrictions on how the property may be used. Sometimes they also draw up contracts, although this is a reflection of market practice and is not something that is recommended from the vendor's and the buyer's perspectives. It is worth noting that agents should not be viewed as a replacement for a lawyer, but it is reasonable to expect that they will conduct at least a first screening of any documentation before a lawyer takes over to perform the conveyancing work.

The other major difference from British estate agents is that, when a property is sold in Croatia, both the seller and the buyer will be charged a fee by the agent. By law, the fee charged on a total transaction should not exceed 6 per cent plus PDV (Croatian VAT), and typically this breaks down to the buyer being charged 4 per cent plus PDV (4.88 per cent in total) and the seller 2 per cent plus PDV (2.44 per cent in total).

Estate agencies prefer to represent both the buyer and the seller in a sale, for obvious reasons, but it is very common that there will be two or even three agents for a sale, as co-operation between agencies has become common over the last couple of years, with some specialising in attracting and servicing buyers and others specialising in sourcing properties. However, this does not necessarily increase the total commission paid on a transaction, as the agents usually have an arrangement between themselves to share the workload and the revenue. Buyers can use this arrangement to their advantage by finding one or two agencies with whom they are happy to work and asking those agencies to use their contacts to find them suitable property. This also overcomes any language barrier where the agent who has the property you wish to buy may not speak English.

For more on dealing with estate agents, see **Selecting a Property**, pp.80–82.

Valuing Property

Valuing anything without something for comparison is a very difficult thing to do and is prone to error. In the UK, when a valuer sets a value for a property, he or she would look at the property and establish the condition, size and other features relative to similar properties in the area that have recently sold. However, in Croatia, this approach is not nearly so effective. Properties are often very different from one another, and there is a long tradition of bequeathing property in a will, so that the same property will belong to the same family for many generations (even for several centuries). Also, in the UK people move house to trade up or to relocate for their job but that rarely happens in Croatia. It is common for people to live in the same house or flat for their whole lives, even after marriage. The existence of so few property transactions makes the business of valuing property difficult, and so it is a good idea to view a property valuation for anything other than a new-build apartment in a resort town as a ballpark figure rather than a precise amount.

Trying to use the information available on the Internet about current asking prices is also prone to error, because many estate agents' websites advertise properties that were sold a long time ago, or whose prices have been changed several times as the property has been on sale for many years. Also, many Croatian sellers raise the asking price from time to time, but as there are so many agents advertising the property they do not inform all the agencies of the new price. This is one of the reasons why it is possible to find the same property advertised at different prices on several websites. The other common reason is that the vendors often tell the agent to 'add your commission on top', and some agents are a little more generous to themselves than others.

Asking prices are usually set by the vendor, who may or may not be willing to take advice from the estate agent. In fact, because there is not a tradition of selling property in Croatia, it is quite common for the price of a property being offered for sale to be set according to the following equation: 'My sister and I own the house 50/50. She wants to build a new house for herself on some land she owns, I want to put my son through college, and the cost of those two things is X. Therefore the price at which we are willing to sell is X.'

There are a few professional valuers in Croatia, although most are based in the capital, Zagreb. When banks lend against properties, they require valuations which are performed by their in-house team. Often the 'in-house team' is in fact a firm of local estate agents.

In the end, unless the buyer is purchasing a new-build apartment that is in an area where there are several similar properties and it is easy to compare prices like for like, it is simply not possible to accurately determine a property's value, so it comes down simply to what it is worth to the would-be buyer.

Which Currency?

Many foreign buyers are confused as to whether their property purchase should be paid in kunas or in euros. The short answer is kunas. However, as this subject comes up repeatedly, it is worth taking a minute to understand the background and the difference between the legal requirement and what is commonly practised.

Since suffering hyperinflation during the final months of Yugoslavia at the end of the 1980s, the Croatian people have been reluctant to keep their savings in kunas, preferring to hold their money in a euro account instead. This creates a dual system in Croatia today where all expensive items, such as cars and property, are quoted and negotiated in euros, but according to Croatian legislation payment should be made in kunas.

This dual system, where one currency (euros) is used in common practice and another (kunas) is required by law, can, and frequently does, create a problem, because the law requiring property transactions in kunas is not universally enforced. Many Croatian vendors expect to receive euros and are often willing to take their chances with being caught, whereas foreign buyers are well advised to remain within the law and to be seen to pay kunas. This especially applies to foreign buyers who set up a Croatian company as a vehicle for owning the property, because their company records and bank accounts will be examined by the tax officers, who will be able to see whether kunas were used for the transaction. Failure to pay in kunas could result in a fine or even in the transaction's being nullified.

Foreigners who wish to buy privately have a better chance of a euro transaction going unnoticed by the authorities as long as the bank payment reference does not say that the money is intended as payment for a property. If it does say

> ### *Transferring Currency*
> Many, but not all, UK banks and foreign exchange companies have a facility to convert money into kunas and send it to a bank account in Croatia. It is worth shopping around, as there are considerable savings to be made by having money arrive in Croatia in kunas rather than use the foreign exchange services of the Croatian banks.
>
> If sending money to a Croatian company account, it is important to emphasise that the name on the inter-bank SWIFT confirmation must match the name of the person who has money-laundering clearance for that company. So for example Robert Smith must not be Bob Smith.

that, then the bank will be obliged to convert the money into kunas and deliver it instead to the vendor's kuna account. Inevitably, the vendor tries to convert the money back into euros and discovers that, because of the differences in the bank's buying and selling exchange rates, they no longer have the amount of money they were expecting. At this point, the vendor will often take the view that the buyer has short-changed him and will ask the buyer for more money to cover the loss.

The solution lies in clarity from the first moment of negotiating a deal to buy the property. If you intend to pay in kunas, then you must state that you will offer the kuna equivalent of euros at some predetermined exchange rate (usually the exchange rate selected is the National Bank of Croatia's euro selling rate on the date of the final contract).

Such is the widespread practice of paying for property in euros that most sellers are unaware of the law on this point, and many estate agents are also unaware of it, or are at least willing to overlook it for the sake of an easier sale.

Making the Purchase

Assembling and Checking Documentation

Although the compiling and checking of documentation is the lawyer's responsibility, commonly the estate agent performs most of the legwork. The twin key objectives are to prove that the person(s) selling the property is/are the legal owner(s) and to demonstrate that the property has been built according to planning permission. It is also important to ascertain what, if any, encumbrances there are on the property or, in the case of land, to confirm that it will be possible to build on it. Finally, if the property is under cultural heritage protection, it will be necessary to go through a process of offering the property to the government under their pre-emptive rights.

Confirming Title

The Land Registry (Zemljišnik)

In Croatia, property ownership is recorded in two registers. The first and most important is held at the Zemljišnik, which lawyers and estate agents call the 'land registry' when discussing it with their English clients.

There is one land registry for each municipality. Sometimes it shares a building with the local commercial court. The land registry keeps what is often regarded as the definitive record of who owns which property and what percentage each owner holds if there are co-owners. When a property changes ownership, the new owner or his representative submits a notarised copy of the document which proves the change of ownership – usually either the sales contract or the inheritance solution if the property was bequeathed in a will.

The land registry produces a printed extract on demand (although with a wait of anything from two to 10 or more days). This **extract** is called a *vlasnicki list* (owner's sheet) and it is the key document in proving ownership. The *vlasnicki list* will show all the current owners of the property, which is defined using a code number such as 174/1. It describes what the property is, gives the size of the house or apartment, any garden and any other buildings (such as a pigsty or stables), and lists each and every owner, with their percentage of ownership shown as a fraction next to their names. Sometimes this fraction can be 1/1 (one owner), or 1/2 (half), or even something like 5,896/12,859 (the person owns 5,896 of 12,859 parts). These situations come about because of successive inheritances where increasingly distant cousins inherit a share of the same property. Adding all the fractions together will equal one.

The important point to establish is that all the names on the *vlasnicki list* are also listed in the sales contract with their fractional ownership correctly noted, and that all parties either intend to sign the sales contract or have given someone a power of attorney to do so on their behalf. If this is not the case, perhaps because one or more of the owners is dead or uncontactable, the property is said to be in an **'unclean'** situation; this creates a significant problem that may take years to resolve.

Also shown on the *vlasnicki list* are any burdens or encumbrances on the property such as a mortgage held against it (this is important, as in Croatia a mortgage remains with a property, not a person). If there is a mortgage, always ensure that proof of repayment is evidenced before signing any contract. This section is also used to show to whom the property has recently been sold. This is helpful and reassuring, as it can take several months from the time when the sales contract or will is delivered to the land registry until the day when the new owner's name is entered into the *vlasnicki list* in the 'owners' section.

If the property comes under **cultural heritage protection** (similar to Grade II listing in the UK), this fact is usually, but not always, noted on the *vlasnicki list*. *See* p.105.

The *Cadastre* (*Katastar*)

The *katastar*, sometimes translated into the Napoleonic version '*cadastre*', is the second register of property ownership. It comes in two parts: a **katastar map** (*katastarski preris*) depicting the outline of the plot, and sometimes the house within the plot; and a **katastar extract** (*izvadak iz katastar*), which provides the name of the owners against the plot numbers. Sometimes one house spans a number of plots.

There is a government drive, started in 2005, to make the *katastar* more accessible, and to this end the *katastar* records for many municipalities are now available for viewing on the Internet. The web address is **www.katastar.hr**, and the property *katastar* number is required to operate it and to view the written material, but not the accompanying map, which must be collected in person from the counter in the relevant *katastar* office.

However, there is a major downside of relying on the *katastar*: it is not in a good condition. The records for an individual property are frequently very out-of-date because for most of the 20th century people did not go out of their way to keep the records up to date.

Clean Title

The reasons for not keeping the ownership records up to date were manifold, but the main ones were fear of confiscation during the early socialist years, emigrant inheritance issues, and having no expectation of ever wishing to sell the property. Under socialism, it was not a good idea for a Yugoslav citizen to have an official record showing that he or she owned several pieces of property, as large property holdings were confiscated in the early years of Tito's rule. The neighbours all knew who owned the property and within the family there was a common understanding of what fraction each individual owned, and whether or not that represented a distinct area of the house or not.

Added to this is the fact that Croatia had a large number of emigrants, second only to Ireland, and that the descendants of these emigrants who now live or are buried predominantly in the USA, Canada and Australia frequently inherited a share of grandpa's Croatian house. Frequently they may not be aware of the fact, and it becomes easy to see why the situation has become so muddled.

In any case, as people rarely sold property, preferring to hand it down from generation to generation, the need for keeping the official records up to date was almost obsolete, although most people did make some effort to keep the land registry updated.

In recent years, the situation has started to change. It is becoming increasingly common for a young couple to try to buy their own home rather than living with the husband's parents for the rest of their lives (although this is still prevalent outside the cities). To do this they need a mortgage, and the banks have tighter lending regulations than a cash buyer might, so the cleaning up of the land registry and the *katastar* records began. When foreign buyers entered the market, they were understandably less willing to adopt the pragmatic approach the locals had previously taken, and so owners who want to sell their property have made efforts to clean up the papers. The European Union, as part of pre-accession spending, has funded the clean-up process, as a fully functioning, efficient property market is one of the key building blocks for economic development. New electronic registers are being developed, with the aim of having all the property records available on the Internet.

The ideal situation would be for the person who is offering the property for sale to be the sole owner and for his or her name to have been entered into both the *katastar* and into the land registry. This is possible, even likely, for a property constructed within the last 40 years or so, but the probability falls when considering old stone village houses, especially the ones which have been empty for some years.

There is a legal process whereby the names of the owners can be removed from the *vlasnicki list* and the *katastar*. It involves appointing a lawyer who will contact each person (sometimes after hiring a private detective to find them), and then the court will give them the option to declare whether they wish to claim their property or not. Most people (when they can be found) do not want to claim it, especially if they did not know they had a claim on it and that claim at best is 1/280th of a tiny ruin somewhere. Sometimes, it is simply more trouble than it's worth to claim it. Other times, they (sometimes rightly) conclude that there is a mistake in the land registry and that they have no rightful claim over the property. If some of the people cannot be found, or they are long dead with no known living successors, then a court representative will be appointed to act on their behalf.

All this takes time, and the legal bill can accumulate. Therefore for some properties the cost of cleaning up the papers outweighs the value of the property, making a sale financially unviable. These properties (called 'dirty' or 'unclean' properties) are unsaleable until some time in the future when the market has risen substantially, to cover this cost.

It is vital to ensure that any buyers in Croatia today (irrespective of whether they are foreigners or locals) have their name entered into the land registry as the new owner. Their vendor's name must be already there, preferably as the owner, but at the very least as a 'burden' (someone who is in the queue to be added to the property). Additionally, some buyers insist on the *katastar* records being clean; others take a more pragmatic approach and do not.

If the *katastar* records are out of date, then to bring them up to date it is necessary to present the *katastar* office with a complete paper trail of all the past owners going back to the one who is currently listed in the *katastar*. This paper trail must consist of the documents by which the previous owners inherited, were gifted or purchased the property. As always in Croatia, these documents must be either originals or notarised copies.

Confirming the Legality of the Building

This section will concern you if you intend to buy land to build on from scratch, and also to remind you to check the legality of any building you buy – i.e. whether the person who built the property has complied with all planning regulations. If a building is to be built on a patch of bare ground according to planning permission, there are up to six stages to be worked through:

- **drafting zoning and general urban plans.**
- **obtaining cultural heritage permission, if relevant.**
- **obtaining a location permit.**
- **obtaining a building permit.**
- **obtaining an usage permit.**
- **obtaining an** *étagère***, if relevant.**

Not all these stages will be applicable to every property, but it is worth taking some time to understand the process in order to be able to discuss with your lawyer any potential matters that might affect you.

Zoning and General Urban Plans

Croatia has recently undergone a process whereby each municipality has been mapped out and a function has been assigned to each constituent zone, in a similar way to town planning in Britain. These plans are called the **general urban plans (GUPs)**. The functions can fall into different categories. For example, some areas have been set aside for a new marina; others for tourism (such as hotels) and others are reserved for residential use.

Probably the most flexible zone is **M1** (mixed use) which means that properties in the zone can be used for commercial premises or a place to live or for tourism. The least flexible areas are those coloured **green** on the maps. These areas are zoned for agriculture, and the only building permitted there would a small toolshed. This land can cost very little – typically 1/20th of the price of land that is zoned for building, so foreign buyers are sometimes tempted to be imaginative with their interpretation of toolshed. However, this is not a good idea, because, when a property falls foul of the planning authorities, they can and do demolish an illegally built property, sending the owner the bill.

The GUPs were due to be finalised by the end of 2005. However, many are not yet completed, as the process of establishing a GUP involves gaining a consensus within the community, and there has been considerable lobbying by landowners to ensure that their land is zoned for building rather than the almost valueless agricultural land. However, there has been progress recently and it would be reasonable to expect that most of the unfinished GUPs will be completed by the end of 2007.

Cultural Heritage Permission

Cultural heritage permission is similar to Grade II listing status in Britain, but applies to whole areas, not just specific buildings. Properties that come under the protection of the Cultural Heritage Department attract an additional level of planning permission, which must be obtained before progressing to the location permit stage. Typically, the officers at the Cultural Heritage Department are concerned to maintain the character of the buildings under their protection, but they are only interested in the external appearance, not with internal renovations. Approval is valid if stamped and signed by the Cultural Heritage Department.

Location Permit (*Lokacijska Dozvola*)

For most people, the first stage of the planning process is to obtain a location permit. This permit gives approval to the outline architect's plan and confirms that the property is being developed in keeping with the GUP.

The location permit is valid for two years from the date of issue and must be stamped by the planning department.

Building Permit (*Gradjevinska Dozvola*)

Once a location permit has been obtained, the next step before building can commence is to obtain a building permit. This step takes the most time, partly because the neighbours are consulted at this stage and there must be a quorum of approval from neighbours before the permit can be issued. However, once the signed and stamped letter of approval from the planning department has been issued, building can commence.

The building permit is valid for two years from the date of issue. There is no time limit on how long it can take to finish a building project but work must commence within two years.

Usage Permit (*Uporabna Dozvola*)

The usage permit is issued at the end of the construction phase and has the same function as a building completion certificate in the UK, in that it certifies that the building has been constructed according to the terms of the building permit. For example, a building on which the developer added an extra floor or built larger than the footprint for which he or she had permission will not have or get a usage permit. As always in Croatia, the document is only valid if stamped with the official seal of the issuing department.

Etagière

An *étagière* is performed if a property is subdivided into two or more legally separated dwellings. It is obtained once the building work is complete. The outcome of the process is that the separate dwellings will have their own *katastar* numbers and can be legally sold separately.

What to Look For in the Documentation Stage

Buyers should expect to be able to see a recent *vlasnicki list*, a *katastar* map and a *katastar* extract. If the vendor bought the property recently and these records are not fully up to date, then it is also reasonable to ask to see a copy of the contract by which the vendor purchased the property, which will probably arrive with the price blacked out. These things are sufficient to prove title.

To prove the legality of the build, a new-build property should have a usage permit and, if it is an apartment or a subdivided house, then it should have its own *katastar* number and not share this with the neighbours, which will be clear on the *katastar* extracts and the *vlasnicki list*.

If the property was built before 1968 and has not been changed externally since then, there will not be a building permit or a usage permit. All properties built before 1968 are automatically deemed legal. The *katastar* holds records of all buildings since 1968 and can on request issue a document which will describe the size and number of floors of the property on that date. If it can be seen that the building still fits the 1968 description, then it is considered proved that the building is legal.

Surveys

There are a few companies who will survey a property and give a professional report on the condition, possibly in conjunction with an estimation of its market value. However, although increasing in popularity, this service is not widely used in Croatia. More typically, a local builder is asked to examine the property and give his opinion as to the condition of the roof, etc., which he or she will do either for a low fee or for free in the expectation of being awarded the work should the potential purchaser go ahead and buy the property.

Signing Initial Contracts

The Pre-contract (*Predugovor*)

The pre-contract stage is similar to the **exchange of contracts** stage in England and Wales – it is the point where the sale becomes binding on both parties and where a **deposit** is paid. The pre-contract is an important stage of the process. It will form the basis of the purchase contract and should cover all points, including the price and the currency in which the price will be paid, and the full names and ID numbers of the vendor(s) and buyer(s). It should describe the property and state precisely what is being sold. It should also name the conditions under which the purchase contract will be signed and the sale finalised.

If either the vendor or the buyer is unable to attend Croatia to sign in person, they can assign a **power of attorney** (a *punomoć*).

Translation of the Contract

No one should sign a contract without fully understanding, and being willing to commit to, the terms of the contract. It is good practice for the buyer and vendor to approve the pre-contract before arriving in the notary's office for the signing, but occasionally this is not practicable, for example if someone has found the property they wish to buy while on holiday and is eager to secure the property before flying home.

The contract will be written in Croatian, but, unless both parties speak Croatian, the notary will insist that the contract be translated into a language which the non-Croatian party can understand. The notary insists upon this because if one of the parties later claims that they did not understand what they were signing, the contract can be overturned in court.

Croatia operates a system of court-certified interpreters. An interpreter will either prepare a written translation if there is time, or will attend the signing in person and translate the contract verbally before signing. The fee for the translator will vary by time spent or according to the number of words, but an estimate for this service is £30 for a verbal translation or £90 for a full written translation of a contract. The notary, the estate agent and the lawyer should all be able to arrange for the contract to be translated with a little notice.

It is not obligatory that the translator is court-certified, although it can be a good idea as they are most experienced in translating and explaining legal terminology. However, a friend who speaks English and Croatian would suffice.

For this contract to be legally binding, the buyer and the vendor must sign the pre-contract in front of a public notary. This requirement for private citizens whether Croatian or otherwise to sign in front of a notary, who will then apply his own seal to the document, is mandatory for all contracts in Croatia. If a private person signs without a notary, the contract cannot be enforced later.

If, however, a company is the buyer or the vendor, then a director of the company may sign and apply the company's seal on the pre-contract without a notary.

The Deposit

The standard deposit applied in most sales is 10 per cent, although it can be varied depending on the agreement reached between the vendor and the buyer. The deposit is commonly paid by the buyer directly into the vendor's bank account, and, because this situation is so common, it is likely that it will be what the vendor will expect to happen. However, an obvious downside is that if the sale fails, the buyer may have difficulty getting his money back. A safer option is for the buyer to deposit the money with an independent third party. who will hold the money in an **escrow account** on the buyer's behalf until the terms of the pre-contract are satisfied. This service is chargeable but is a safer way of holding the deposit. However, before deciding to take this route, some thought should be given to the vendor's expectations and that he or she may well be offended if he or she considers that the buyer does not trust him.

Pre-Emptive Rights

Those properties that fall under the protection of the Cultural Heritage Department must be offered to the government, under their pre-emptive rights, before a sale is made. The legislation is in place to give the government the opportunity to buy up properties of architectural value at the market rate. There are houses and flats which fall into this category in the old parts of UNESCO-protected Trogir, Dubrovnik and the properties in Diocletian's Palace in Split, but also many of the red-tiled old stone houses in fishing villages that characterise the coast. Under the legislation, the current owner is required to find a buyer and, once a deal has been agreed and the pre-contract signed, he or she is obliged to give the local council, the county and the Republic of Croatia the opportunity to buy at the price stated in the pre-contract.

In reality, these government bodies never or at least very, very rarely, actually exercise these rights, but the owner is not permitted to sell his property until the rights have been offered or allowed to expire. The rights are offered in writing and sent by registered post. Each of the three bodies has 30 days to respond. If they have not responded within 30 days, the owner is free to sell the property for the price it was offered at after a further 30 days. However, if they respond within 30 days asking for more information, such as more photographs of the property, then the period of 30 + 30 days begins again when the information is submitted. Typically, properties that fall under this cultural heritage protection require 60 days between the pre-contract and the final sales contract; this is comparable to the month which is the standard time for 'normal' sales.

If the property is sold without these rights being offered, the government has the right to cancel the sale at any point up to three years after the sale, should it decide that it wishes to take up its rights.

By law it is the owner of the property who is obliged to make the pre-emptive rights offer to the government, but often in practice the estate agent or the lawyer makes the offers and manages the process on the owner's behalf.

Applying for Permission to Buy Privately or Setting up a Croatian Company

Although this is described at this point in the timeline, a Croatian company can be set up at any point before the signing of the final sales contract; but it is actually preferable if it is done before the pre-contract. The following sections deal with how to apply for permission to buy privately and how to set up a Croatian company. First read pp.94–7 to help you make the decision about which option to take.

Private Purchase: Applications for Permission to Buy

Although Croatia has a reciprocity agreement with Britain whereby the citizens of each other's country are permitted to buy property in the other country, Croatia requires British citizens to obtain permission first. The British are not being singled out for such treatment; most foreign nationals are required to follow this route. It can take a long time but approval is almost always granted eventually. However, there are a few categories of foreign citizens for whom private purchase is not an option because the relevant treaties are not in place, including Russian citizens and those who live in certain states of the USA.

The 'permission to buy' requirement only applies to private purchasers who wish to buy the property in their own name, and not to those who set up a company and use the company to buy the property.

The application by a private individual for permission to buy a property in Croatia is made to the Ministry of Justice. Although it is possible to make the application without assistance (and how to do this is explained below), it is common practice for foreign buyers to appoint a lawyer to do this work on their behalf. Sometimes the lawyers will include the application and the follow-up in their conveyancing fee but sometimes they do not, so it is a good idea to check at the outset when appointing the lawyer.

Estate agents also do this work on behalf of their clients, and often the work is included within the brokerage commission, but again it is a good idea to check rather than assume.

Anyone who appoints a lawyer or an estate agent to do this work should ask him or her for the postal receipt to prove that the application was made. Such applications should be sent by registered post and, as such, the post office should provide a receipt proving delivery.

DIY Applications to the Ministry of Justice

Since July 2006, the Ministry of Justice has been the authority for giving consent for private purchase. Prior to that date, the Ministry of Foreign Affairs carried this responsibility, and you will still find many references on the web and in printed literature to MFA permission, which can cause confusion, so it is worth bearing in mind that this is now out of date.

The decision on giving consent for acquiring titles over real property in Croatia to foreigners is made during the administrative proceedings of the sale, and a written request should be handed over directly at the court admission desk or mailed to the Ministry of Justice of the Republic of Croatia, Civil Law Administration Department, Dežmanova 6, 10000 Zagreb, Croatia.

The following documents must be attached to the written document:

- an original document or certified copy providing the legal basis for acquiring a title (purchase agreement, gift agreement, lifelong support agreement, etc.).

- an original document or certified copy, less than six months old, providing evidence of the current ownership of the person disposing of the property (usually the seller, but it may be being gifted or willed) over the real property in question, or the original or a certified copy of the land registration extract that is no more than six months old.

- confirmation (by original no more than six months old) issued by the local government body in charge of the urban and physical planning (county offices) that the real property lies within the boundaries of the construction area envisaged in urban planning.

- proof of citizenship for foreign buyers (certified passport copy) or proof of the legal entity status (court register extract), if the buyer is a foreign legal entity.

- if there is an authorised agent, the original or a certified copy of the power of attorney; he or she will be contacted to submit other deeds or documents if necessary during the procedure.

Apart from the documents and deeds listed, it is necessary to attach a proof of the administrative fee payment to the application. According to Article 21 of the Amendment to the Law on Administrative Fees and Taxes (*Official Gazette* no.163/03), tariff number 74.a, the following levels have been set for administrative fees:

- 50 kunas for the application.
- 100 kunas for the decision on acquiring real property.
- 20 kunas for any addition to the application (in case certain documents are missing).

The administrative fees iof 100 kunas will be charged in stamp duties of corresponding monetary value, while the amounts exceeding 100 kunas must be paid by postal money order to the Republic of Croatia Budget account no.: 1001005-1863000160, putting no. 24 (model) in the first box of the payment slip, and filling in the second box of the payment slip with 5002. When a Croatian citizen is making the payment, his or her ID. no. (JMBG) has to be added to number 5002, while the number 721 has to be added after number 5002 if a foreign national is paying the set amount. The applicant, or his or her authorised agent, needs to enclose the filled-in payment slip (or duty stamps) with all other documents.

The Ministry of Justice accepts calls from foreign owners on Wednesdays only.

Call **t** +385 (0)1 371 0779. The caller is required to quote his or her Ministry of Justice issued case number (UPE); these numbers are different from the case numbers that were previously issued by the Ministry of Foreign Affairs before August 2006.

Establishing a Croatian Company

There are two ways to set about establishing a Croatian limited company: hire a company to do the work, or do it yourself. The following sections explain both options.

Company Set-up Services

Lawyers, many estate agents and even some accountants offer a company set-up service varying in cost from as little as £1,000–2,000. Comparison of these services is difficult because some offer an all-in service, which includes notary fees, translation fees, courier fees, company stamps, setting up bank accounts and the payment of all taxes, such as the court fees. Whether the person setting up the company has to be physically present in Croatia is another variable.

Typically, it takes three to four weeks from start to finish to set up a company, including the work which the accountant does to gain exchange control clearance. However, this time will increase if documents have to be apostilled and then posted from the UK (*see* p.92).

All company set-up services require the same basic information in order to get started:

- **the full name(s) of the company founder(s).**
- **the names of the intended director(s) of the company (typically but not necessarily the founder(s)).**

How to Decide the Percentage Ownership of a Company

In Britain, there is a concept of joint ownership which is widely used in cases where couples have joint bank accounts or jointly own a property. However, this does not exist in Croatia, where instead people are treated as individuals rather than as married (or unmarried) unit. So, if a couple wish to jointly own a property or a company in Croatia then the closest they can get to this is for one person to own 50 per cent and the other person own the other 50 per cent.

This 50/50 split works for most couples, but there is one further caveat to take into consideration: if you decide to move to Croatia then you will need a visa. One such visa which is relatively easy to obtain is a business permit, which can be applied for if you own 51 per cent or more of a Croatian company. So if you are a married couple and you wish to move to Croatia, then you would be well advised to keep your options open and ensure one of you owns a majority share in your company. Spouses can obtain a spouse's visa if their other half has a business permit.

- the percentage share of each of the owners (*see* box, below).
- the UK or other home address(es) of the company founder(s)'.
- the passport number(s) and place of issue (in the UK, this is just 'UKPA') of the company founder(s)'.
- the intended registered business activities.

It is a good idea to list every possible activity you might wish your company to perform in the future. It costs nothing to add another few activities at this point, but adding another activity after the court papers have been drawn up and submitted to the commercial court will require a complete redrafting of the paperwork by the notary and will cost upwards of £600. These are examples of the sorts of business activities that a company might perform:

- real estate (this covers the sale of the property in the future).
- the buying and selling of goods.
- preparation of food and provision of nutrition services, preparation and serving of drinks and beverages and provision of accommodation services (this enables the company to let the property).
- provision of services in nautical tourism, rural, health, congress, sports, hunting and other forms of tourism; provision of other tourist services.

Company Name

The name for the company must be in either the Croatian language or one of the dead languages (Latin, Greek, etc.) and it can only consist of letters, not numerals. It must be sufficiently different from all other company names in the county in which the company will be registered for it not to be confused with any other company. However, it is better to make it different from any other Croatian company, irrespective of the place of registration, as there is always a possibility that the commercial court judge may reject the application if he or she finds grounds for confusion.

The founder's surname is acceptable. The words 'Croatia' and 'Croatian' may not be used, except with government permission.

Company Address

The company must have a Croatian address. It can be the address of the property you mean to buy, but before using this option it is a good idea to be very sure that the property sale will go through because, if the sale fails for any reason, your company will be registered at an address to which you have no access.

For this reason, many people elect to use their accountant's address, especially as this has the added benefit that all bills, including the one from the Ministry of Finance for the stamp duty on the property, can be directed straight to the accountant's office, which will enable him or her to pay it within the time limit. However, this service may well be chargeable, as the accountant will be taxed on the rent the tax officer will decide he or she should have collected from your company for the office space. For this reason, it is a good idea to have a short contract between your company and the accountant in which you sublet the smallest possible space – perhaps one square metre for a set annual fee.

Other options include using the address of the company that is performing the company set-up, although this service will be chargeable for the same reasons that the accountant would charge for it.

It is important to get this correct from the start, because changing the address later will require another trip to the notary and another request to the commercial court and will thereby incur additional expense in the region of £600.

HITRO: The Do-It-Yourself Method

The HITRO website states: 'HITRO.HR is a service of the Government of the Republic of Croatia intended for quick communication of citizens and business subjects with the state administration.'

HITRO services are provided in FINA offices. FINA ('The Financial Agency') is similar to National Girobank in the UK. However, unlike the UK where it can be found in post offices, FINA offices are in separate buildings. There is a FINA office in most large and medium-sized towns, although not all FINA offices have a HITRO service. The locations of HITRO are listed on the HITRO website (**www.hitro.hr**). By attending the HITRO counter in FINA, you can initiate the process of establishing a Croatian limited liability company without professional assistance. Details of the procedure and the documentation required is provided in English on the HITRO website (*see* above).

One thing which you should pay special attention to before visiting the HITRO counter is the selection of your proposed company name. *See* left for the rules to be applied in making this choice.

Although the establishment of the HITRO service is a laudable attempt by the Croatian government to simplify the company set-up process and to become more business-friendly, in line with the country's move towards accession to the European Union, in practice it can be a somewhat confusing and daunting process. Navigating the paperwork and forms as well as obtaining clear advice in English or other foreign languages can be problematic. Although the website is in English, the forms are in Croatian and you should not rely on the counter staff at FINA being able to provide help in English.

In general, most foreigners who choose to buy property in Croatia via the company route tend to use the services of lawyers or estate agents to help with their company set-up, and it is advisable to use the services of an agency or lawyer who has conducted this service for other foreigners and therefore has experience, because there are some small differences in the documentation required for foreign citizens. These professionals should be able to provide helpful and practical advice, which will be invaluable and will help to simply the process and to move it along as swiftly as possible. Speed can sometimes be important, as the company set-up process can take three or four weeks (when things go smoothly).

Setting Up a Business Bank Account

Part of the process of establishing a fully operational company is to open a business account at a bank in Croatia, and HITRO does not handle this part. It is a three-step process.

The **first step** is to deposit the foundation capital for the company with a bank in an escrow account. After this you should wait for the court approval for your application to establish a company. Once the approval has been granted, the **second step** is visit the bank in person, to initiate the opening of the permanent business account and arrange the transfer of the foundation capital into the permanent account. The **third and final step** is performed by your company accountant, who will obtain exchange control clearance from the Croatian central bank (to prevent money-laundering). Once these three steps have been completed, you will be able to transfer money from your account in the UK to the business account and go on to complete the purchase of the property.

The following items should be brought to the bank in order open the company business bank account:

- **the court registry decision about the registration (submit a copy; the original should only be presented for inspection).**
- **the notice of classification from the National Institute for Statistics (submit a copy; the original should be presented for inspection).**
- **the company seal (official company stamp).**
- **ID (e.g. your passport).**

The Sales Contract (*Ugovor*)

The sales contract is also called a purchase agreement, a sales and purchase agreement or a purchase contract, but more usually it is informally called 'the final contract'. This is the key document. The sale of the property is completed on signing this document and adding the notary's certification. Payment of the balance and any deposit held in escrow with a notary should be paid to the seller. Once the contract has been signed and notarised, the notary should be asked to make several certified copies. Both the vendor and the buyer should retain one copy each. The remaining copies should be delivered to whoever has been appointed to notify the sale to the land registry and the *katastar* and to the tax office. If the property was purchased via the company route, it is useful to give the company accountant a copy of the contract, too.

The sale process is now complete, and any legal fees and estate agent's fees will now become due if they have not already been paid. The remaining work involves updating the ownership records and informing the tax office of the sale. Although the buyer carries the responsibility of ensuring the remaining work is done, it is typically carried out by the estate agent or lawyer, especially if the buyer is unable to speak Croatian.

Immediately after the Purchase

Submitting Documentation to the Land Registry

The land registry (Zemljišnik; see p.100) will require a notarised copy of the sales contract, a covering letter requesting that the records be updated to reflect the change in ownership and a fee of 250 kunas. If the property is being purchased privately by a foreign buyer, the land registry will also require the Ministry of Justice approval letter.

Submitting Documentation to the *Katastar* Office

The *katastar* office (see p.101) will require two notarised copies of the sales contract, two original copies of a covering letter requesting that the records be updated to reflect the change in ownership, a copy of the *vlasnicki list*, and a fee of 70 kunas. If the buyer does not attend the *katastar* office in person but sends a representative instead, the representative will be required to bring a valid power of attorney (*punomoć*) to prove that he or she has the authority to act on the buyer's behalf.

If the *katastar* records do not show the preceding owner's name, then the buyer will also be asked to provide evidence linking the preceding owner with whichever name is on the *katastar* record. This is usually a paper trail of sales contracts and inheritance transfers.

Paying Real Estate Transfer Tax

Second-hand (resale) properties are subject to a real estate transfer tax of 5 per cent. This is the same thing as stamp duty in the UK, but, unlike in the UK, it does not have to be paid on the day of the property purchase and is not based on the contract price. Instead, the local tax officer assesses the value of the property independently at a later date and the tax bill is charged at 5 per cent of the tax officer's valuation (this is a grey area, as some tax offices simply take the contract value to be the taxable value, but it is the local tax officer's valuation which is binding). Therefore, it is a good idea to assist the tax officer to make an accurate valuation by taking several photographs of the property designed to show the condition at the time of purchase *before* embarking on any improvement works. There is an appeal process if the tax valuation is higher than the contract price, but you will need to seek legal advice from your lawyer with regard to the chances of success. Appealing does not mitigate your legal requirement to pay. You will still have to pay the 5 per cent as valued, and hope to be able to claim some money back.

The buyer has a legal requirement to inform the local tax office of the property purchase within 30 days or risk a fine. The tax office will require the following documents when declaring the purchase:

- **two notarised copies of the sales contract.**
- **a completed form (which can be collected at the office); this form must be completed in Croatian.**
- **a copy of the *katastar* map.**
- **a copy of the *katastar* extract.**
- **a copy of the document by which the preceding owner came into ownership of the property (purchase contract, inheritance transfer, etc.).**

A tax bill is sent soon after the valuation, and payment is required within 30 days, after which penalties will be incurred.

Summary and Disclaimer

Although this information has been compiled from what the author believes to be reliable sources, there is no substitute for doing thorough research and taking any necessary professional advice before committing to purchase a property in Croatia. With a sensible approach and good advice, buying property in Croatia is no more difficult than buying property in many other countries, and some procedures are simpler than elsewhere. The greater the understanding of the process, the greater the likelihood of avoiding the pitfalls that can hinder the unwary buyer.

Financial Implications

Taxation

All tax systems are complicated, and the Croatian system is no exception. Fortunately, most people will only have limited contact with the more intricate parts of it. This chapter can only provide a general introduction to Croatian taxation; it is intended to enable you to have a sensible discussion with your professional advisers and, perhaps, help you work out the questions that you need to be asking them. **It is not intended as a substitute for obtaining proper professional advice.**

Many owners of holiday homes in Croatia will have only minimal contact with the system. In fact, many Croatian residents also have minimal contact with the tax system. Evasion is rife, but it is dangerous. It has become a joke and, in reality, while it is widespread it is probably not quite as common or extravagant as is reported.

It is helpful to have some sort of understanding about the way in which the system works and the taxes that you might face. You also need to be particularly careful about words and concepts that seem familiar to you but which have a fundamentally different meaning in Croatia. Of course, the rules change every year especially in the build-up to joining the EU.

Your situation when you have a foot in two countries – and, in particular, when you are moving permanently from one country to another – involves the consideration of the tax system in both countries with a view to minimising your tax obligations in both. It is not just a question of paying the lowest amount of tax in, say, Croatia. The best choice in Croatia can be very damaging to your position in the UK. Similarly, the most tax-efficient way of dealing with your affairs in the UK could be problematic in Croatia. The task of international advisers is to find a path of compromise that allows the client to enjoy the major advantages available in both countries without incurring any of the worst drawbacks. There is no perfect solution for most tax questions. That is not to say that there are not a great many bad solutions into which you can all too easily stumble.

What should guide you when making a decision about which course to pursue? Each individual will have a different set of priorities. Some are keen to obtain the biggest advantage out of their situation. Others recognise that they will have to pay some tax but simply wish to moderate their tax bill. For many, the main concern is a simple structure that they understand and can continue to manage without further assistance in the years ahead. Just as different clients have different requirements, so different advisers have differing views about the function of the adviser when dealing with a client's tax affairs. One of your first tasks when speaking with your financial adviser should be to discuss your basic philosophy about the payment of tax and management of your affairs, to make sure that you are both operating with the same objective in mind and that you are comfortable with your adviser's approach to solving your problem.

Residency for Tax Purposes

The biggest single factor in determining how you will be treated by the tax authorities in any country is whether you are resident in the country for tax purposes. This concept of tax residence causes a great deal of confusion, and can be different in different countries. You will see below that the Croatian definition of tax residence is different from the one that applies in the UK, and this sometimes confuses British and US foreigners. Tax residence is a question of fact. The law in every country lays down certain tests that will be used to decide whether you are tax resident there or not. If you fall into the categories stipulated in the tests, then you will be considered tax resident whether you want to be or not, and whether it was your intention to be tax resident or not, and whether or not another country also considers you tax resident.

It is your responsibility, if required, to make your tax declarations each year. The decision as to whether you fall into the category of resident is, in the first instance, made by the tax office. If you disagree, you can appeal through the courts. Because people normally change their tax residence when they move from one country to another, the basis on which decisions are made tends to be regulated by international law and to be reasonably, but not totally, consistent from country to country.

You will have to consider two different questions concerning tax residence:

- **Whether you will be treated as tax resident in the UK.**
- **Whether you will be treated as tax resident in Croatia.**

Tax Residence in the UK

It is outside the scope of this book to go into any details about UK taxation but these basic points should help you to make sense of Croatian taxation.

In the UK there are two tests that will help determine where you pay tax. They assess your domicile and your residence.

Your **domicile**, in UK terms, is the place that is your real home, the place where you have your roots. For most people it is the place where they were born. Changes in domicile can have far-reaching tax consequences and can be a useful tax reduction tool, but are not easy to make.

Residence falls into two categories. Under UK law there is a test of simple residence – actually living here other than on a purely temporary basis – and of ordinary residence. A person will generally be treated as **resident** in the UK if he or she spends 183 or more days per year in the UK. A visitor will also be treated as resident if he or she comes to the UK regularly and spends significant time here. If he or she spends, on average over a period of four or more years, more than three months here, he or she will be treated as tax resident.

A person can continue to be **ordinarily resident** in the UK even after he or she has stopped actually being resident here. A person is ordinarily resident in the

UK if his or her presence is a little more settled. The residence is an important part of his or her life. It will normally have gone on for some time.

The most important thing to understand is that, once you have been ordinarily resident in this country, the simple fact of going overseas will not automatically bring that residence to an end. If you leave this country in order to take up permanent residence elsewhere then, by concession, the Inland Revenue will treat you as ceasing to the resident on the day following your departure. But they will not treat you as ceasing to be ordinarily resident if, after leaving, you spend an average of 91 or more days per year in this country over any four-year period.

Until 1993 you were also classified as ordinarily resident in the UK if you had accommodation available for your use in the UK even if you had spent 364 days of the year living abroad. This rule was cancelled and no longer applies.

Tax Residence in Croatia

An individual is considered as a tax resident in Croatia if they have a permanent residence or a habitual abode in Croatia, or if they are registered in the Croatian civil registry.

A **habitual abode** is defined as a continuous or time-related stay in Croatia which lasts at least 183 days in one or two calendar years. Where interruptions to the stay take place, such as nipping back to the UK to stock up on curry powder and tea bags, for the purposes of calculating tax residency they will not affect the individual's status where the interruption lasts no longer than one year. '**Domicile**' is the place where an individual has his or her main centre of interests.

However, a **permanent residence** is one which is owned by the individual, or placed at the individual's disposal, for an uninterrupted period of not less than 183 days in one or two calendar years. Your actually staying in the apartment is not essential; you will still be tax resident. Having this second test for tax residency makes Croatia relatively unusual. Most countries only consider the number of days you actually spend in the country, whereas the second test – the number of days you have the *use* of a house or flat in Croatia – is similar to the pre-1993 UK rule (*see* above) and would apply to many more people than the first, as most people who buy property in Croatia do so for leisure or rental purposes rather than for it to serve as a main residence. In fact, the only obvious category of people who would be excluded from being tax resident is those who own a Croatian company and have bought the property listing their company as the owner. Their company would be tax resident, of course, so the Croatian government would still get its taxes paid relating to the property, if there were any due.

The key, though, is whether you have any taxes due, i.e. whether you have a tax liability, not whether you are tax resident. The rule of thumb is that if you make money through your Croatian property then you will be liable for paying tax on the money you make, but if you don't, then there should not be a tax bill. The most common ways people earn money on their property are by making a profit when they sell it and/or by letting it to tourists. Both of these situations will generate a tax liability on the money made, as will be explained later.

There is just one more thing to relate before we move on. Croatia's tax legislation is as new as the country itself. There are a lot of taxes and some are quite high, but in their formulation the Croatian government does not appear to have fully considered people who don't live in Croatia but have tax bills in the country. High taxes mean that Croatia does not attract attention as a tax haven, but the relatively unsophisticated tax legislation does offer opportunities for investors. Gaining **proper tax advice** is a good idea wherever an investor invests, but it would definitely be money well spent before investing in Croatia.

Tax Residence in More than One Country

Remember that you can be a tax resident in more than one country under the respective rules of those countries. For example, you might live in Britain but own a house in Croatia, or you might spend 230 days in the year in Croatia and 135 days in the UK. In this case you could end up, under the rules of each country, being responsible for paying the same tax in two or more countries, such as capital gains on the sale of your Croatian property. This would be unfair, so many countries have signed reciprocal **double taxation treaties**, and the UK and Croatia have such a treaty. It contains 'tie-breakers' and other provisions to decide, where there is the possibility of being required to pay tax twice, in which country any particular category of tax should be paid. The basic principle of the double taxation treaty is to protect people being taxed twice for the same activity. *See p.131.*

Taxes Payable in the UK

The significance of the residence rules is that you will continue to be liable for some UK taxes for as long as you are either ordinarily resident or domiciled in the UK. Broadly speaking, if you leave the UK to live in Croatia:

- **You will continue to have to pay tax in the UK on any capital gains you make anywhere in the world for as long as you are ordinarily resident in the UK – i.e. spend more than three months there in any one year – or domiciled in the UK. If you go to live permanently in Croatia with no intention of returning, and inform the UK authorities, you can apply to no longer be considered UK-domiciled, though changing your domicile is very difficult.**

- **You will continue to be liable for UK inheritance tax on all of your assets located anywhere in the world for as long as you remain domiciled in the UK. This will be subject to double taxation relief (*see* p.131). Other, more complex rules also apply in certain circumstances.**

- You will always pay UK income tax (Schedule A) on income arising from land and buildings in the UK – wherever your domicile, residence or ordinary residence.
- You will pay UK income tax (Schedule D) on the following basis:
  - Income from 'self-employed' work carried out in the UK (Cases I and II) – normally taxed in the UK if income arises in the UK.
  - Income from interest, annuities or other annual payments from the UK (Case III) – normally taxed in the UK if income arises in the UK and you are ordinarily resident in the UK.
  - Income from investments and businesses outside the UK (Cases IV and V) – normally only taxed in the UK if you are UK domiciled and resident or ordinarily resident in the UK.
  - Income from government pensions (fire, police, army, civil servant, etc.) – in all cases taxed in the UK.
  - Sundry profits not otherwise taxable (Case VI) arising out of land or building in the UK – always taxed in the UK.
- You will pay income tax on any income earned from salaried employment in the UK (Schedule E) only on any earnings from duties performed in the UK unless you are resident and ordinarily resident in the UK – in which case you will usually pay tax in the UK on your worldwide earnings.

If you are only buying a holiday home and will remain primarily resident in the UK, your tax position in the UK will not change very much. You will have to declare any income you make from your Croatian property as part of your UK tax declaration. The calculation of tax due on that income will be made in accordance with UK rules, which will result in a different taxable sum from that used by the Croatian authorities.

Since your property is located in Croatia, you will also have to pay taxes to the Croatian tax authorities. The taxes you will have to pay are discussed below. The UK Revenue & Customs will give you full credit for the taxes already paid in Croatia. On the disposal of the property, you must disclose the profit made to the Inland Revenue, which again will give full credit for Croatian tax paid. Similarly, on your death, your assets in Croatia must be disclosed on the UK probate tax declaration but, once again, full credit will be given for sums paid in Croatia.

Should You Pay Tax in Croatia?

Under Croatian law it is your responsibility to fill in a tax return in each year when you have any taxable income unless that income is:

- taxed in full at source, i.e. employment income.
- outside the scope of Croatian tax.

There are six categories of personal income tax law, covering:

- **employment income.**
- **self-employed income.**
- **income from property and property rights** (e.g. rental income).
- **income from capital.**
- **income from insurance.**
- **other income.**

All, apart from the employment income, will entail filing a tax return.
There are three key points to remember:

- **Lots of Croatian people don't pay the taxes they owe, but the same people would disapprove if they suspected a foreigner was evading paying taxes to the Croatian government**
- **The rules are applied more strictly every year.**
- **If you are caught not paying the taxes you owe, the penalties are substantial and the nuisance can be even more substantial. In Croatia, late payment of tax is subject to interest at 15 per cent a year. Certain other kinds of default or violation of the corporate tax laws are subject to penalties up to 200,000 kunas. The deadline for completing and submitting a tax return is at the end of February in the following year.**

There is a lengthy document written by the Ministry of Finance (available in PDF format on the web, **www.porezna-uprava.hr/en/publikacije/p_prirucnici_brosure.asp?id=b03d1**) that sets out all the rules of the Croatian tax system. It is generally pretty clear and, even better, it is written in English!

It is probably simplest to arrange for an accountant to complete and file your various tax returns, as these are complicated and in Croatian. There are many different deadlines for payment of the various taxes.

The Croatian tax system is composed of two main types of taxes: direct taxes and indirect taxes. The distinction between the two is broadly the same as in the UK or USA. Non-residents will pay applicable indirect taxes in, generally, the same way as a resident, but they are treated very differently when it comes to direct taxation.

Indirect Taxes Payable in Croatia

Value Added Tax or VAT (PDV)

PDV is charged on any supply or service deemed to be made or rendered within the Croatian territory. The ordinary PDV rate is set at 22 per cent. There is a reduced rate of 10 per cent for services related to organised stays such as hotel accommodation and the agency fees for those services. Additionally, certain products are zero-rated, such as educational books and some medicines.

PDV at 22 per cent is also due on the sale of new-build properties when the PDV-registered developer sells them for the first time. Although payment of PDV for such property sales is the responsibility of the developer, the sale prices of such properties are often increased to reflect the heavy tax charge.

Real Estate Transfer Tax

Similar to stamp duty in the UK, real estate transfer tax is due on specific contracts if made in Croatia and on contracts, including those made abroad, regarding the transfer or leasing of immovable property (real estate including land, houses and apartments) in Croatia. Real estate transfer tax is applied when a resale property is sold. Where a newly built or renovated property is purchased from a PDV-registered developer for the first time, real estate transfer tax is only due on the value of the land portion being purchased.

When transferring immovable property, cadastral and land registry taxes also apply, although the sums involved are fairly negligible. These relate to the formal transfer of ownership in the public register.

Import Taxes

With a rapidly improving range of goods in the shops, the temptation to import goods into Croatia diminishes each year. However, many new property owners still find it difficult to find furniture and soft furnishings without a shopping excursion over the border to the likes of IKEA, or many simply wish to import their own furniture from home. These actions are subject to excise duty. As always in Croatia many people successfully flout the law, but, if you are caught, the shopping trip can be expensive. Exemptions are available to those who are moving to Croatia and have been recently granted a temporary residency permit, but only for used goods; see **Settling In**, pp.141–42.

Cars are also relatively expensive in Croatia compared with most of the rest of Europe, as Croatia does not make cars and all cars are imported. Excise duty for cars ranges from £500 to £8,000, and additionally some cars also fall into the luxury products category, incurring a further 30 per cent import cost.

Anyone who wishes to import goods legally would do well to employ the services of a *Spedicija* company, whose job it is to liaise with customs officers to help ease the bureaucracy.

City Surtax

Municipalities and cities may levy an additional tax, called city surtax. Currently, the city of Zagreb has the highest city surtax rate, at 18 per cent. City surtax is calculated on the amount of personal income tax payable.

Inheritance and Gift Tax

Inheritance and gift tax exists in Croatia but is rarely paid, as there is a wide range of people who are exempt from paying this tax, including the spouse, parents, children, siblings, sons-in-law and daughters-in-law and nieces and nephews of the deceased. Also exempt are the church, public institutions or charitable institutions.

However for any group not exempted, inheritance tax is charged at 5 per cent on the movable estate over the 50,000 kuna (approx £4,600) threshold.

As property is not movable, the transfer of property through inheritance does not incur inheritance tax but it is subject to the 5 per cent real estate transfer tax. However, the spouse, parents, children, siblings, sons-in-law and daughters-in-law and nieces and nephews of the deceased are all exempt along with the ex-wife or ex-husband if the property formed part of the divorce settlement.

Withholding Taxes

There are two main withholding taxes on certain payments made to foreign entities: withholding tax on interest and withholding tax on royalties. There is no tax on dividends (since 1 January 2005) and so no dividend withholding tax.

Interest Payments

Interest payments from bank accounts and deposits, certain bonds and similar securities are subject to withholding tax at rates of 15 per cent but reduced to 10 per cent for British citizens under the terms of the double taxation treaty between Croatia and the UK. These taxes, if any, on interest received by Croatian residents generally consist of an advance payment of income tax due by the recipients. As such, gross interest must be included in the recipient's tax base and the withholding tax deducted from the aggregate taxable income. However, non-residents are not charged withholding tax on Croatian government bonds or corporate bonds. Also there is no withholding tax on loans granted by a non-Croatian bank.

Royalties

Royalties paid to Croatian-resident corporations are subject to withholding tax of 15 per cent. Royalty payments to British citizens not resident in Croatia are subject to a 10 per cent withholding tax.

Taxes on Capital Gains

As this book is about buying property in Croatia and there are two main routes to doing so, this section deals with the capital gains tax that applies to people who own their property privately, and with the company profit tax that applies to those who own their property via their Croatian limited company.

Private purchasers are subject to capital gains tax on any profit made if they sell the property within three years of purchase (which of course begins from the point of legal ownership including the Ministry of Justice permission, *see* pp.95–7, 33 and 109–11, not the point where the sales contract is signed). If you sell your property after three years of ownership, or if the property was your main residence, then no capital gains tax is due. The capital gains tax is charged at the marginal rate of tax according to the individual, but for almost everyone it works out at 25 per cent.

Company purchasers are subject to profit tax which is charged at 20 per cent but without any time limit. If the only thing you do is set up a company and use it to buy a house or apartment, then later sell the house or apartment for a profit, the government will take 20 per cent of that profit. If you make losses or have costs on some other part of the business, then the profit you will make will be lower, and so will the tax.

There is one other point of which buyers should be aware. At the time of writing (summer 2007) there is no capital gains tax on the sale of a company. Possibly using something of a loophole in the system, buyers have been buying a property on behalf of their company and then selling the company and all its assets (the property) for a profit without incurring any tax liability. Although there are clearly significant tax savings to be made by following this path, it should not be relied on, as with one change of legislation the loophole could be closed. In any case, anyone intending to exploit this opportunity would be well advised to seek legal and tax guidance first.

Direct Taxes Payable in Croatia

The Croatian tax system is immensely complicated, and is made worse because it is so different from what you will be used to. What follows can only be a very brief summary of the position.

Remember that Croatia is (taken overall, not just in relation to income tax) a high-tax society. Whether for this reason or out of an independence of spirit, many people suffer from selective amnesia as far as the taxman is concerned and significantly under-declare their income. This is dangerous. The penalties are severe. There are, however, quite legitimate tax-saving devices that you can use to reduce your liabilities. These issues are best addressed before you move to Croatia, as there are then many more possibilities open to you.

There is no Croatian wealth tax.

Croatian personal income tax law recognises six categories of income:

- **employment income.**
- **self-employment income.**
- **income from property and property rights.**
- **income from capital.**

- income from insurance.
- other income.

Tax on Employment Income

Taxable remuneration from employment includes all remuneration, whether monetary or non-monetary, including benefits in kind provided to an employee. Statutory pension insurance contributions paid by the employee reduce taxable income. The taxable income of individuals is also reduced by a personal allowance and an allowance for dependent family members, voluntary pension contributions, life insurance premiums with the character of savings and premiums for additional and/or private health insurance. Payments of these items can decrease the tax base of an individual by a maximum of 2,000 kunas.

Obligatory employer's health insurance, insurance against accident at work and employer contributions are not part of the employee's taxable income.

The remuneration and benefits paid by a Croatian employer are generally taxed through monthly payroll tax withholding.

Personal income tax is paid at the following rates:

- **15 per cent on taxable income up to twice the taxpayer's basic personal allowance (3,200 kunas per month).**

- **25 per cent on taxable income between double and five times the taxpayer's basic personal allowance (3,200–8,000 kunas per month).**

- **35 per cent on taxable income between five and 14 times the taxpayer's basic personal allowance (8,000–22,400 kunas per month).**

- **45 per cent on taxable income exceeding 14 times the taxpayer's basic personal allowance (over 22,400 kunas per month).**

Income tax is further increased by municipal tax (so-called 'city surtax') ranging from zero per cent to 18 per cent. The rate of surtax depends on the individual's place of residence.

Taxable income for a particular tax year includes:

- **gross salary paid during the tax period to 31 December.**

- **pensions received on the basis of previously paid compulsory pension insurance contributions.**

- **benefits in kind (e.g. housing and rental allowances, relocation expenses, private use of employer-owned or -provided cars, boats and buildings, as well as interest-free loans or loans at an interest rate lower than 4 per cent annually).**

- **insurance premiums that employers pay to private pension plans, health insurance plans and life insurance, where the employer has no statutory obligation to make contributions or pay premiums.**

- **benefits and awards above the non-taxable level.**

These benefits qualify as non-taxable earnings:

- reimbursements of travel expenses for coming to work (the actual cost of travelling by public transport).
- a daily allowance for business trips within Croatia (up to 170 kunas per day, plus travel and accommodation expenses).
- a daily allowance for business trips abroad.
- an occasional allowance for Christmas, Easter, annual vacation, etc. (up to 2,000 kunas annually).
- reimbursement for use of employee's personal car for business purposes (up to 2 kunas per kilometre).

Tax on Self-employment Income

With high unemployment (around 18 per cent), Croatia is understandably reluctant to grant work visas to foreigners except in exceptional circumstances. It is feasible to get a work permit to work for another company, but not likely. Most foreigners who live and work in Croatia are therefore self-employed, often running a small business such as one dealing with yacht charter, property management, property development, holiday lettings or estate agency. This section will apply to those people. Labour is cheap, especially student labour which has a low tax base, so there are occasional references to what can be deducted when employing someone else.

Taxable self-employment income includes income from small business activities, independent professions (doctors, lawyers and similar), agriculture and forestry. The tax on income earned from self-employment is calculated based on the difference between the business receipts and the business expenses within a tax period. Taxpayers engaged in self-employment activities are obliged to pay Croatian pension and health insurance contributions.

Individuals receiving income from self-employment are obliged to file annual income tax returns and meet the filing and payment deadlines (*see* p.131). They are also obliged to make monthly advance tax payments in accordance with the tax authority's assessment.

A taxpayer may elect to pay corporate profit tax rather than personal income tax. The tax administration gives a ruling on the basis of a request for such a choice at the end of a current year for the next calendar year. The ruling is binding on a taxpayer for five subsequent years (in certain circumstances shorter periods may be approved).

Tax on Income from Property and Property Rights

Taxable income from property and property rights includes income earned from rentals, leases, the letting of flats, rooms and beds to travellers and tourists and money received from the sale of property and property rights.

The amount of tax due on income earned through the letting or lease of property can be decreased by up to 30 per cent for expenses. The tax rate is 15 per cent with no personal allowance. The local tax office will decide the amount of tax due and give you a deadline for payment. This may appear strange to people who have only lived and earned their income in a country where the tax laws have evolved over centuries and payment of taxes is widely regarded as unavoidable, such as the UK. In this respect Croatia is wholly unlike the UK. It is a new country and, although the national taxes are the same throughout Croatia, it should be noted that each municipality has its own tax office and that there can be variations on how the tax legislation is interpreted and enforced. This is one of the points which the EU has raised and asked for specific improvement on in Croatia's EU entry negotiations, so it would be reasonable to expect the situation to change over the coming months and years.

Where income from property arises from the letting of apartments, rooms and beds to travellers and tourists, where the taxpayer is not registered as a PDV taxpayer, tax is paid according to the tax authority assessment. Only companies can be PDV-registered, so any private owner should expect to pay tax in this way. Any foreign property owner who has used the company route to buy should seek financial advice and assistance from their company accountant when choosing whether or not to apply for PDV registration.

Income generated from the disposal of property and property rights, if the property or property right has been sold within three years of the date of purchase and the taxpayer did not use it as his or her residence, is taxable at the rate of 25 per cent and paid as one-off payment under 'other income'. Income from property and property rights is only taxed if the taxpayer has not already paid self-employment income tax on this income.

Although unrelated to this section, which deals with personal taxation and not company taxation, it would be worth pointing out that when a company sells a property, this tax is not due (*see* 'Indirect Taxes: Taxes on Capital Gains, pp.125–6'). Instead the profit is subject to normal company profit tax of 20 per cent, which takes into account all the company's expenses and revenues throughout the tax year. The company tax does not qualify for the three-year exemption and is payable however long you have owned the property.

Tax on Income from Capital

This includes bank interest income, share option income from the purchase or allocation of own shares, withdrawal of assets, and the use of services by company owners for their private purposes at the expense of the current year's profit – an example would be if you stay in a holiday home owned by your company, thereby causing your company to lose the opportunity to let out the holiday home and receive rental income during the weeks in which you are occupying it; your stay would be regarded as a 'benefit in kind', to use UK terms, and may be taxable at rental rates.

The tax levied on capital income is withheld at source without provision for taxpayers to claim expenses or personal allowances.

The rates levied on capital income are:

- **15 per cent on profit-shares divided by the management and employees of a business enterprise on the basis of shares granted or purchased via stock option schemes.**

- **35 per cent on income from interest, withdrawals of assets and use of services.**

Since 1 January 2005, receipts from dividends, and shares in profit based on shares in capital, have not been considered to be income.

Tax on Income from Insurance

Tax levied on income from insurance policies, for example life insurance, is withheld at source without provision for taxpayers to claim expenses or personal allowances. Tax is levied at the rate of 15 per cent.

Tax on Other Income

Other income includes, for example, royalties, receipts received by athletes, agents, artists, referees and sports delegates, interpreters, consultants, expert witnesses and similar activities. Rewards and scholarships to pupils and students paid above any tax-free thresholds are also deemed 'other income'.

Tax levied on 'other income' is withheld by the payer of the income at the rate of 25 per cent, without provision for taxpayers to claim personal allowances.

The taxable amount can be decreased by 30 per cent for expenses, providing the income derived relates to royalties, income from professional journalism, artists' and athletes' activities and income by non-residents arising from art, entertainment, sport, literary and visual-art-related activities connected with the press, radio, television and entertainment events.

Other income is subject to Croatian social security contributions.

Health Insurance

For any person who is not in Croatia on a 90-day tourist visa – i.e. for those who are either resident or who have even just received their first one year temporary stay permit – it is mandatory to have health insurance. This is not something which can be privately purchased from companies such as BUPA or PPP; it must be purchased from the Republic of Croatia and should be thought of as similar to the UK's National Insurance contributions. All foreigners in Croatia must pay it, irrespective of whether they are in employment. Even pre-school children have to pay, doubtless from their piggy banks as the bills are sent direct to the children, not to their parents!

For those who are in employment, it is calculated at 15 per cent of their gross salary per month. For those who are not employed, the tax is calculated as though they have earned the minimum wage. As a guide, in 2006, the basic cost was 325 kunas (approx £30) per month.

New Residents

New residents are liable to tax on their worldwide income and gains from the date they arrive in Croatia. Until that day they will only have to pay Croatian tax on their income if it is derived from assets in Croatia.

The most important thing to understand about taking up residence in Croatia (and abandoning UK tax residence) is that it gives you superb opportunities for tax planning and, in particular, for restructuring your affairs to minimise what can otherwise be penal rates of taxation in Croatia. To do this you need good advice at an early stage – preferably several months before you intend to move.

Tax Returns and Payments

The tax year runs from 1 January to 31 December and the deadline for submitting the tax return is 28 February in the subsequent year. Each municipality has its own tax authority, and the tax return should be submitted to the one in the taxpayer's place of residence.

Most people in Croatia do not have to submit personal annual tax returns unless they fall into one of the following categories

- **they had more than one employer in the same tax year.**
- **they received income from self-employment activities or from property.**
- **they received income directly from abroad.**
- **the tax authority requested they make a tax return.**
- **their employer failed to perform the tax calculation accurately or pay the employee's tax bill on the employee's behalf.**

The local tax authority will issue a tax assessment, and payment of any outstanding liability is required within 15 days of receipt. Failure to file a completed tax return on time or late payment of taxes can incur a high penalty of 500–50,000 kunas.

The Double Taxation Treaty

The detailed effect of double taxation treaties depends on the two countries involved. Although treaties may be similar in concept, they can differ in detail.

The major consideration is whether you are a tax resident in Croatia or not. Resident taxpayers with foreign-sourced income are liable to pay tax. Under

Croatian regulations, taxes paid abroad on income earned abroad from employment or from other sources may be deducted against Croatian tax. However, the tax credit cannot exceed the foreign tax paid or the Croatian tax payable on income earned abroad.

Only the effect of the Croatia-UK treaty is considered here. These are the main points of relevance to residents:

- **Any income from letting property in the UK will normally be outside the scope of Croatian taxation and, instead, will be taxed in the UK, as income from immovable property is taxed in the location of the property.**

- **Pensions received from the UK are not deemed as income in Croatia and therefore are not taxable. The Croatian income tax regime does not tax income consisting of interest from savings in domestic and foreign currency accounts or income earned on credits and loans, income from securities, gains from selling securities unless such sales are considered to be the taxpayer's business activity, or income earned from dividends and shares in profit.**

- **UK government pensions will continue to be taxed in the UK but are not taxed in Croatia, nor do they count when assessing the level of your income or when calculating the rate of tax payable on your income.**

- **You will normally not be required to pay UK capital gains tax on gains made after you settle in Croatia except in relation to real estate located in the UK.**

- **If you pay tax on an inheritance outside Croatia, the same will apply.**

Double tax treaties are detailed and need to be read in the light of your personal circumstances. A good place to start with regard to the Croatian tax system is **www.porezna-uprava.hr/en/porezi/v_poreza.asp?id=b01d1**. This gives a comprehensive overview, in English, of the tax regime and likely liabilities.

Investment Incentives

It is worth remembering that, as in all high-tax societies, there are substantial incentives available for people and businesses investing in Croatia. The rules are fairly complex and have a twofold purpose. They are designed to stimulate economic activity in areas that have been suffering economic depression, and to help those areas particularly affected by the war between 1991 and 1995.

In general, investment incentives are usually organised as corporate tax credits, so tax rates can be reduced for up to 10 years on completion of various conditions (*see* the table opposite). However, the tax benefits cannot exceed the investment amount.

Tax Benefit Rates for Companies with 10 or more Employees

Investment Amount	Tax Benefit Rate	Period	Must Employ
At least 4 million kunas	10%	10yrs	10 employees
More than 10 million kunas	7%	10yrs	30 employees
More than 20 million kunas	3%	10yrs	50 employees
More than 60 million kunas	0%	10yrs	75 employees

Other concessions and exemptions are generally related to:

• companies established in regions under special state care, employing more than five persons permanently – up to 75 per cent corporate tax reductions over a period of 10 years starting in 2005.

• companies established in the territory of the city of Vukovar (on the eastern border with Serbia) and employing more than five persons permanently – exempt from any corporate income tax over a period of 10 years starting in 2005.

• companies established in mountain regions and employing more than five persons permanently – up to 75 per cent corporate tax reductions over a period of 10 years starting in 2005.

• businesses whose registered and only business activity is research and development – these are not liable to pay profit tax.

Summary

Questions arising from taxation issues are inevitably complex. This chapter is an attempt to lay out the major terms of the Croatian tax code as it is likely to apply for the majority of UK buyers of Croatian property. At its simplest, a private buyer (as opposed to a buyer using a Croatian-registered company) will incur a Croatian tax liability if they sell their property within three years of purchase for a greater sum than they paid for it (after three years this capital gain is tax-free).

When a buyer wishes to let out their property, i.e. will incur rental income, they would be advised to purchase using a Croatian company, which can be easily set up. Any rental income earned will be taxable at corporate rates, and any gain on the property at point of sale will incur a corporate profit tax liability (which is lower than the private buyer's capital gains tax).

As anywhere in the world, it is always wise to seek professional advice regarding such matters, especially if you envisage your circumstances being different from or more complex than normal.

Inheritance

The Croatian Inheritance Rules

The Croatians cannot do just as they please with their property when they die. Inheritance rules apply, which for Croatians are much more restrictive than the rules under UK law. Certain groups of people have (almost) automatic rights to inherit a part of your property. Fortunately, if you are not Croatian you can dispose of your property in whatever way your national law allows. For British people this is, basically, as they please.

Making a Will

It is always best to make an Croatian will. If you do not, your UK will should be treated as valid in Croatia and will be used to distribute your estate. This is a false economy, as the cost of implementing the UK will is much higher than the cost of implementing a Croatian will, and the disposal of your estate set out in your UK will is often a tax disaster in Croatia.

If you are not a resident in Croatia, your Croatian will should state that it only applies to immovable property in Croatia. The rest of your property – including movable property in Croatia – will be disposed of in accordance with English law and the provisions of your UK will. If you are domiciled in Croatia (*see* 'Residency for Tax Purposes', pp.119–21) you should make a Croatian will disposing of all your assets wherever they are located. If you make a Croatian will covering only immovable property in Croatia, you should modify your UK will so as to exclude any immovable property located in Croatia.

Always use a lawyer to advise you on the contents of your will and to draft it. Lawyers love people who make home-made wills. They make a fortune from dealing with their estates because the wills are often inadequately drafted and produce lots of expensive problems.

A person who dies without a will dies intestate and the results are complicated. Will the UK rules about what happens in this event apply (because you are British) or will the Croatian rules apply? This gives rise to many happy hours of argument by lawyers and tax officials at your (or your heirs') expense.

It is much cheaper to make a will.

Investments

Most of us don't like making investment decisions. They make our heads hurt. They make us face up to unpleasant things – like taxes and death. We don't really understand what we are doing, what the options are and what is best. We don't know who we should trust to give us advice. We know we ought to do something, but it will wait until next week – or maybe the week after. Until then our present arrangements will have to do. If you are moving to live overseas you must review your investments. Your current arrangements are likely to be financially disastrous – and may even be illegal.

What Are You Worth?

In financial terms, most of us are worth more than we think. When we come to move abroad and have to think about these things it can come as a shock.

Take a pencil and list your actual and potential assets in the table below. This will give you an idea as to the amount you are worth now and, just as importantly, what you are likely to be worth in the future. Your investment plans should take into account both figures.

Asset	Value (kunas)	Value (£)
Current Assets		
Main home		
Holiday home		
Contents of main home		
Contents of holiday home		
Car		
Boat		
Bank accounts		
Other cash-type investments		
Bonds, etc.		
Stocks and shares		
PEPS, Tessas, ISAs		
SIPPs		
Value of your business		
Future Assets		
Value of share options		
Personal/company pension (likely lump sum)		
Potential inheritances or other accretions		
Value of endowment mortgages on maturity		
Other		
TOTAL		

Who Should Look After Your Investments?

You may already have an investment adviser in the UK and you may be very happy with his or her experience and the quality of the service you have received, but this person is unlikely to be able to help you once you have gone to Croatia. Moreover, he or she will almost certainly not have the knowledge to do so. He or she will not know about the Croatian investments that might be of interest to you. Even if he or she has some knowledge of these things, your investment adviser in the UK is likely to be thousands of miles from where you will be living.

Choosing an investment adviser competent to deal with you once you are in Croatia is not easy. You cannot simply select a new local (Croatian) adviser once you have moved, as many Croatian advisers know little about the UK aspects of your case or about the UK tax and inheritance rules that could still have some importance for you.

By all means seek guidance from your existing adviser. Ask for guidance from others who have already made the move. Do some research. Meet the potential candidates. Are you comfortable with them? Do they share your approach to life? Do they have the necessary experience? Is their performance record good? How are they regulated? What security, bonding and guarantees can they offer you? How will they be paid for their work – fees or commission? If commission, what will that formula mean they are making from you in 'real money' rather than percentages?

Above all be careful. There are lots of very dubious 'financial advisers' operating in the popular tourist areas of Croatia. Some are totally incompetent and some are crooks, seeking simply to separate you from your money as cleanly as possible. Fortunately there are also some excellent and highly professional advisers with good track records. Make sure you choose one of these.

Where Should You Invest?

British people must decide whether they should keep their sterling investments. Many have investments that are largely sterling-based. Even if they are, for example, a Far Eastern fund, they will probably be denominated in sterling and they will pay out dividends in sterling.

You will be spending Croatian kunas. As the value of the kuna fluctuates against the pound sterling, the value of your investments will go up and down. That, in itself, isn't too important because the value won't crystallise unless you sell. What does matter is that the revenue you generate from those investments (rent, interest, dividends and so on) will be paid according to the fluctuations in value.

Trusts

Trusts are an important weapon in the hands of a person or people going to live in Croatia and allow you:

- **to put part of your assets in the hands of trustees so that they no longer belong to you for wealth tax or inheritance tax purposes.**
- **to receive only the income you need (rather than all the income generated by those assets) so keeping the extra income out of sight for income tax purposes.**

They are therefore a very flexible vehicle for investment purposes.

How Trusts Work

After leaving the UK (and before moving to Croatia) you reorganise your affairs by giving a large part of your assets to 'trustees'. This is normally a professional trust company located in a low-tax regime. Needless to say, the choice of a reliable trustee is critical.

The trustee holds the asset not for their own benefit but 'in trust' for whatever purposes you established when you made the gift. It could, for example, be to benefit a local hospital or school or, more likely, it could be to benefit you and your family. If the trust is set up properly in the light of the requirements of Croatian law, then those assets will no longer be treated as yours for tax purposes. On your death the assets are not yours to leave to your children (or whoever) and so do not (subject to any local anti-avoidance legislation) carry inheritance tax. Similarly, the income from those assets is not your income. If some of it is given to you it may be taxed as your income, but the income that is not given to you will not be taxed in Croatia and, because the trust will be located in a nil or low-tax regime, it will not be taxed elsewhere either.

The detail of the arrangements is vitally important. They must be set up precisely to comply with Croatian tax law. If you do not do this they will not work as intended.

Trustees can manage your investments in (virtually) whatever way you stipulate when you set up the trust. You can give the trustees full discretion to do as they please or you can specify precisely how your money is to be used. There are particular types of trusts and special types of investments that trusts can make that can be especially beneficial in Croatia.

Trusts can be beneficial even to Croatian-resident people of modest means – say £350,000. It is certainly worth investing a little money to see if they can be of use to you, as the tax savings can run to many thousands of pounds. If you are thinking of trusts as an investment vehicle and tax-planning measure you must take advice early – months before you are thinking of moving to Croatia. Otherwise it will be too late.

Keeping Track of Your Investments

Whatever you decide to do about investments – put them in a trust, appoint investment managers to manage them in your own name or manage them yourself – you should always keep an up-to-date list of your investments and assets and tell your family where to find it. Make a file. By all means have a computer file, but print off a good old-fashioned paper copy as well. Keep it in an obvious place known to your family. Keep it with your will and the deeds of your house, preferably in a safe-deposit box with your bank or your solicitor. Also keep the originals of bank account books, share certificates and so on in the same place, or a note of where they are to be found.

For a lawyer it is very frustrating – and expensive for the client – when after a parent's death the children come in with a suitcase full of correspondence and old cheque books. The lawyer has to go through it all and write to what may well be a series of banks lest there should be £1,000,000 lurking in a forgotten account. There never is, and it wastes a lot of money.

Conclusion

Buying a home in Croatia – whether to use as a holiday home, as an investment or to live in permanently – is as safe as buying one in the UK.

The rules may appear complicated. Our rules would if you were a Croatian person coming to this country. That apparent complexity is often no more than lack of familiarity.

There are tens of thousands of British people who have bought homes in Croatia. Most have had no real problems. Most have enjoyed years of holidays in Croatia. Many have seen their property rise substantially in value. Many are now thinking of retiring to Croatia.

For a trouble-free time you simply need to keep your head and to seek advice from experts. If you don't like lawyers, remember that they make far more money out of sorting out the problems you get into by doing it yourself than they do by giving you this basic advice!

Settling In

07

Now that you have bought your very own Croatian property, it is time to start the enjoyable process of settling into your second home. The following chapter contains the practical information you will need to establish your new life, including how to pay your first electricity bill, open a bank account and register with the local GP. All these things may seem very daunting at first, but Croatians are extremely welcoming, so, with the help of this guide, your transition from visitor to resident should be complete in no time at all.

Making the Move

As you pack up your home, whether for a summer, for a year or for good, there will be plenty on your mind but make sure the following points are included on your 'to do' list:

- Double-check that you have the necessary visa for entry into Croatia and the paperwork needed to apply for residence and work permits once you arrive (*see* **First Steps and Reasons for Buying**, 'Visas and Permits', pp.22–31).

- Ensure that your passport is valid for six months beyond your intended stay in Croatia. It is a good idea to keep photocopies of your passport in case the original is lost or stolen.

- If you are taking a pet, obtain either an EU Pet Passport or proof of a rabies vaccination, an international certificate of health from your local vet, and your pet's microchipping details. *See* 'Taking Your Pet to Croatia', pp.165–6, for more details.

- Notify your bank and credit card company if you intend to use any of your bank cards or credit cards overseas. You may also want to check the charges for accessing services from foreign countries, such as cash withdrawals from ATM machines, and verify that direct debits are in place to pay any regular bills while you are away.

- If you are intending to take large sums of cash with you, remember that there is no limit on foreign currency taken into the country but a ceiling of 15,000 kunas if you take local currency. Amounts worth more than 40,000 kunas must be declared to customs officers at the border.

- If you are moving permanently to Croatia, notify your credit card companies and mailing lists of your change of address.

- Set up a forwarding service with the UK Post Office so that all mail is directed to your new address.

- Take a supply of different-denomination British postage stamps with you in case you need to send stamped self-addressed envelopes back to the UK.

- Make sure you can obtain all the British tax forms you may need before they are due.

• Set up a British account with an overseas courier service in order to save money if you are likely to do a lot of shipping.

• Terminate or suspend the utility contracts to your home in the UK.

• Check that your health insurance provides cover for your stay in Croatia and any other country you will be visiting. Arrange a last round of dental and medical appointments before you leave.

• If you suffer from any medical conditions or complaints, including allergies, have a brief explanation translated into Croatian.

• If you take any prescription medicines, including the Pill, take an ample supply with you to last the entire duration of your stay or until you have registered with a local doctor and established an alternative. You may want to arrange repeat prescriptions with your UK doctor and have someone send the medication to you in Croatia.

• Stock up on any creams, ointments or beauty products that you may not be able to find in Croatia and don't want to live without.

• Make sure you have plug adapters for all your electrical appliances, including any computers, that you are bringing from the UK.

• If you are taking a computer with you, make sure you have all the English-language software you will need and an English computer keyboard, as Croatian ones are different.

Removal Companies

If you are planning to take furniture, household goods and a large number of personal possessions with you to Croatia, by far the easiest option is to hire an international removals company to do it for you. Not only will they pack the items in your UK home and deliver them directly to your new address in Croatia, but they will deal with all the Croatian customs requirements and guide you through the necessary paperwork.

The website **www.croatia.shipping-international.com** has a directory of removal firms and shipping agents that provide services between the UK and Croatia; **www.europemovers.com** allows you to compare services and prices of a number of different international removal firms. Also see **References**, p.192.

If you decide to hire a van and transport your belongings yourself, be prepared to spend a day waiting at the Croatian border for customs officials to work through their paperwork. All goods imported into Croatia, whether used or new, are subject to a customs tariff, which is usually around 10 per cent of their value, plus a 22 per cent PDV tax. You will also be charged an administration fee of 500–1,000 kunas. If you have been granted a temporary stay permit or permanent residence by the Croatian government, however, you are eligible for customs duty relief and can avoid paying these charges. The customs duty relief allows you to import household articles that you have owned and used for at least 12 months, including furniture, art, bikes, motorcycles, small amounts of food or provisions and caravans. In order to qualify you need to present:

- a temporary stay permit or permanent residence papers.
- a written statement declaring the date of your residence transfer to Croatia and that you haven't benefited from customs duty relief before.
- an inventory of all items, including evidence that they have been owned and used by you for the last 12 months.

If you have a work or business permit, the customs duty relief also allows you duty-free importation of goods connected to your work, such as office stationery, materials and tools. In this case you have to present your business or work permit as well as an inventory of business items including their trade name, quantity and value.

If you don't have any kind of permission to stay in Croatia but intend to set up residence in the country within six months of your arrival, you are still eligible for customs duty relief as long as you pay a financial bond, which is returned to you once you have been granted a relevant permit.

Once awarded, the customs duty relief is valid for up to 12 months, allowing you to make repeated trips to ferry your belongings from the UK. You can find further details about all the outlined regulations on the website of the Customs Directorate of the Croatian Republic (*Carinska Uprava*) at **www.carina.hr**.

Learning and Speaking the Language

Croatia is an easy country for English-speakers to be lazy linguists. The majority of Croatians have learnt English from a young age and are happy to speak it. At the very least, most people you meet will know enough English words to enable you to communicate with them. However, Croatians are unfailingly delighted if you have made the effort to learn even the basics of their language. No matter how rudimentary your Croat skills, if you try, you will receive abundant encouragement – and even admiration; Croatians are the first to point out that their language is a difficult one to learn.

Spoken by over six million people, Croatian is a southern Slavic language that uses the Latin alphabet (rather than Cyrillic) but with four extra letters. As well as Croatia, it is an official language of Bosnia-Herzegovina and, as a result of an historical anomaly, of small regions in Austria and Italy. Since it first emerged as a modern language in the 14th and 15th century, Croatian has often been the victim of political manoeuvrings. Most recently it was declared, along with Serbian, as simply a dialect of Serbo-Croat rather than a language in its own right. With the demise of Yugoslavia this idea was dismissed, and Croatian has become an important part of Croatia's national identity.

Dialects

There are three main Croatian dialects in use in various parts of the country, and they are differentiated from each other by the three separate ways of saying 'What?' In the Štokavian dialect it is said '*Što?*', in Kajkavski, '*Kaj?*' and in Čakavski, '*Ča?*'. There are other disparities between the dialects in grammar and pronunciation which make them very distinct from each other, but 'What?' is the most obvious. Štokavian is the standard literary dialect used across Croatia in books and the media, but on the streets of Zagreb you will hear Kajkavski being spoken. This was once the official dialect of Croatia but it is now mostly confined to Zagreb, Zagorje, Karlovac, Sisak and the surrounding areas. Čakavski is the oldest of the three dialects and is dominant in Istria, the Dalmatian littoral and on the islands.

The matter of dialect is further complicated by the fact that each of these three major idioms has numerous sub-dialects as well as mixing with each other. For example in certain areas Čakavski and Štokavian have blended to create a separate dialect: Šćakavian.

There are obvious reasons why English-speakers find Croatian a demanding language to learn. The first is pronunciation. Croatian demands open vowels (for example, 'a' is spoken as 'ah'), flamboyantly rolled 'r's and sounds that it seems an English-speaking jaw was never intended to grapple with. A classic example is the common 'lj' sound. As explained by an online language tutorial, rather than incorrectly separating the L and the J, 'the tongue has to be stuck to the palate all the way from the upper front teeth to the throat and the sound produced simultaneously with the unsticking of the tongue from the palate'.

Fortunately Croatian words are spelt phonetically, so once you have mastered the basic sounds of the letters you should be able to read aloud the written word correctly. This is when the language's second challenge presents itself – and unfortunately it is unavoidable. You cannot speak Croatian without understanding its grammar. Right from day one of learning the language, it plays a fundamental role in the meaning of sentences and even individual words. The connotation of a single word can be subtly but distinctly altered by changing its prefix or ending. Unlike English, Croatian uses seven different cases, each of which gives a word a different ending. Croatian also provides verbs with a prefix that denotes 'the degree of completion of the action'. As one determined student of the language put it, 'Imagine every word in the English language. Make it either masculine, feminine or neutral and give it several endings which change depending on its meaning and where it is in a sentence, and you begin to get an idea.' Despite the challenges, there is immense satisfaction to be gained (not to mention the respect of your neighbours) from persevering. The best way to learn is to keep practising and don't be worried about making mistakes. Croatians are incredibly forgiving of bad grammar, as nobody knows better than they do about its complexity.

Case Study: Language Barrier

Paul Bradbury, an ex-aid worker from Manchester, settled on the island of Hvar nearly four years ago. One of his first priorities was to learn the Croatian language. 'Every morning I'd go to my local café and have a mock conversation with the waiter who was studying English. People get scared about the Croatian language so don't bother to learn it, but it is really appreciated if you know at least a few words.' Paul found that the island's tightly knit community was far more welcoming to those who made an effort to get involved. As an ex-teacher, he decided to start English classes for local school children in his spare time, but he says that smaller gestures are just as effective at smoothing the integration process. 'When you come to Croatia, bring something traditional from home like a bottle of whisky,' he advises, 'then go and introduce yourself to your neighbours and share it with them. Even if you don't speak the language it will be appreciated.'

Having established his new life, Paul now lives the dream that many potential expatriates aspire to. Every morning he gets up and sits on his terrace in the sunshine looking out over a sea view before starting work on a wireless laptop. 'It's a much slower pace of life than I ever thought I'd be happy with,' he admits, 'but I've got good friends here, and my family, and I lead a much healthier lifestyle than I ever would have done back in the UK.'

A quick search on the Internet will reveal dozens of Croatian language courses in Croatia, but most of them are based in schools in Zagreb. If you don't live near a city, ask around locally. It won't take long to find a willing tutor. In the UK, you can enrol in a class (again, the Internet will provide a number of options in your local area), or employ a tutor to come to you. The website **www.language-school-teachers.com** has a directory of Croatian language tutors located all over the world as well as in the UK. Unless you are blessed with superhuman self-discipline, try to avoid the teach-yourself options. Added to the obvious difficulty of finding time to regularly put aside for language studies, Croatian is a language that you really need to hear and speak and be taught. It is not impossible to teach yourself – but there are wiser options. For some basic pre-trip words and phrases you can find downloadable audio files on the Visit Croatia website (**www.visit-croatia.co.uk/croatianfortravellers**).

See **References**, pp.195–8, for a basic pronunciation guide and a few useful phrases to try out.

Shopping

Like most other European countries, out-of-town shopping centres and ever-expanding hypermarkets are emerging like mushrooms around the larger towns and cities of Croatia. Luckily this trend doesn't seem to have dampened the bustling commerce of the town centres, where specialised, often family-run shops and businesses still rule the roost.

Opening Hours and Payment

During the summer, shops tend to open from 8am to 8pm or later on weekdays and until 2 or 3pm on Saturdays. Some shops maintain the Mediterranean tradition of closing in the afternoon from 12 noon to 4pm to avoid the worst of the day's heat, but this is becoming less and less common. In winter, opening hours are much shorter, with shops opening at 10am, closing around 6pm and taking an hour for lunch. In both winter and summer the majority of shops stay shut on a Sunday, allowing the town centres to be taken over by weekly outdoor markets.

Major credit cards like American Express, MasterCard and Visa are universally accepted, and you may well be asked for a PIN number as well as a signature when you pay. Croatian shopkeepers are obliged to charge PDV (VAT) tax on everything they sell, but in an effort to clamp down on VAT evasion Croatian law makes it the responsibility of the customer to check they have paid the proper tax on the goods they buy. Make sure you are issued with an appropriate receipt for all your purchases.

Grocers, Food Shops and Household Essentials

You will find that in all but the tiniest of Croatian hamlets there will be a well-stocked village shop selling all the bare essentials (but without much variety). In the larger villages and towns the local shop is joined by a butcher and at least one bakery, where you can usually buy hot snacks to take away as well as bread and pastries. The proliferation of bakeries in Croatia is a national phenomenon bordering on obsession. A bakery seems to wait around every corner to tempt

Tax-free Shopping

If you spend more than 500 kunas in one shop on one day, you are entitled to a refund of the PDV tax as long as you leave the country within three months of your purchase. To claim the refund you must ask the shopkeeper for a PDV-P form which you fill in and get stamped on the spot. As you leave Croatia, hand the PDV-P form to customs officials at the border, who will verify it for you. You can then either return to the shop within six months to retrieve your refund or send the verified receipt to the shop by post and provide bank details so that they can pay the money directly into your account. Either way, the process is long-winded and inconvenient. It is much easier to shop in one of the 2000 Global Refund affiliated shops that display a 'Croatia Tax Free Shopping' sign. This means that you can claim your PDV refund as you pay, at the expense of a small service charge. There is more information on **www.globalrefund.com**.

Writing History

The humble pen is something all of us use almost every day and yet very few people know much about its origins. In 1906 the Croatian inventor Slavoljub Eduard Penkala produced a revolutionary mechanical pencil. Today, adjustable pencils with lead refills are taken for granted, but, at the time, the idea of a pencil that needed no sharpening was ground-breaking. The 'Penkalas' were an instant success across Europe and brought Penkala international fame.

The following year he cemented his position as the father of all writing instruments by producing yet another radical innovation, the fountain pen. The original models were filled with ink by a pipette but leaked if they were turned upside-down. This is why Penkala added the clip, which has become a permanent feature of fountain pens ever since.

In the years that followed, Penkala introduced coloured leads for his mechanical pencils and dry ink for his fountain pens as well as several other inventions including the first thermos flasks, a rotary toothbrush and a pocket torch. His creative life was cut short when he died of pneumonia at the age of 51, but Penkala had already, in a small but significant way, changed the world forever.

you with its cakes and biscuits, and you can rely on them to be open for a quick bite when everywhere else is resolutely closed.

In the larger towns these staple stores are interspersed with specialist shops dedicated to just one product such as cooking oils or wine, but the big-name supermarket chains are also beginning to appear. Franchises like Konzum, Plodine and Mercator run small, town centre grocery stores as well as larger out-of-town hypermarkets. Like any modern hypermarket, these tend to be open late and offer a range of household products as well as food.

Outdoor Markets

Every Croatian town will have its own outdoor market, with locals from the surrounding area gathering to sell their home-grown produce. Sometimes these are daily affairs but more typically they happen once a week on a Sunday morning and, after a brief frenzy, are all over by 2pm. Stalls are piled high with a vast array of fruit and vegetables, some of it still coated in the earth from which it was pulled, bottles of olive oil, jars of honey scented with walnuts, almonds or apricots, home-dried ham and pats of soft, and slightly sour, traditional cheese – all of it cheaper and fresher than the produce in the supermarkets. Fish stalls with seafood so fresh it is sometimes still squirming form their own sub-market, while other stallholders selling anything from flowers to leather belts frequently swell the throng. The best outdoor market can be found in the centre of Zagreb, where Dolac market has been trading since the 19th century, and in Split, where the food market takes place every day outside the Roman palace walls near the harbour, with a separate, more central fish market.

Clothing Stores

Out-of-town shopping malls are only just beginning to surface in Croatia. The largest in the country was opened towards the end of 2006 in Zagreb and features 85 shops, restaurants and cafés, which is relatively small compared to the monster-malls we've become accustomed to in the UK. This means the best place for shopping is still the city centre. In the main pedestrianised streets of cities like Pula, Rijeka and Split you will quickly notice several familiar fashion chains as well as a large number of independent boutiques. The great news is that clothing, footwear and accessories, even from big-name brands like Benetton, are around 20 per cent cheaper than in the UK.

Home Utilities

Although Croatia is in the process of modernising its public utilities, most companies and providers are state-run or operated by a single private company that has a nationwide monopoly. In spite of this, prices are significantly cheaper than equivalent services in the UK.

If you have a **problem with your bills or service** you will find that each utility company has its own complaints procedure to follow, but if you are getting nowhere you can also seek advice from the **Croatian Association for Consumer Affairs** (*Hrvatska udruga za zastitu potrosaca*) or **HUZP**. The HUZP offers individual consumer support and handles 800–1,000 complaints every year. Their website (**www.huzp.hr**) has no English translation, but you can get information in English by contacting the HUZP directly:

Hrvatska udruga za zastitu potrosaca (HUZP)
Trg Kralja Petra Kresimira IV br.2
Zagreb 10000
t +385 (0)1 46 333 66
huzp@zg.t-com.hr

Payments

Utilities are charged monthly or bi-monthly. You receive a bill which displays the amount you owe, a deadline for payment and your **customer number**, which is used in every transaction you make with the utility company. It is worth making a note of your customer numbers for each utility company and keeping them in one place along with vital contact details so that all this information is easily at hand when you need it. You can **pay the bill** by cash, by credit card or by electronic transfer in one of several ways:

  • **in person – with cash or credit cards at the utility office, post office, local FINA (Croatian Financial Agency) office or at branches of certain banks.**

• **by automatic transfer from your bank or credit card company – known as a direct debit in the UK, this is sometimes called a 'permanent payment order' in Croatia; the bill is paid automatically every month, which is especially convenient if you are not in the country all year round.**

• **online via the Internet – through an account number for bill payments so that you can pay your bill by electronic transfer; this is handy if you use Internet banking. You can also submit gas and electricity meter readings online, in English, to calculate your monthly bill. To do this you need to quote your customer number.**

If you want to **terminate your utility contract** you usually need to give at least 30 days' notice and to contact the company in writing to explain why you are ending your contract. You will be asked to provide notarised evidence of the reason given (for example, if you are selling the property you must provide documents that prove the change of ownership) and a final meter reading before your contract is officially terminated.

Electricity

The company responsible for supplying electricity to your Croatian home is **HEP-Operator distribucijskog sustava** or **HEP-ODS**, a subsidiary of Croatia's state-owned electricity company **Hrvatska Electropriveda** or **HEP**. There are HEP-ODS offices, known as *elektra*, in the main towns of each region, and this is where you go to arrange connections, request contracts and pay bills. The contact details of all *elektras* can be found on the HEP-ODS website (**www. hep.hr/ods**).

Across Croatia, the standard electricity supply is 220V (similar to the UK), but power outlets are the two-pin continental type and many old houses, particularly in rural areas, are supplied with a maximum power of just 3Kw. As a comparison, the average British household uses a power supply of around 15Kw. You may therefore be restricted in the amount of electricity you can use at any one time – boiling a kettle while using your computer might well be enough to overload your system and blow a fuse.

When buying property you must contact HEP-ODS within 30 days of the transfer of ownership to apply for a new contract. To do this you will need copies of notarised documents that record the change of ownership and a recent meter reading. You have the choice of several different tariffs, including a lower night rate, but your alternatives are limited by the type of meter fitted at your property – single-tariff meter, multi-tariff meter, pre-payment card meter, etc.

If the property is not already connected to the electricity network, you need to apply to HEP-ODS for connection approval followed by a 'supply and use of network' contract. Once the contract is signed you are issued with an installation registration form, which can only be certified by a licensed electrician when they have completed the internal wiring and external connection work at

Case Study: Following the Rules

'In the UK we're used to having the civil service there to help us,' says IT contractor Noreen Brittman, 'but here in Croatia the civil service is not there to help – it's there to enforce the rules' – rules that Noreen and her husband, Peter, have found tend to be interpreted differently depending on whom you ask.

In 2005 the couple bought a four-storey house in a village outside Trogir on the Dalmatian coast and hired a local builder to help them divide it into two two-bedroom and two one-bedroom apartments. As soon as the first apartment was renovated they moved in, squeezing all their worldly possessions into just three rooms. 'We lived downstairs,' recalls Noreen, 'while the Bosnian builders lived in one of the unfinished apartments upstairs.' The building was already connected to local electricity and water mains but there was only one meter to share between all four apartments. 'We eventually got the electricity company to agree to put in separate meters, but only after going to their office first thing every morning and demanding that somebody speak to us. They themselves didn't seem at all sure about how it all worked, and in different offices we got different versions of what we should do.'

All four apartments are now complete and the couple have moved into one of the larger two-bedroom apartments in preparation for selling on the other three. 'We're planning to build a villa,' says Noreen, 'because it's more cost-efficient to build from scratch than to renovate. It will make our builder much happier!' However, the couple is reluctant to leave the area and the community that they have become a part of so quickly. 'Every so often we get little presents of cherries or lemons, and even though I don't speak the language I have conversations across the back fence using fingers and toes!' laughs Noreen.

your property. Finally, you take the certified installation form to your local *elektra* and arrange a time and date for a HEP-ODS representative to 'energise' the connection.

Monthly electricity **bills** are based on estimated consumption unless you opt for a self-reading contract, in which case you are obliged to submit a meter reading each month (which can be done online) and a bill is issued based on your reading. In either case, if you are unhappy about the amount you have been charged, you have 15 days from the issue date to contest the bill.

Gas

There are two **mains gas** suppliers operating in Croatia, but both of them are limited to regions of inland Croatia. The majority of apartment buildings in Zagreb and Osijek are connected to a district heating system run by gas. This system is operated by **HEP Toplinarstvo** (**www.toplinarstvo.hep.hr**), with monthly bills issued on the basis of regular meter readings. **HEP Plin** (**www.plin.hep.hr**) controls a network of gas pipelines in large areas of Slavonia and around Zagreb. The gas is used mostly for interior heating and hot water and is billed every month (every two months in summer). Both HEP Toplinarstvo and HEP Plin are subsidiaries of the larger HEP company and charge a flat rate of 1.9 kunas per cubic metre for gas. If you need to contest a bill you have eight days from its date of issue to make a complaint. If your complaint is upheld, you will receive a refund by the date of your next bill, plus interest.

Liquefied petroleum gas (LPG) is commonly used for cooking and heating appliances across Croatia, particularly on the islands. LPG is supplied in refillable tanks that are usually tucked away at the back of a property. You will find LPG vendors in almost every town, where you can buy various sizes of gas cylinder or exchange empties. Many of these vendors also offer a regular delivery service at an extra cost.

Water

Water quality in Croatia is good, and it is safe to drink mains water straight from the tap across the country. The water is supplied by the national mains operator Croatian Water or **Hrvatske Vode** (**www.vode.hr**), which charges each property a flat rate for the water it uses plus an annual charge to cover the cost of waste-water disposal.

All Croatian properties connected to the water mains have **water meters**, so you only pay for what you use. Some of the islands have their own systems that source water from natural springs or from rainwater collection plants but many properties are not connected to any mains water system at all. It is a similar story in remote rural regions, where connection to the mains would be prohibitively expensive. Many properties use rainwater **tanks** and some even have **wells**. If you buy a property with a well, make sure to have the water quality checked before you use it and to confirm that the water rights belong to you.

Boilers

Check that the water boiler in your new property is big enough to handle the hot-water needs of the entire house. This will save long, frustrating waits between showers for hot water, as the boiler struggles to keep up with demand.

Septic Tanks

Commonly used in rural areas and on the islands, septic tanks collect all the sewage and waste water from the property. The waste is then treated with bacteria so that it can be disposed of safely when the tank is emptied. The size of the tank determines how often it must be emptied, so make sure yours is large enough for your needs.

Swimming Pools

When choosing a property with a swimming pool, it is worth remembering that your water usage is metered. Make sure you have factored into your annual budget the cost of filling the pool, emptying it (if necessary) and keeping it regularly topped up.

Telecommunications

Home Phones

Ten years ago, Croatia's fixed line telephone network was operated by the government-owned company, Croatian Post and Telecommunications (HPT). In 1999 the company was split into two separate entities, with Croatian Telecom (HT) taking charge of not only the fixed line networks but the growing mobile network within the country as well. Five years later, Croatian Telecom was bought by the German company Deutsche Telekom (best known in the UK as T-Mobile) and renamed **T-HT** (**T-Hrvatski Telekom**) to symbolise the takeover. T-HT inherited both fixed line networks and mobile networks from Croatian Telecom, so it created two new subsidiary companies to take care of each part of its business. **T-Mobile** deals with the mobile networks, while **T-Com** takes care of fixed line networks, broadband services and digital TV.

Although it is a private company, T-Com currently has a monopoly on all fixed line telephone services in the country. It operates two fixed line networks, an analogue service called HALO and a digital network called ISDN that has a raft of optional additional features such as caller identification, voicemail, call waiting and conference calling capability.

To sign up with T-Com you must visit one of the '**T-Centres**' that are scattered across the country. You'll be asked to select a network (HALO or ISDN) as well as a tariff option. Some of the tariff packages offer cheap international calls. If you need a telephone line installed at your new property you have to submit an application and wait a few days before a technician arrives to install it for you. Contact details for all T-Centres and further information on the services offered by T-Com can be found on the T-com website (**www.t-com.hr**) or you can ring the T-Com information line on **t** 0800 9000.

Croatian telephone numbers that start with 08 are public information numbers and are free. Numbers that start with 06 charge a toll. National **telephone directories** are sold at T-centres but you can access this information for free online at the T-HT website (**www.t.ht.hr**). There are also two countrywide **directory enquiries** numbers: **t** 988 for local and intercity numbers and **t** 902 for information on international numbers.

Calling abroad, even to continental Europe, is expensive in Croatia, so you may want to sign up with an international operator, whose cheaper-rate services are accessed by typing a prefix number before your international call. It could also be worth investigating Internet communication services, such as Skype (**www.skype.com**), which are completely free no matter where in the world you are calling. Pre-paid **phonecards** (*telefonske kartice*) are also widely available in Croatia. They can be bought in various denominations (25 to 100 kunas) from post offices and newspaper kiosks and can be used in public phone boxes to make both local and international calls. Local calls are charged at 0.8 kunas per minute, while international calls cost between 3 and 10 kunas per minute depending on what country you are calling.

Mobile Phones

A mobile phone has become a natural extension of the body in Croatia just as it has done in the UK and other parts of Europe. Every town will have a plethora of shops that deal exclusively in accessories for your phone. The coverage in Croatia is impressive and works on a GSM 900/1800 frequency, so if you have your UK phone switched to international roaming it will work in all parts of the country. However, the charges for making 'roamed' calls are high and quickly accumulate into a painful phone bill. There are cheaper ways of using your mobile phone in Croatia. If you are able to 'unlock' your phone you can replace your UK SIM card with one bought locally. The new SIM card will cost around 120 kunas including a certain amount of call time (usually 100 kunas), and you will be given a new Croatian phone number. If you cannot unlock your existing phone, you might want to consider buying a new handset in Croatia. A complete pay-as-you-go package, including handset, call time and SIM card, starts at 400 kunas. Even if you throw the handset away at the end of your trip, you are likely to have saved money on the cost of making 'roamed' calls.

There are two mobile network providers in Croatia: the sister company of T-Com, **T-Mobile** (**www.t-mobile.hr**), and private enterprise **Vipnet** (**www.vipnet.hr**). Both offer a range of subscription and pre-paid services and there is very little to choose between them. T-Mobile numbers begin with 098 while all Vipnet numbers start with 091.

The Internet

Surprisingly, given the popularity of mobile phones, not all Croatian homes have access to the Internet and wireless technology hasn't taken off yet. Rijeka remains the only place in the country where you will find wireless hotspots. Cybercafés are the easiest way to get online, and you will find at least one in every town. They are often open late and charge between 10 and 20 kunas per hour plus a few kunas extra if you want to print, or download pictures onto a CD.

If you have your own computer and want an Internet connection in your home you need to sign up with an internet service provider (ISP). There are several ISPs operating in Croatia, offering either basic dial-up services or faster broadband connections. The most popular are Vip Online (**www.vipnet.hr**), T-Com (**www.t-com.hr**), Global Net (**www.home.globalnet.hr**) and ISKON (**www.iskon.hr**, website in Croatian only). Most of these companies offer a combined Internet and telephone package that can often work out cheaper than arranging them separately, and lower night rates between 7pm and 7am.

Post Offices

The national postal service in Croatia, **Hrvatska Pošta (HP)**, is generally considered to be reliable and provide good value. There are HP offices centrally located in every town but they can sometimes be hard to find with just a small yellow spiral symbol on the front. In Croatia, HP offices are much more than simply a place to buy stamps. Here, you can exchange foreign currency, pay household and credit card bills, send telegrams and make local and international phone calls. HP also runs an international courier service, called EMS. You can find out more about EMS as well as track parcels, find postcodes and the location of your local HP office on the HP website (**www.posta.hr**).

You can also buy **stamps** (*marke*, singular *marka*) at newsagents and tobacco kiosks. Letters are charged according to weight and airmail costs extra.

Media

After declaring independence in 1991, Croatia entered an eight-year regime under its first president, Franjo Tuđman (Tudjman). The Tuđman era saw a gradual and increasingly blatant censorship of the country's media by the government. Popular national newspapers were sold off to supporters of the president or placed under considerable pressure to support the regime, while state-run TV and radio stations became little more than a thinly disguised mouthpiece for the government. The death of Tuđman in 1999 signalled the end of his government and an end to the restrictions placed on the media. Things gradually improved over the following years, and today the media operates in a climate of relative freedom.

Newspapers and Magazines

Newspapers are relatively expensive in Croatia. Of the national dailies, *Jutarnji List*, *Večernji List* and *Vjesnik* are the most popular. *Vjesnik* has a long-standing reputation for being pro-government and slightly stuffy, while *Jutarnji List* ('Morning Paper') has a liberal, more populist editorial policy. *Večernji List* ('Evening Paper') is the biggest Croatian tabloid and tends to mix showbiz gossip with nationalistic politics. Its main competition is *24 Sata* (24 hours), a daily sensationalist tabloid launched in 2005 that already claims the third-largest circulation of any newspaper in Croatia.

More respected politically are the national weeklies, *Globus* and the *Feral Tribune*. *Globus* is a glossy political magazine with a reputation for investigative journalism while the *Feral Tribune* is a satirical paper famed for poking irreverent fun at the political élite. The *Feral Tribune* gained tremendous respect as one of the only newspapers to hold out against menacing pressure from the Tuđman regime, maintaining the consistently critical and mocking voice for which it was famed throughout the period. In addition to the national papers there are dozens of well-regarded regional papers and news magazines that cover country-wide as well as local news.

It's not unusual to see English newspapers in Croatian news-stands, and the best English-language Croatian papers can be found online. There is a daily English-language news bulletin provided by news agency Hrvatska izvještajna novinska agencija at **www.hina.hr** and also by the Croatian Information Centre at **www.hic.hr**. The popular weekly news magazine *Nacional* has an English version of its news website (**www.nacional.hr**).

Television

Television is the main source of news and information for most Croatians. Croatian Television, **Hrvatska Radiotelevizija** (**HRT**), operates two terrestrial channels – HRT 1 and HRT 2 – as well as a satellite channel – HRT Plus. The channels feature a lot of American sitcoms and movies with Croatian subtitles (good news for English-speakers), as well as football matches, political panel shows, game shows (like the Croatian version of *Who Wants to Be a Millionaire?* and *The Weakest Link*) and cultural documentaries. You can find listings for all the HRT channels on their website (**www.hrt.hr**).

HRT is partly financed by advertising, but 60 per cent of its funding comes from licence-fee revenue. Similar to the system in the UK, everyone who owns a television (or radio set) must pay for a **TV and radio licence**. The fee is set every year at 1.5 per cent of the average net annual salary and is currently around €100 per year. As well as HRT there are two other national commercial broadcasters, **Nova TV** and **RTL Televizija**, and up to a dozen regional commercial stations.

Cable TV is available in parts of the bigger cities, but **satellite** subscription services are more popular, allowing reception of several European channels including the BBC.

Radio

HRT is the oldest broadcaster in southeast Europe, transmitting its first radio programme on 15 May 1936 (the very first item broadcast was the Croatian

National Anthem). Today it broadcasts three national radio channels. **HR 1** features news and current affairs, while **HR 2** is more entertainment-based, with news bulletins every half hour and **HR 3** is mostly classical music. It also operates seven regional radio stations that mix music with local news and issues. You can find frequencies and listings for all HRT stations on their website (**www.hrt.hr**). Added to this are a number of commercial radio stations at both a national and a local level, mostly producing a mix of popular Croatian and international music of all types. Among the most popular are **Radio 101** (101MHz), **Otvoreni Radio** (105.6MHz and 92.6MHz) and **Narodni Radio** (107.1MHz and 107.5MHz).

If you have a short-wave radio you can receive the BBC World Service from anywhere in Croatia.

Money and Banking

If you only intend to spend a short part of each year in Croatia, using your British bank account shouldn't be a problem. You can use your bank cards in the ubiquitous Croatian ATMs, pay for goods and services using your existing credit or debit cards and arrange your finances in the UK remotely using Internet banking. Doing this is quick, easy and convenient, but you will be charged a small commission for each transaction you make.

If you bring cash with you to Croatia, don't exchange your currency in the UK. Exchange rates are typically 10 per cent higher if you exchange your cash once you arrive in Croatia.

Banks and Bank Accounts

If you are planning to spend a lot of time in Croatia or intend to set up a Croatian company you will need to open a Croatian bank account. The new account will allow you greater access to your funds, a Croatian debit or credit card so that you can make payments and cash withdrawals without incurring any additional charges, access to telephone and Internet banking services, and the ability to set up standing orders to pay regular bills.

There are two main types of account. The most basic is a **personal account**, which will receive transfers from other accounts and regular foreign currency deposits such as pension or benefit payments from abroad. You can draw on the account for expenditure within Croatia and make small withdrawals or transfers. All you need to do to open this type of account is to visit your nearest bank with your passport, fill in a form, and the account will be open within a week.

If you require additional services such as bank cards, standing orders and Internet or telephone banking, you will need to open a **current account**. Most banks insist that you have some form of formal residence in Croatia before you can open this type of account, and you will need to provide proof of your Croatian address and a statement about why you wish to open an account as well as evidence of your residence status.

You will quickly notice that there is a large number of **banks** to choose from. Apart from the state-owned Hrvatska Poštanska Banka (HPB), all Croatian banks are owned by larger Austrian, Hungarian or Italian companies. Each bank has its own rules on the eligibility of foreign clients and offers slightly different services, so it is worth shopping around and doing some research.

When deciding where to open your Croatian bank account, find out:

- **What accounts and services are you eligible for as a non-resident?**
- **Does the bank offer a foreign currency account that can be linked to your current or personal account for the easy transfer of foreign currency?**
- **Does the bank charge a fee for opening and/or closing accounts?**
- **Does the bank charge a fee for the services you are likely to be using?**
- **How convenient is the bank's nearest local branch?**
- **Are there English-speaking staff at the bank's local branch?**
- **What are the opening times of the local branch?**

General **opening times** for most Croatian banks are Monday to Friday from 8am until 7pm, but some branches also open on Saturday mornings.

Many of Croatia's main high-street banks offer accounts specifically for non-residents or provide foreign currency accounts and have informative websites translated into English. Here is a selection of them:

- Erste + Steiermärkische (**www.erstebank.hr**).
- Hrvatska Poštanska Banka (**www.hpb.hr**).
- Hypo Alpe Adria Bank (**www.hypo-alpe-adria.hr**).
- OPT (**www.optbanka.hr**).
- Privredna Banka Zagreb (**www.pbz.hr**).
- Raiffeisen (**www.rba.hr**)
- Splitska Banka (**www.splitskabanka.hr**)
- Zagrebaška Banka (**www.zaba.hr**).

Working and Employment

Unemployment is a major problem in Croatia, with around 17 per cent of the labour force out of work, and employment opportunities for foreign nationals are therefore very limited. If you intend to compete for Croatian jobs you may well find that prospective employers feel morally obliged to offer vacant positions to Croatians in preference to non-nationals.

However, opportunities do exist in those industries that demand skills that Croatians can't supply. The country's ever-expanding tourist industry employs growing numbers of foreign nationals every year. Many resorts are in need of seasonal water-sports instructors, and yacht charter companies are continually looking for qualified skippers and crew. If you have nautical skills, try **www. croatiacharter.com**. Real estate is another booming business rich in openings for European expatriates who can help other foreign nationals to buy Croatian property – a process they have more than likely been through themselves; there are several vacancies advertised at **www.adriaticpropertyservices.com**.

Teaching English as a foreign language is a viable career in Croatia's numerous private language schools, and translation skills can be valuable in many industries if you also have a certain level of competence in Croatian. Lancon English Language Consultancy (**www.lancon.hr**) recruits translators and TEFL teachers.

Finally, there are plenty of worthwhile volunteer positions ranging from environment conservation to community work. You can find details at **www.volunteerabroad.com/listings** and at the Volunteer Centre Zagreb (**www. vcz.hr**).

Before you undertake any form of employment in Croatia you must apply for the appropriate work or business permit (*see* **First Steps and Reasons for Buying**, 'Visas and Permits', pp.22–31). If you have been awarded permanent residence you can use the Croatian Employment Service (**www.hzz.hr**), which can provide labour market information and vocational guidance from any of its local offices. Other places to look for current vacancies are listings websites **www. moj-posao.net** and **www.4icj.com**, which both give information in English.

If you gain employment within a Croatian company, there are some points of law that it is wise to be aware of:

- **Working hours and overtime**: The working week is limited to 40 hours with a maximum of 10 hours a week overtime, which must be remunerated at an acceptable level.

- **Holidays**: As well as 13 days of public holiday, employers are obliged by law to permit at least 18 working days of paid leave a year.

- **Maternity leave**: Mothers are awarded full pay for the duration of their maternity leave, which begins 28 days before the expected birth (45 days if there have been complications during the pregnancy) and continues until the child is six months old. There is the option to extend the leave for a further six months or for the father to take over by claiming parental leave 42 days after the birth.

- **Sickness and disability**: Employees are entitled to between 70 per cent and 100 per cent of their salary for the first six months of incapacity (which can include donating organs and nursing a sick child under three years old). If the incapacity is due to injury at work or an occupation-related illness, the affected employee is immediately awarded full pay.

- **Pensions:** The retirement age is 65 for men and 60 for women. If enough insurance has been paid (*see* pp.160–63), early retirement is possible at the age of 60 years for men and 55 years for women.

- **Dismissal policies:** Employees have a high level of protection under Croatian law and it is very difficult for employers to fire a member of staff. They are obliged to prove that they cannot offer re-training or another post as an alternative to dismissal.

Croatia's employment laws are some of the most favourable in Europe for employees, but there is a considerable gap between legislation and reality. The European Foundation for Improvement of Living and Working Conditions recently reported that 85 per cent of Croatia's labour force worked in excess of 48 hours a week and 11 per cent worked seven days a week. Of those figures, 50 per cent received no overtime pay.

Health and Emergencies

Croatia has a public health system run along similar principles to the National Health system in the UK. The Croatian Institute for Health Insurance, **Hrvatski zavod za zdravstveno osiguranje (HZZO)**, organises the collection of compulsory health insurance payments from Croatian salaries, which finances public hospitals, medical treatment and prescription drugs.

The standard of care in Croatia is good, with hospitals staffed by a well-trained and dedicated workforce of medical professionals. However, facilities are often antiquated, budgets overstretched and waiting lists for non-urgent treatments as long as those back home. Hospitals and clinics in the larger cities are generally more modern and better equipped than those in rural areas and on the islands, where only the most basic medical care is available. You can find a list of hospitals and clinics around the country at **www.daily.tportal.hr** (Info/Healthcare). To contact the **emergency ambulance service (HITNA POMOC)** from anywhere in the country, simply call **t** 94.

All foreigners of any nationality are granted free emergency care at Croatian public hospitals but as an EU citizen you are also entitled to a limited amount of free healthcare provision as well. If you are staying in Croatia for short periods during the year but are still tax resident in the UK and paying UK National Insurance, make sure you have a **European health insurance card (EHIC)**. You can get hold of a form at your local post office, apply online at **www.ehic.org.uk** or ring **t** 0845 606 2030. Despite the fact that Croatia is not yet part of the EU, the EHIC along with a UK passport will allow you to claim free hospital treatment, emergency dental care and consultations with a GP. You will still have to pay for prescription drugs but at a reduced cost, and you may be able to reclaim the cost once you have returned to the UK – so keep any receipts.

If you intend to live and work in Croatia for more than a year, you will be obliged to pay regular **national health insurance contributions** and will, therefore, be entitled to the same level of free public healthcare as a Croatian citizen. You cannot opt out of these mandatory contributions, but if you are paying tax in the UK you may be exempt as a result of the double taxation law (*see* p.131). In either case, if you intend to spend a lot of time in the country it is wise to **register** with your local doctor, particularly if you have young children or existing medical complaints.

There are a growing number of private medical facilities in Croatia and many foreign nationals choose to take out **private medical insurance** rather than use the public system. The US embassy website (**www.usembassy.hr**) has a list of English-speaking doctors and dentists in Croatia who work in the private sector. You can also get reciprocal private health plans from the UK, which give you access to private hospitals and healthcare abroad; try **BUPA International** (**t** (01273) 208181).

Croatia is generally a healthy place to be. There are no compulsory **vaccinations** but some doctors recommend typhoid, hepatitis A and rabies inoculations as a precaution. It is also wise to make sure you are up to date with all your general vaccinations before you leave the UK, for example influenza and pneumococcal shots for the elderly, hepatitis B for healthcare workers, and diphtheria and tetanus. The most common medical complaints are insect bites (take plenty of repellent, particularly in wetland areas where mosquitoes can be a problem) and sunstroke or sunburn (sun cream, UVB-resistant sunglasses and a sunhat are essential). You should also be aware of tick-borne encephalitis. This is a serious illness transmitted by the bite of infected ticks and is a danger if you intend to hike or camp in forested areas of inland Croatia during the summer months. Precautions include wearing trousers and long-sleeved tops and checking yourself regularly for bites. There have also been outbreaks of avian flu in migratory swans in Croatia but there have been no cases in humans thanks to the Croatian government's stringent control measures. There is more information about both avian flu and tick-borne encephalitis on the UK Foreign and Commonwealth Office website (**www.fco.gov.uk**).

Social Services and Welfare Benefits

Your eligibility to claim benefits through the Croatian social security and welfare system depends crucially on how many years you have been paying contributions into the system. How long you have lived in the country, whether you have been granted permanent residence and whether you are self-employed or employed by a Croatian company will also have a bearing on what support you are entitled to. The best way to proceed is to get advice on your individual circumstances from the office of **Republicka Fond Mironvinskog**

I Invalidskog Osiguranji, the national insurance scheme of the Republic of Croatia, which should be able to tell you what contributions you need to make, how to pay them and what benefits the payments will make available.

Hrvatski Zavod za Mirovinsko Osiguranje (HZMO)
Radnika Hrvatske
41000 Zagreb
Mihanoviceva 3
t +385 (0)1 4595 500
www.mirovinsko.hr

Within the next few years Croatia will join the EU and the country's eligibility rules will align with those of other member countries. This will make it easier for EU citizens to claim benefits through the Croatian system and for National Insurance contributions paid in your home country to be taken into account in Croatia.

Croatian Benefits

Depending on your personal circumstances, you may be eligible to apply for the following benefits offered by the Croatian welfare system:

- **Disability allowance:** If you have been granted permanent residence but have suffered a disability as the result of a work injury or an occupational disease while employed in Croatia, you may be eligible for disability benefits. Otherwise you must have made social insurance contributions in Croatia for at least one-third of your working life in order to qualify.

- **Unemployment benefit:** Depending on how many years they have paid social insurance contributions in Croatia, permanent residents between the ages of 15 and 65 may apply for unemployment benefits if they have had at least nine months of employment in the last 24 months.

- **Family allowance:** Permanent residents who have lived in Croatia for the previous three years can apply for family allowance regardless of their employment status. Children under 15, full-time students under 19 and disabled young people under 27 all count for benefits purposes.

- **Sickness and maternity benefits:** There is no minimum period of social insurance contributions to be eligible.

- **Pensions:** If you have made social insurance contributions in Croatia for 15 years you are eligible for a state pension once you reach retirement age (65 for men, 60 for women), but if you have made contributions for 35 years you are eligible for a state pension at an earlier retirement age (60 for men, 55 for women).

UK Benefits

Depending on your work situation in Croatia, you should still be able to claim certain benefits from the UK despite living permanently overseas. Before you leave the UK you should inform the HM Revenue and Customs National Insurance Contributions Office of the date you intend to leave the country and of your new Croatian address. They will send you a form that you will need to send back to the same office when, or if, you return to the UK.

National Insurance Contributions Office
International Services
HM Revenue and Customs
Benton Park View
Newcastle-upon-Tyne
NE98 1ZZ
t 0845 915 4811
www.hmrc.gov.uk

There are two kinds of welfare benefit in the UK: 'contributory' and 'non-contributory'. If you have paid (or been credited with) sufficient National Insurance contributions to qualify, then you will be eligible for the former benefits, otherwise you are limited to the latter. In the UK there are various classes of National Insurance contributions. The categories are:

- **Class 1**: paid by employees and their employers and consisting of a percentage of income.

- **Class 2**: a flat-rate payment paid by self-employed people.

- **Class 3**: voluntary payments made by people no longer paying Class 1 or Class 2 contributions; their rights are protected for a limited range of benefits.

- **Class 4**: compulsory 'profit-related' additional contributions paid by self-employed people.

These differing types of NI payments qualify you for various benefits, as shown in the table below.

Entitlement to UK benefits for different NI contributions

	Class 1	Class 2/4	Class 3
Maternity allowances	Yes	Yes	No
Unemployment benefit	Yes	No	No
Incapacity benefit	Yes	Yes	No
Widow's benefit	Yes	Yes	Yes
Basic retirement pension	Yes	Yes	Yes
Additional retirement pension	Yes	No	No

Not only must you meet the eligibility criteria in order to claim benefits, but some benefits are also means-tested, so that the amount you are paid depends on your personal financial situation. Otherwise benefits are paid at a flat rate, regardless of an individual's wealth.

Accidents at Work or Occupational Diseases

Any benefits you receive from the UK benefits system as a result of an accident at work or an occupational disease should still be payable to you in Croatia.

Incapacity Benefit

Any National Insurance benefits you receive from the UK benefits system as a result of invalidity should still be payable to you in Croatia. Attendance allowance, severe disablement allowance and disability living allowance are not usually payable if you live abroad permanently.

Widow's and Other Survivor's Benefits

Any benefits you receive from the UK benefits system as a result of being widowed should still be payable to you in Croatia.

Pensions

If you are already retired and you only ever paid National Insurance contributions in the UK, you will receive your UK retirement pension in Croatia. You will be paid without deduction (except remittance charges) and your pension will be updated whenever pensions in the UK are revised. If you have established an entitlement to a retirement pension in several EU countries by working in them, all the pensions will still be payable to you in Croatia. These, too, will be paid without deduction (except remittance charges) and your pension will be updated whenever the pensions in those countries are revised.

If you have not yet retired and you move to Croatia (whether you intend to work in Croatia or not), your entitlement to your UK pension will be frozen and the pension to which you are entitled at that point will be paid to you at UK retirement age. This freezing could be a disadvantage, especially if you are still relatively young when you move to Croatia. This is because you need to have made a minimum number of NI contributions in order to qualify for a full UK state pension. If you have not yet done this but are not far off, it may be worth making additional payments while you are residing overseas. You may choose to pay either continuing Class 2 or Class 3 contributions.

Voluntary National Insurance Contributions

You may pay Class 2 contributions if:

- **you are working abroad.**
- **you have lived in the UK for a continuous period of at least three years during which you paid NI contributions and you have already paid a set minimum amount of NI contributions.**
- **you were normally employed or self-employed in the UK before leaving.**

You may pay Class 3 contributions if:

- **you have at any time lived in the UK for a continuous period of at least three years.**
- **you have already paid a minimum amount of NI contributions in the UK.**

Class 2 contributions are more expensive but potentially cover you for maternity allowance and incapacity benefits. Class 3 contributions do not. In both cases you should apply in the UK using form CF83.

Retirement

This chapter has already contained a great deal of information about benefits, healthcare and pensions. Those who retire in Croatia are still eligible for a full UK state pension (if they have made sufficient NI contributions), *see* previous section, and if they have made sufficient contributions to the Croatian national insurance scheme they are also eligible for a Croatian state pension. First read **First Steps and Reasons for Buying**, pp.20–22. This section addresses some of the other issues that may arise as you plan for your retirement in Croatia.

The retirement age in Croatia is 65 for men and 60 for women. If enough insurance has been paid, early retirement is possible at the age of 60 years for men and 55 years for women.

Receiving Pension Payments

Your UK state pension can be paid directly into your bank account wherever you are in the world. In Croatia you are especially fortunate, as all pension and state benefit payments from abroad are currently tax-free. If you qualify for a Croatian state pension but intend to return to the UK or move elsewhere, these benefits are also payable abroad, so you won't lose out.

Private pension schemes may not be so flexible, and often stipulate that payments must be made into a UK-based bank account. If your scheme does agree to pay money directly into your Croatian bank account, watch out for steep transfer fees and fluctuating exchange rates. Keep transfer fees to a minimum by arranging quarterly rather than monthly payments and look into currency dealers, who will transfer funds at a pre-agreed and fixed exchange rate to avoid costly fluctuations.

Death

The death of a British citizen in Croatia must be reported to the British Embassy Consular Section in Zagreb. This may be done in Zagreb or at one of the consular offices in Split or Dubrovnik. To report the death you will need to provide proof of your identity, produce the deceased's passport and have a copy of the death certificate (*izvadak iz matice umrlih*). The death certificate is produced by the Croatian Registry of Vital Statistics (Maticni ured) after receiving a report from either the hospital doctor or the coroner who attended after the death.

For information about inheritance issues and making a will, *see* **Financial Implications**, 'Inheritance', p.134.

Cars and Other Private Transport

The regulations for driving a foreign-registered car into Croatia were covered earlier, along with the rules of the road that you will need to know as you drive around the country (*see* **Selecting a Property**, pp.57–8 and 61–5). Officially you are only allowed to drive a British-registered vehicle on Croatian roads for a maximum of 90 days, so you must leave the country and come back again every three months. However, this is very rarely checked.

If you wish to keep a car permanently in Croatia there are a few other issues to consider.

Insuring a Car

If you arrange insurance for your British-registered car in Croatia you can opt for expensive fully comprehensive (*casco*) insurance or the mandatory basic insurance (the equivalent of third party insurance), which is cheaper. If you have basic insurance you are restricted to driving within Croatia only – you cannot drive across any of the borders into neighbouring countries or across Europe.

Some people choose to continue to insure their car from the UK, but this too has its drawbacks. First, it means that you must return to the UK with the car once every 12 months to get an MOT, because the car must be taxed in the UK for the insurance to be valid. Secondly, standard UK insurance policies restrict periods overseas to 90 days within any 12-month period. After that period you are only covered by the lowest-level third-party insurance.

Buying a Car

By buying a car in Croatia you will not only have Croatian numberplates (which will make getting insurance cover a lot easier) but the car will also be left-hand drive, which has safety advantages when driving on Croatian roads. Cars are expensive in Croatia, however, and you should not be surprised if you are asked for as much as twice the price of an equivalent model in the UK.

An alternative is to buy a left-hand drive vehicle from elsewhere in Europe. Germany is recommended as the place to go to find a wide range of good quality cars at reasonable prices. You can find a selection online at **www.autoscout24.de**. Not only will you save money on the purchase but because you are taking the car to Croatia, which is currently outside the EU, you can reclaim the German VAT of 16 per cent.

Importing a Car

Any car imported permanently into Croatia must be left-hand drive and less than seven years old from the date of manufacture. If you import the car as a non-resident you will be charged import duty, 22 per cent PDV and an extra administration charge called '*trosarina*'. All these charges, except the *trosarina*, are waived if you have been granted any form of temporary or permanent residence within the previous 12 months. If you have been issued a business visa you won't have to pay any charges at all and will be issued with temporary Croatian registration plates, which have green letters. These green plates are only valid for the same period as your business visa, so you will need to re-apply for them at the same time as you apply for an extension on your visa.

Taking Your Pet to Croatia

Travelling between the UK and Croatia with your pet has become a lot easier since Croatia signed up to the Europe-wide **Pet Passport** scheme a few years ago. An EU Pet Passport is an official document that contains a description of the pet, the contact details of its owner, information about any vaccinations or medical treatment the pet has had and the all-important proof of vaccination against rabies. It allows your pet to travel between any of the countries that have signed up to the scheme without having to go through quarantine.

You can obtain a Pet Passport by applying at your local veterinary clinic at least six months before you intend to travel. The scheme is only open to cats and dogs, and your pet must be fitted with a microchip and vaccinated against rabies before a passport can be issued. If you want to know more about the scheme, or need to read about the special regulations for travelling with other pets including birds, rabbits, rodents, fish, invertebrates and reptiles, there are full details on the website of the UK Department for Environment, Food and Rural Affairs (**www.defra.gov.uk/animalh/quarantine/index.htm**).

A valid EU Pet Passport that shows your pet has had a rabies vaccination between six months and one year before the date of arrival is all you need to bring your cat or dog into Croatia. If you do not have an EU Pet Passport, you will need an international certificate of health from your vet, your pet's microchip details and evidence that your pet has had a rabies vaccination between six months and one year before travelling.

If you decide that you want to bring your pet back to the UK, or have a new pet that you wish to bring into the UK for the first time, there are some requirements in addition to the EU Pet Passport. The following procedures must be carried out in the order shown, and by a government-authorised vet:

- **Have your pet microchipped (if you have not already done so) to ensure that it can be accurately identified.**

• Arrange for your pet to be vaccinated against rabies.

• Arrange a blood test which will show whether the vaccine has provided a satisfactory level of protection against rabies. The blood test must give a positive result at least six months before you travel to the UK.

• Apply for the issue of a EU Pet Passport (or update the existing passport).

• Have your pet treated for ticks and tapeworm at least 24 hours but not more than 48 hours before you travel, and obtain an official certificate of treatment from the vet to show that this has been done.

• Sign a declaration of residence which states that your pet has not entered any countries not included in the UK Pet Travel Scheme (PETS) in the previous six months. For a list of countries included in PETS, *see* **www.defra. gov.uk/animalh/quarantine/pets/territory.htm.**

• Arrange for your pet to travel to the UK on an approved route using an approved transport company. For a list of approved routes and companies, *see* **www.defra.gov.uk/animalh/quarantine/pets/territory.htm.**

For more information about travelling out of or in to the UK with a domestic animal you can contact the PETS helpline by calling **t** 0870 241 1710 or emailing pets.helpline@defra.gsi.gov.uk.

Crime and the Police

Croatia has a much lower crime rate than the UK, and than most other parts of Europe. Violent crime is extremely rare and petty theft occurs only in the larger tourist resorts during high season. However, the British Embassy in Zagreb issues the following advice and warnings:

• **Carry your passport at all times. You must be able to show some form of official identification if required.**

• **Personal and valuable items should not be left unattended, particularly on the beach.**

• **If travelling by train, special care should be taken to guard valuables, especially at night.**

There have been reports of an increase in the number of forged Croatian kuna banknotes being discovered, especially 200 and 500 notes. Take care when purchasing kunas; you should only do this at reliable outlets, such as banks and cashpoints.

There have been a number of reported incidents of gangs robbing car occupants after either indicating that they are in trouble and require assistance, or pulling alongside a car and indicating that there seems to be something wrong and they should pull over. You should therefore be extremely cautious should something similar to the above occur.

Croatia has adopted a law expressing zero tolerance on alcohol consumption by those in charge of yachts and other boats. If you intend to take charge of a boat in Croatia, you should not consume alcohol. The penalties for being caught in charge of a boat with alcohol in your bloodstream are likely to be heavy.

There have been a number of cases of yacht or boat skippers being arrested and taken to court for entering a non-designated entry port when arriving in Croatia, without informing the authorities, which has resulted in the skippers being heavily fined. If you are considering sailing to Croatia you should be aware of the rules on entry to Croatia. Enter only at a designated port or harbour; if this is not possible due to a problem, contact the local harbour master, or the police before entering a non-designated port/harbour.

The Croatian **police force** is part of the Ministry of the Interior and is split into 20 regional administrations with over 200 local police stations. You can find the telephone numbers and addresses of all the local police stations in the country on the Ministry of the Interior website (**www.mup.hr**), but you can contact **emergency police services** by calling **t** 92 free of charge from any phone across the country, including mobiles. Croatian police are generally courteous and professional. Many speak English but it is often useful to take someone with you who can translate if you need to visit a police station.

If you are a victim of a crime in Croatia, report it to the local police as soon as possible and obtain a copy of the police report. If your British passport has been lost or stolen you must report it immediately to the British Embassy in Zagreb. The embassy cannot issue full replacement passports but can provide either a temporary passport for multiple travel, valid for one year, or an emergency passport, which is valid for one journey back to the UK. The emergency passport can also be issued in Split or Dubrovnik. If you need a replacement of your full British passport you can apply in Zagreb, Split or Dubrovnik, but the application must be sent to the British Embassy in Vienna and may take 6–8 weeks.

Education

Education in Croatian state schools is free and compulsory up to the age of 15. Children enter **primary school** (*osnova škola*) at the age of five or six and for the first four years are taught by one teacher covering all subjects. Over the next four years they are taught by different teachers for individual subjects, including maths, Croatian, history, geography and science.

At 14, students move on to **secondary school** (*visoka škola*) and have a choice of highly specialised institutions that broadly fall into one of three categories: **art school** (*umjetnička škola*), **vocational school** (*strukovna škola*) and **university prep school** (*gimnazija*). Art schools focus on music, dance, visual art and design, while vocational schools concentrate on trades and crafts and involve a period of practical training. University prep schools are further categorised into general, linguistic, classical and scientific depending on their specialism, and their sole focus is preparing their students for further education.

At 18 students move on to **university** (*sveučilište*). Zagreb is Croatia's oldest and most well-established university but there are others in Split, Dubrovnik, Zadar, Osijek and Rijeka (which also has a campus in Pula). Tuition fees for permanent residents range from nothing to around £500, whereas the annual cost for foreign students can be as much as triple that figure. Undergraduate courses take from four to six years and foreign students are obliged to complete a two-term course in Croatian at the beginning of their studies.

See also **First Steps and Reasons for Buying**, 'Educating and Raising Children', pp.19–20.

Recent History and Politics

Croatia is an extremely young nation. It gained independence in 1991, but the road to full sovereignty has been far from smooth. In the months after independence was declared, tensions between ethnic Serbs and Croats within the country became critical – aggravated by agitations from neighbouring Serbia and the remnants of the Yugoslav People's Army (JNA). Croatian Serbs feared for their future in an independent Croatian state and began to take control of Serb-majority areas by force. The ensuing 'Homeland War' was marked by brutal ethnic cleansing on both sides and crimes against humanity that shocked the world. The war came to an end in 1995 but Croatian politics continued to be hampered by its events, particularly by the issues of refugee return and co-operation with the International War Crimes Tribunal in The Hague. Warrants were issued by The Hague in 2001 for leading Croatian generals who were accused of war crimes but had been decorated for their actions during the Homeland War and were generally regarded as national heroes by the Croatian public. Owing to what the international community saw as reluctance on the part of the Croatian government to extradite the indicted Croatian generals, the country was blocked in its attempts to become a potential member of NATO and the EU. Particularly contentious was the fate of General Ante Gotovina, who spent four years in hiding. His arrest in Tenerife in 2005 by Spanish police brought the crisis to a close and finally paved the way for Croatia to begin accession talks with the EU. The latest estimates are that Croatia will join the European Union by 2010, an event that currently dominates government policy and is the single biggest factor in shaping the nation's future. Ante Gotovina is currently awaiting trial in the Hague.

The Croatian government is run on a unicameral system, which means that there is only one house of representatives. The parliament (*Sabor*) is made up of between 100 and 160 members who are elected for a four-year term. Most of the members are elected from multi-seat constituencies within Croatia, but

Land Mines

One legacy of the 1991–1995 Homeland War is the estimated 240,000 landmines that remain in Croatia. De-mining operations are ongoing, but there are still affected areas in eastern Slavonia, along the Sava in the Lonjsko Polje, in parts of Krajina, upland areas of Lika and Dalmatia and on remote parts of the islands of Vis and Lastovo. All suspected landmine areas are fenced off and clearly posted with warning signs, but there are occasionally accidents when people either ignore or are oblivious to the danger. In 2003 a Dutch tourist was badly injured on the island of Vis after wandering into a landmine area despite several signs, and in 2006 there were seven reported incidents (none involving tourists), including one fatality. The Croatian Mine Action Centre (Hrvatski centar za razminiranje; HCR) has a detailed map of mine-affected areas on its website (**www.hcr.hr**) and offers the following advice:

• Respect mine warning signs.

• Do not go to mine-suspected areas.

• Do not touch explosive devices or suspicious objects.

• Mines are hidden and hard to see; watch your step.

• Do not try to de-mine. Leave it to professionals.

there are a small number of seats reserved for representatives of ethnic minorities and of the Croatian diaspora. The head of state is the president, who is elected by popular vote for a five-year term. The president has limited executive powers (except in times of war) but his main roles are as commander-in-chief of the armed forces, representing Croatia both at home and abroad, advising on foreign and national security policy, and convening the *Sabor*. The president appoints the prime minister, with the permission of the *Sabor*, and invites him to form a government (*vlada*). The prime minister has two deputy prime ministers and 14 ministers responsible for various sectors of government.

Since the last *Sabor* elections in 2003 the governing party has been the Croatian Democratic Union or **HDZ** (Hrvatska demokratska zajednica). The HDZ was first elected into power in 1990, an event that effectively ended Communist rule in the country (the date of the election is celebrated annually in Croatia today as a public holiday called Statehood Day). The HDZ was elected into power again in 1992 and 1995 but lost its majority in the 2000 elections. **Ivo Sanader** became the new leader of the HDZ later that year and shifted the party from its traditionally right-wing, nationalist stance to a more modern, centrist position. As a result, the party won the 2003 parliamentary elections and Sanader is currently serving as prime minister. **Stjepan ('Stipe') Mesić** of the Croatian People's Party (Hrvatska narodna stranka; **HNS**) is the country's president. Mesić is a well-respected politician who appears to be genuinely held in affection by the Croatian people. He was elected as president in 2000 and re-elected for a second term in 2005.

Religion

For decades after the Second World War Croatia was part of a Communist state in which any outward displays of religious belief were suppressed by the authorities. With the fall of Communism in the late 1980s and Croatia's independence in the 1990s, the Croatian people flooded back to the Church and revelled in the freedom to openly celebrate their faith once more. Despite the fact that, even now, Croatia still has no official state religion, the country is overwhelmingly Roman Catholic. Even the smallest town or village has at least one church and you will find standing room only during Sunday Mass among a congregation that consists of young and old alike. In the cities, shoppers and office workers will stop in the street to say a quick prayer at street-side shrines devoted to a particular saint or, more commonly, to the Virgin Mary. The Church is treated with respect, as are the nuns and clergy that you will often see going about their business, but the more traditional values and attitudes of the population, upheld by the church for so long, are starting to soften. Abortion is legal and homosexuality is tolerated (although not generally flaunted).

In addition to Christmas and Easter, major Catholic feast days such as Assumption and Corpus Christi are celebrated as public holidays throughout Croatia and there is a plethora of patron saints that each have their own festivals. Every town will have at least one patron saint that it will honour annually with processions, Masses and a civic holiday. Some of these festivals involve unique rituals, such as the opening of St Simeon's coffin in Zadar or the blessing of throats in the name of St Blaise in Dubrovnik.

In common with the rest of the Balkans, religion in Croatia is closely related to ideas of ethnic identity. Some 87 per cent of the population in Croatia declare themselves to be Roman Catholic, while the minority Serbian population (five per cent) are predominantly Orthodox. This has led to friction in the past between the two groups, particularly during the recent 'Homeland War' of the 1990s. Islam was first introduced to Croatia as a result of the Ottoman Turk invasions between the 15th and 19th centuries and there is currently a small but active Muslim community in Croatia, making up 1.5 per cent of the population. By far the smallest representation is the Jewish community, which was decimated by the Holocaust. Out of over 23,000 Jews living in Croatia before the Second World War, only 5,000 survived, and today the nationwide community has shrunk to half that number.

Food and Drink

It is difficult to identify exactly what constitutes truly Croatian cuisine. Gastronomy varies so widely as you travel from region to region that it is impossible to point out a single 'national' dish, and even within the same region there

Curious Gastronomy

Roman cuisine wouldn't suit every palate, but in certain parts of Croatia popular snacks of the 3rd and 4th century BC have survived as regional delicacies. In the Kvarner area, Whit Sunday is eagerly awaited as the first day of the hunting season for the dormouse. In ancient Rome, dormice were dipped in honey and poppy seeds and eaten as a dessert. Today they are considered as game, and the meat is coated in cornflour before being grilled over charcoal or fried.

Further south, eels have been caught in the Neretva river every autumn and spring since the days of the Roman emperors. The female eels are the most sought-after because they are twice as long as the males and, while spring eels are favoured for their taste, the autumn eels are fatter and juicer. Once caught, the meat is skewered onto a spit in small strips to be slowly roasted over a fire.

Frogs are a delicacy most commonly associated with France, but you will find them being enjoyed in traditional dishes across most of Croatia, stewed with snails and mushrooms, fried and wrapped in ham or simply cooked in rosemary and red wine. Frogs are particularly popular around the end of April, when the Night of Frogs (Žabarska noć) is celebrated in northern parts of Dalmatia.

might be several distinctly different versions of the same delicacy. Just as Croatia's heritage is coloured with the legacy of successive invaders from the Greeks to the Hungarians, so its cuisine has been inspired by the flavours and techniques of the Mediterranean and central Europe.

The main force behind Croatian cooking is always local produce. The country is blessed with some of the finest fresh ingredients, such as olives from the islands, oysters from Ston and strawberries from Zagreb; the best dishes are often the most simple ones that exploit locally sourced produce.

One of the most celebrated dishes in the Istrian region is the *fritaja*, or omelette, which is cooked plain with only one seasonal addition. In spring this might be wild asparagus while in autumn it is likely to be truffles. Istria is famous for its truffles, particularly the tuber *magnatum pico* (white truffle), which can fetch over €3,000 per kilo. From autumn until the end of the year every restaurant in the region offers at least one truffle dish, most commonly unadorned pasta or gnocchi topped with wafer-thin slices of black or white truffle – a dish kept deliberately simple so that you can savour the flavour of the precious fungus.

The regional speciality in neighbouring Kvarner is spit-roasted lamb (*janjetina na ražnju*), frequently cooked on stalls at the side of the road. The meat is served with spring onion and is delicately flavoured by the aromatic herbs that the sheep graze on as they wander across the barren islands of the Kvarner Gulf.

On the island of Pag the sage bushes are coated in sea-salt by the *bura* wind, giving the cheese produced from the sheep's milk a distinctive flavour. *Paški sir* or Pag cheese is hard, tangy and presented on menus across the country,

Živjeli (To Life!)

Despite the fact that parts of Croatia have been producing wine for centuries, it is only in the last few years that Croatian wines have begun to earn a solid reputation on the international market. Look out for Graševina, a floral white from Slavonia, and Pošip, a dry-white from the island of Korčula, which are both well regarded. The red wine Dingač from the Pelješac peninsula has a reputation as a pleasingly rich wine, which is unfortunately less-pleasingly expensive. Lighter in flavour, and expense, but equally respected, is Teran from the wine regions of western Istria. Teran is often drunk in Istrian bars as 'supa'. The wine is warmed in a ceramic jug called a *bukaleta* and mixed with a spoonful of sugar, a pinch of ground pepper and a splash of olive oil. The wine isn't drunk, but sipped like a soup using a slice of toasted bread as a spoon.

typically served with home-cured *pršut* ham. *Pršut* is prepared by flattening the back legs of slaughtered pigs under rocks or in a wooden press before salting and hanging out to dry in the same *bura* wind that gives Pag cheese its unique flavour. *Pršut* can take months to cure, smoke and mature to perfection but then most Croatian dishes demand serious preparation time.

Pašticada is a traditional Croatian beef stew that requires days of attention before it is cooked. Tender beef is marinated at length before being slowly stewed in a fruit- and spice-laden gravy, left to stand and finally served with freshly cooked gnocchi. Throughout inland Croatia such meaty dishes take on distinctly central European influences, particularly in Zagreb where paprika-seasoned goulashes form the basis of Purger Cuisine, a legacy of Croatia's Habsburg era. The inland regions take the blending of sweet and hot paprika as seriously as Italians take the blending of their coffee beans. These skills are put to the best use in the preparation of *kulen*, a type of sausage traditionally using pork of Black Slavonian pigs reared on acorns. Like *pršut*, the sausage is carefully smoked and cured for months according to jealously guarded local recipes and there is even a hotly contested national *kulen* competition called the Kuleniada.

Prepared with similar passion is the *brudet* of Dalmatia. Dalmatia can offer the finest shellfish and seafood plucked fresh from the Adriatic but the *brudet* is an elaborate fish stew originally designed to make the most of whatever odds and ends were left over from the catch. It seems that everybody has their own secret recipe but they usually include some shellfish, vegetables, herbs and spices. Some of the more eccentric versions use seawater, and one form of *brudet*, called *falši*, replaces the fish with a stone collected from the sea bed.

Letting Your Property

08

A large percentage of British people who buy homes in Croatia also let them at some point or another. These people can be categorised in two ways. The first category is made up of people who see the property primarily, or even exclusively, as an investment proposition, and wish to let it regularly. These people want to make money by letting their property and will try to find a steady stream of tenants to fill the house all year. The second category consists of people who are primarily buying a holiday home and are not interested in making a profit from letting it, but are hoping to cover all or some of their purchase costs through rental income.

There are fundamental differences in the ways these two groups should approach the house-buying process. For the first group this is a business. Just as in any business, the decisions they make about where and what to buy, whether and how to restore the property and what facilities to provide will be governed by the wish to maximise profit. They should put themselves in the position of the person or people to whom they want to let their property, and consider exactly which part of the market they expect to appeal to – whether, for example, it might be couples looking to enjoy Adriatic culture and cuisine or a family wanting a cheap beach holiday – and predict and cater for features clients like these would expect. They should choose an area, buy a property, convert it and equip it solely with their prospective tenants in mind.

The second group will have to bear in mind some or most of the same considerations, but overall can make far fewer concessions to their tenants. Their property is first and foremost a holiday home for themselves, and they will be ready to compromise on the more businesslike aspects of house-buying (and so reduce potential income) in order to maximise their own enjoyment of it. They will have to make some changes to accommodate visitors – extra bedding, setting aside some wardrobe space where they can lock away their own things while the house is let – but these should be as few as possible. Where they draw the line will be determined by just how much income they need to get out of the property.

The section that follows relates mainly to the first group. If you identify more with the second category, you can pick and choose from the ideas within it, and there are also some points that are more directly relevant to your situation.

But whichever group that you feel you fall into, there is a very important point to remember: in either case, you are most unlikely to cover all of your expenses and capital and interest repayments on a large mortgage from letting your property, however efficiently you do so.

First Steps and Questions

It is essential to sit down and establish your financial objectives before starting to let your property, since many other decisions will depend on them – what kind of tenants to aim for, whether to use a management company, and so on. You should also work out what your outgoings are likely to be – fitting out the house, general and garden maintenance and paying someone to clean the house and greet tenants may all take a chunk out of any rental income. You can employ an agent or management company to manage the lettings for you, but this will cut into the income you can expect to get from letting the property.

Questions to Ask Yourself before Starting to Let

- **What are your financial objectives?**
- **Do you plan just to cover your costs or do you want to maximise the income from your property?**
- **Do you want to use the property yourself – if so, when? If you'd like to use it at Easter and in the summer – that's exactly when other people will want to be there as well.**
- **Do you want to be there on set dates, or can you be flexible and only go on weeks with no bookings?**
- **What kind of people do you want to have in your house – are children OK? What about a hen party or a group of amateur sailors?**
- **What advantages does your property have – is there anything that makes it stand out? What amenities is it near?**
- **Will you have the time (or inclination) to manage the lettings yourself? This can entail a substantial amount of work.**

Location, Choice of Property and Rental Potential

If you advertise any property well, you will always get some tenants. You will only begin to get repeat customers and a spreading circle of recommendations from previous tenants – one of the best ways of building up your customer base, since it saves on repeat advertising – if the house or flat itself, the area around it and the things to do there really satisfy or, better still, exceed people's expectations of an enjoyable time.

Choosing the Right Area

The choice of area in which to buy your rental property is by far the most important decision that you will make. In the coastal regions of Croatia, along the Adriatic, it is fairly easy to let a property regularly enough to make it a commercially viable proposition. A traditional wooden house in a mountainous inland region may find fewer tenants each year, however, and it will be harder to generate enough business to make a substantial commercial return on your investment. If you are interested in a house such as this, then you are probably already aware of its rental limitations and should view any rental income as a bonus that may help with some of your expenses, rather than any kind of nest egg.

The factors to take into consideration when deciding on an area are slightly different from those you might look at when just thinking about buying a place for yourself. They will also vary depending on your target clientele and your preferred way of administering the property. Most are related to the tourist traffic of an area, its attractions and services, and also to the practical services it has available that you can call on to help manage the letting.

Attractions

Climate is, naturally, a major factor (*see* p.70 and **References**, 'Climate Charts', p.210). Anywhere in the country, including inland regions and the islands, can be relied on to have good, sunny weather during the prime tourist season from May to late September, but for letting purposes you may prefer to be in an area where you can expect blue skies in March, April and October and mild weather through the winter, to extend your letting season. To maximise your income, you might choose to use the property yourself in these fringe months at the beginning and end of the peak season to leave the property free during the summer when it can earn the highest rental.

Croatia hasn't yet caught on as a city-break destination, but an apartment in Zagreb or Dubrovnik could have a year-round appeal as a socially desirable place to be – regardless of the weather. Similarly, there may be scope to develop a small market for longer-term lets in areas with particularly mild climates during the winter.

Of equal importance are the attractions of the area, both natural features, such as spectacular beaches, and cultural attractions, like the dramatic architecture of Split. Easy access to a good beach is crucial, but it helps if there are other activities available, such as sailing, diving and other sports facilities. For some clients, proximity to a historic town oozing character would be a major asset, while for others it might be more important to be near one of Croatia's national parks. The point is that there must be *something* to bring people to your area so that they will need to use your accommodation. The mere fact that

Case Study: Summer Holidays

Carol Pringle and Paul Whitlie own a three-storey house in the perfect Dalmatian bay of Viniśće. The property is perfectly located for a holiday let, being within walking distance of the sea, a busy marina, a supermarket, a village post office and a string of waterfront café-bars and restaurants. The couple let the top floor as a studio apartment for two to four people and the first floor as a two-bedroom apartment sleeping four to six people, while they themselves live in the ground-floor apartment. The rental income allows them to live in Croatia for eight months of the year, but Carol describes their existence as 'shoestring'. 'The Croatian season is too short,' complains Paul. 'It gets going in May but the weather is great here as early as March, and the season is over by the end of September when it is still just as warm. For us to be able to afford to stay here, the season needs to get longer.'

Despite the uncertainty, the couple don't doubt for a minute that they have made the right move. 'The local people in Viniśće make us feel very much at home,' says Carol, 'from the old woman with her goats, to the local shopkeeper always smiling and trying to communicate with us and our postman shouting "Hello!" as he passes on his old scooter.'

Paul interrupts, 'And the weather's a darn sight better than in the UK too!'

the house has a great view will not, of itself, be enough to attract a significant number of tenants.

Added to these activities are the more everyday attractions of an area, which for most people loom as large as the more spectacular features in their enjoyment of a holiday let. Most people who rent self-catering accommodation will want to be able to stock up on food, drink and other necessities without too much trouble and, since they won't want to cook all the time, will also want to be able to eat out. They will appreciate it greatly – and your property will be much easier to let – if your house is within easy distance (preferably walking distance) of at least a few shops and a choice of bars and restaurants.

Access

As important as climate and the charms of the locality is the ability of tenants to get to your property. This has two sides to it. The area where your flat or house is located must be reasonably accessible from the places where your prospective tenants live; and the property itself must be easy to find.

Most British visitors will want to be able to get to the property from a local airport with direct flights from a UK airport close to where they live (for details of airports and routes to Croatia, *see* **Selecting a Property**, 'Travelling to Croatia', pp.54–60). It is worth repeating here travel industry figures that show that 25 per cent of all potential visitors will not come if it involves travelling for more than an hour from a local airport at either end of their journey, and that if the travelling time rises to 1½ hours this will deter around 50 per cent of people. Of course, this does not mean that if your home is over an hour's drive from an airport you will never let it – with charming rural houses, for example, a different set of rules applies, and their very remoteness can be an attraction in itself. For more conventional homes, though, there is no doubt that finding interested tenants will be simpler if you are within the magic hour's distance of an airport.

Nor should owners underestimate the importance of being able to find the property easily. Navigating the country lanes in the depths of central Istria could be tiresome, just as trying to locate a flat while snarled up in Dubrovnik's congested one-way system would not be a great start to a holiday. Giving tenants decent maps and guidance notes on getting there is essential.

Letting Agencies and Target Markets

Strange as it may seem, deciding *how* to let your property is one of the first decisions that you are going to have to make, even before you actually buy it. This is because, if you decide to use a professional management or letting agency, it will alter your target market and therefore the area in which you ought to be buying (*see* 'Management Agencies', pp.185–8).

If you are going to let your property through a professional agency, then it is worth contacting a few before you make a final choice of location, to see what they believe they can offer in the way of rental returns. They will also be able to advise you on what type of property in that area is likely to be most successful as rented property.

If, on the other hand, you expect to find tenants yourself, then you need to decide on your primary market. Most British people who let their property themselves in Croatia do so mainly to other British people because that is the market they are familiar with and where they have the most connections.

Choosing the Right Property

Picking the right property is just behind choosing the right area in terms of letting potential. Not all properties let to the same extent – villas and flats that most potential clients find attractive let up to five times more frequently than others that do not stand out for any reason. New properties are generally cheaper to maintain than older ones; however, they are not likely to be as attractive to potential tenants. Most people going on holiday to a rural part of Croatia are looking for a character property (preferably with a pool), while most going to the coast are looking for proximity to facilities and the beach.

If you intend to let out your property, it is very useful, therefore, to pick a home that is pretty (if it isn't one of those big enough to be called spectacular). Most people will decide whether to rent a holiday home after they have seen only a brief description and a photograph, and of these two the photo is by far the more important. When buying a house for rental purposes, make sure it photographs well.

The number of bedrooms is also important. In cities, properties with fewer (one or two) bedrooms are easier to let than bigger apartments. On the coast or in the countryside, where the majority of your guests may well be families, three-bedroom properties are the most popular.

Paying the Right Price

When buying a property as a business you will want to pay as little as possible for the property consistent with getting the right level of rental return. If you are only buying the property as a business proposition, this price/rental balance (or return on investment) and your judgement of the extent to which the property will rise in value over the years are the main criteria on which you should decide which property to buy.

If you are going to use the property not just as a rental property but also as a holiday home, there is an additional factor to take into account: the amount of time you will be able to use the property yourself consistent with getting a certain level of rental return.

For example, if you bought a one-bedroom property on the island of Krk, that property might be let for 25 weeks a year and produce a return after expenses of, say, 6 per cent; however, if you bought a two-bedroom property in a coastal resort near Dubrovnik and let that for just 15 weeks per year, you might also generate 6 per cent on your investment. Both would be performing equally well, but the Dubrovnik property would allow you and your family to use it for a much greater part of each year. This and the fact that it had a second bedroom could make it a more attractive proposition. These figures are simply examples, rather than indications as to what will actually be obtainable at any particular moment. Whichever way you look at it, though, paying the minimum necessary for the property is the key to maximising investment performance.

In cities, as mentioned above, you will generally get a better return on your investment in properties with fewer (one or two) bedrooms – which will be cheaper to buy – than on bigger apartments.

Equipping the Property

Having selected an area and a property, you will then have to fit out the villa or flat with all the features that tenants will expect. If you advertise the property well, you will get tenants. You will only get repeat tenants and recommendations from existing tenants if the property meets or exceeds their expectations in terms of the facilities it offers and its cleanliness.

It should, of course, be well maintained at all times, and the external decoration and garden and/or pool area should be kept in good condition – apart from anything else, these are the parts that create the first impression as your guests arrive. Other than that, the facilities required will depend to some extent upon the target audience that you are trying to attract. If, for example, you are trying to attract walkers or sailors, they will appreciate somewhere to dry their clothes quickly so that they can be ready to get wet again the following day.

The following is a quick checklist of the main points to be taken care of when preparing any property for holiday tenants:

Documents

Make sure that all guests are sent a **pre-visit pack**. This should include notes about the area and local attractions and a map of the immediate area (all usually available free from your local tourist office), detailed notes explaining how to get to the house, initial emergency contact numbers, and instructions what to do if they are delayed for any reason.

Inside the property there should also be a **house book** or **information pack**. This should give much more information and recommendations about local attractions, restaurants and so on – collect as many local leaflets as you can – and a comprehensive list of contact numbers for use in the case of any conceivable emergency. The more personal recommendations you can give (best bakery, best café, etc.), the more people will appreciate it. The house book should include detailed instructions about how to work any equipment, switch on the heating and any idiosyncrasies of the house, and the whereabouts of manuals for the washing machine, cooker and dishwasher. It should also include an inventory of the equipment in the house.

Provide some space in it too, or in a separate book, to be used as a **visitors' book**. As well as being a useful vehicle for obtaining feedback, this builds up positive feelings about your home, and can also be a means of making future direct contact with visitors who might have been supplied by an agency.

Greeting

It is best if someone is present, either at the property or at a nearby house, to welcome your guests when they arrive. They can sort out any minor problems or any particular requirements of the guests.

Welcome Pack

Make sure that basic groceries such as bread, milk, tea bags, coffee, sugar and a bowl of fruit are left in the house to welcome your guests on arrival.

Cleanliness

The property must be spotlessly clean, above all in the kitchen and bathroom. You will probably employ a local cleaner, to whom you may well need to give some training and/or a detailed schedule, as people's expectations when going into rented accommodation are often much higher than their expectations in an ordinary home.

Kitchen

This must be modern, even if traditional in style, and everything should (of course) work. The fridge should be as large as you can manage since, in hot weather, your tenants will need to keep a wide range of things chilled. The kitchen should have a microwave, and you should check regularly that there is sufficient cutlery and cooking equipment and that it is all in good condition. Providing a cookbook giving local recipes is a nice touch.

Bathroom

Or, these days, more usually bathrooms plural – an en-suite bathroom for each bedroom is the ideal. Make sure there is soap in the bathrooms, and guests will also much prefer it if you provide towels as part of the service.

Laundry Facilities

A washing machine and tumble-dryer are now standard.

Bedrooms

These should have adequate storage space. Most importantly, they should also have clean and comfortable beds, as nothing except dirtiness produces more complaints than uncomfortable beds. The only beds that last well in a regularly used property, in which the people sleeping will be all sorts of different sizes and weights, are expensive beds such as those used in the hotel industry. Beds should be protected from obvious soiling by the use of removable mattress covers, which should be changed with each change of tenant.

All clients much prefer you to supply bedding as part of your service rather than expecting them to bring their own.

Living Areas

Furniture and upholstery should be comfortable and in good condition; the style is a matter of personal preference, but a simple local style usually works well. There should be adequate means of cleaning, including a vacuum cleaner.

Heating

In Croatia, the importance of an effective heating system that covers the whole house depends on where the property is located. Some regions can get quite cool in the winter and you should keep this in mind.

Air-conditioning

While it is certainly a substantial asset, air-conditioning is not yet considered obligatory except in the most expensive lettings. It can be expensive to both run and maintain.

Swimming Pool

If you are catering to a British clientele, a pool is highly desirable, and in rural areas a long distance from the sea it will significantly increase your letting potential. A pool should be of reasonable size and well maintained.

Marketing the Property

Properties do not let themselves, and anyone wishing to let their Croatian home regularly will have to do some marketing. In the early years you will have to do more than later on, because you will have no existing client base.

As in any other business, the cheapest type of marketing is catching repeat clients, so a bit of money spent on making sure the property lives up to, or exceeds, expectations (and brings them or their friends back next year) is probably the best spend that you will make. Otherwise, there seems to be no correlation between the amount spent on marketing and the results achieved, and this is a field in which much money spent is often wasted.

Bear in mind that any form of marketing of a holiday property is only as good as the quality of the response you give to people making enquiries. Owners would often do better spending less money on advertising and paying more attention to following up leads they have already generated.

These are some key points to remember in relation to marketing any kind of short-term lets:

- **Choose the method of marketing most appropriate to your property.**
- **Follow up all enquiries and leads immediately. Contact the people involved again after a couple of weeks to see whether or not they have made up their minds.**
- **Send any contacts your details again next year at about the same time, even if they have not stayed with you, as they may be planning another trip.**

If you have decided to let your property yourself, there are several well-tried means of publicising your property in the British and Irish markets. If you also wish to tap into the Croatian market, you can advertise the property in Croatian papers and listings. However, your Croatian must be good enough to deal with enquiries and you will be faced with a lot of long-distance telephone charges if you end up having to conduct business from back home. For this reason, many people in this case prefer to use a local letting agency (*see* pp.185–8).

Directories and Web Directories

If your property is attractive, then you are likely to get good results from the various directories and joint information-and-booking services that deal with self-catering properties to let in Croatia. Most are now available on the Internet and have ceased producing paper brochures and magazines. Some provide a full booking service and take part in managing lettings, while others, which are cheaper to use and give owners more freedom to manoeuvre, just give you space for photographs and the presentation of your property. Travel industry websites like **www.travelgate.co.uk** and **www.uk-villasabroaddirectory.co.uk** have lists of the many such companies now operating. The monthly magazine *Private Villas* (**t** (020) 7955 3811; **www.privatevillas.co.uk**) is useful for upmarket properties but its advertising is handled through its sister site **www.daltons holidays.com**.

Advertising in this way only really works if the services are inexpensive, because a private owner with only one property to let has only one opportunity of letting each week, and so a directory that produces, say, 50 enquiries for the first week in July is not particularly helpful.

Press Advertising

The problem with traditional methods of advertising is their scattergun approach and, usually, their cost. As mentioned above, if you have just one property you only need a very small number of responses, and you cannot afford to pay a large amount in advertising fees for each week's let. Except for very upmarket properties, traditional advertising is too expensive, and is mainly used by property companies and agencies. For individual owners, better places to advertise are the small-ad pages in the travel sections of newspapers like the *Sunday Times* and the overseas property press.

Some people have been successful advertising in apparently unconnected special interest magazines – such as literary or historical or sporting publications – where their ad did not get lost among 20 others. On the other hand, you can also get good results – and cheaply – by putting a card on your local supermarket noticeboard.

The Internet

The Internet offers tremendous opportunities for bringing a specialist niche product – such as an isolated villa – to the attention of a vast audience at very little cost. For no extra effort, it can allow people to find out about your Croatian home not just in Britain but throughout Europe and the rest of the world. For independent owners offering property for holiday lets, it is strongly recommended that they set up their own website. For many, it quickly becomes their primary means of finding new tenants.

Your website will be your principal brochure, with space to show lots of pictures and other information about the house and the area around it. It is much cheaper to have someone print off a copy of this brochure from their own computer than it is for you to have it printed and sent by post. If you don't have

Case Study: A Success Story

Mark Francis has a portfolio of three rental properties in Croatia. The first is a 400-year-old stone house in Hvar town close to the main square, the second a modern two-bedroom apartment in Split just 50 metres from the sea, and the third a two-bedroom house spread over three floors in Split old town. Despite renovating all three properties himself, he says the hardest part was getting the rental licence. 'Inspectors come out to check the property. There are lots of furniture commitments and bizarre regulations that you need to know about, and the inspectors seem proud of the fact that nobody passes the inspection first time.' However, on his third attempt Mark was awarded a rental licence and began to let his property by advertising locally, creating his own website and joining a large property website. 'On Hvar we get mostly Italian holiday-makers during the summer because there are direct ferry links from the island to Italy. It starts to get quiet by September but the sea is still warm, the weather is good and the tourists are gone, so I fill the place with friends and family. We get another boost around Xmas and New Year with Croatians from Zagreb and then business goes dead until Easter.' Although his business is a success, Mark says it is hard work. 'Croatia is becoming harder rather than easier, especially as a foreigner. The state needs to do more to help out.'

the skills to design a site yourself, it is now quite easy to find web designers, in the UK or Croatia, who will create a basic site for you at low cost.

Your property should also be listed on some of the many Croatian property websites that can be found around the Internet, links to which are either free or relatively cheap. You will soon find out which ones work for you and which ones don't; some of the best are those that are regionally based, since people find it easy to get to what they want with fewer distractions.

As well as being a publicity medium, the website can also be a means of taking bookings. You will have to decide how sophisticated an electronic booking system you want or whether you are happy just to use the Internet to make contacts. Your website will, of course, have your e-mail address on it.

Even if you do not set up a website, anyone letting out property regularly really should have access to e-mail, which is increasingly becoming people's favourite means of communicating and making bookings. Remember to check it at least once a day.

Doing Deals

There are two kinds of 'mutual aid' deals that can be helpful to independent owners, both of which work best in slightly out-of-the-way areas. If your property, for example, is in a rural area where there is somebody offering a very local tourist service, it can be a good idea to make contact with the people running that service and try to arrange for the clients taking their hikes, cultural tours, cookery classes or religious pilgrimages to stay over in your property. This can significantly increase your lettings, particularly at off-peak times. If you agree to pay the tour organisers a commission of around 20 per cent you will still be well ahead.

The second type of deal involves co-operating with other people in the area who let properties, assuming there are any. One of the frustrations of marketing your property is when you have four lots of people who all want to rent it for the same week. Getting together with others in a mutual assistance group will allow you to pass excess lettings to one other.

Using Your Own Contacts

All these methods aside, personal, direct contacts are still among the best means of marketing a property in Croatia. If you want to use a second home for a fair amount of time yourself, you will perhaps only want to let for, say, 20 weeks each year. Given that many people will take it for two weeks or more, you will probably therefore only be looking for around 10–15 lettings annually, and if you put the word out these should not be hard to put together from friends and from friends of friends.

People who work for large organisations have an advantage in this respect, since they can publicise it internally. Even without people from work, most owners will be able to find enough friends, neighbours and relatives to rent a nice property in Croatia for 10 weeks each year, which will leave only a relatively small number of tenants to be found by other means. With most of your lettings you will have the additional advantage of knowing the people who are going to rent the property, which reduces the risk that they will damage it or fail to pay you.

When letting to family or friends, or indeed work colleagues, you will have to learn how to raise the delicate issue of payment. Given that you are not going to be running up any marketing costs and probably not much in the way of property management cost, you should be able to offer them a bargain price and still generate as much income as you would have done by letting through an agency. Make sure that you address this issue when you accept the booking, as doing it later can be very embarrassing.

Management Agencies

On the whole, the people who are most successful over a period of time in letting their second homes are those who find their tenants themselves. This, however, requires a level of commitment that many people simply cannot afford. For non-resident owners who cannot dedicate much time to keeping track of their property, it is far simpler to use a local letting agency.

Agencies – at least good ones – will be able to attract Croatian clients as well as those of different nationalities, particularly German and Italian. You will have to pay them a sizeable commission, but they will argue that this will be recovered by the extra lettings that they make during the holiday season. This may or may not be true. Larger agencies, who publish glossy brochures, are best contacted well in advance, such as early autumn in the previous year, if you want a property to be advertised for the summer season; smaller agencies will take on properties at any time.

In all the desirable areas you will find agencies that manage and let holiday properties, many of them local estate agents, and there are also many that operate from the UK. If you decide to use one of them, the choice of agency is critical. Some are excellent, both in Croatia and in the UK, and some are simply crooks; between the two there are some that are simply bumbling and inefficient. At worst, agencies may hold on to rents for long periods of time, or let your house while telling you it is empty and pocket the rent themselves; others may just charge a signing-on fee to agree to put your property on their books and do nothing to let it. In the past, many have assumed that foreign owners based thousands of miles away will never find out about anything they do. This is a field where it is important for owners to be cautious and demanding of any agents they engage.

Selecting an Agency

When selecting a letting agency there are various checks to make:

- **Find out if it is a registered Croatian agency and whether or not staff are professionally experienced. Many letting agent services are offered as an adjunct to estate agents, who should have staff with relevant experience.**

- **Check the premises, and make an initial judgement about whether or not staff seem welcoming and efficient, and if there's evidence of significant letting activity.**

- **Check how capable they seem to be, especially if you're making contact before actually buying your property. Ask what type of property the agency staff think would be best for letting purposes in this area, how many weeks' rental they think you will be able to obtain annually, and how much income they think they could generate for you after deduction of expenses and their own fees.**

- **Ask for references, preferably from other overseas clients, and follow them up. Telephone other owners and ask if they are happy with the overall performance of the agency and whether the financial projections given to them have been met.**

- **Take a look at what marketing the agency does. If it relies only on passing trade, then except in the most popular areas it will not get good results.**

• Ask to see a sample information pack sent to a potential client. You will be able to judge a lot from this; think about whether or not this is the image you want to give of your property.

• Ask to inspect two or three properties that the agent is already managing. If they are dirty or badly cared for, then so will yours be, and it will not attract lettings.

• Check carefully what kind of contract the agent offers you; it is also sensible to get it checked by a lawyer before you sign, as some give you far more rights than others. Make sure that the contract entitles you to full reports showing when the property was let and for what money; these must give a breakdown by week, not by quarter- or half-year. You should insist on a full breakdown of all expenses incurred in connection with the property, and ensure the contract gives you the right to dismiss the agency on fairly short notice.

Controlling the Agency

After you have appointed a letting agency, you need to keep a check on what it is doing. You may not wish to seem so suspicious, but there are too many horror stories around to allow anyone to get complacent. You should do the following:

• Check the reports you receive from the agency and that the money you receive corresponds to the amounts shown in them.

• Let the agency know, in the nicest possible way, that you and all of your friends in the area check each other's properties every time you are there, and compare notes about which are occupied and the performance of your letting agencies. If they believe you, this is a good deterrent to unauthorised lettings.

• Telephone your property every week. If someone answers the phone, make a note, and make sure that there is income shown for the week of the phone call.

• From time to time, have a friend pose as a prospective customer and send for an enquiry pack.

• If you get the chance, call to see the property without warning, to check its condition.

Formalising the Letting

If you let through an agency, it will draw up fairly standardised rental contracts for you and your tenants to sign. If you handle all your lettings your-self, unless you let only to family and close friends, it is still advisable for you to give tenants a written contract in line with Croatian law, the model for which should preferably be drawn up, with the advice of your lawyer, when you first begin letting.

From the point of view of landlords, the safest type of letting is a short holiday let of furnished property. To be classified as furnished, the property must have all of the basic items required to live in a home, including, at least, a bed, a cooker, a table, a refrigerator, some chairs and so on. A place without these things could be treated as an unfurnished property, in which case, from the legal point of view, tenants could claim that there was a permanent rental contract, potentially giving them the right to an extension after the contract's first term. Otherwise, a holiday let is one that takes place in a recognised holiday season.

A properly drafted tenancy agreement will take all these factors into account and protect you in the event of a dispute with your tenants and, in particular, if any of them wish to stay on at the end of the tenancy. In the rental contract you should also stipulate what things are going to be covered by your insurance and what are not – typically, for example, tenants' personal possessions would not be covered under your policy.

References

Directory of Contacts

Major Resources in Britain

Embassy of the Republic of Croatia in the United Kingdom
21 Conway Street
London W1T 6BN
t (020) 7387 2022
f (020) 7287 0310
croemb.london@mvpei.hr
www.croatia.embassyhomepage.com
www.mfa.hr

Croatian National Tourist Office
2 The Lanchesters
162–4 Fulham Palace Road
London W6 9ER
t (020) 8563 7979
f (020) 8563 2616
info@cnto.freeserve.co.uk
http://gb.croatia.hr

British Resources in Croatia

Embassy of the United Kingdom
Ivana Lučića 4
10000 Zagreb
t +385 (0)1 6009 100
f +385 (0)1 6009 111
british.embassyzagreb@fco.gov.uk
www.britishembassy.gov.uk/croatia

Visa and Consular Section
Von Humboldta 4
10000 Zagreb
t +385 (0)1 6009 122
f +385 (0)1 6009 298

British Consulate Split
Obala Hrvatskog Narodnog Preporoda 10/III
21000 Split
t +385 (0)21 346 007
f +385 (0)21 362 905
british-consulat-st@st.htnet.hr

British Consulate Dubrovnik
Buniceva Poljana 3
20000 Dubrovnik
t +385 (0)20 324 597
f +385 (0)20 324 597
honcons.dubrovnik@inet.hr

British Council
Ilica 12, pp 55
10001 Zagreb
t +385 (0)1 4899 500
f +385 (0)1 4833 955
Zagreb.info@britishcouncil.hr
www.britishcouncil.org/croatia

Foreign Embassies in Croatia

Embassy of Australia
Kaptol Centar
Nova Ves 11/3
10000 Zagreb
t +385 (0)1 4891 200
f +385 (0)1 4891 216
australian.embassy@zg.t-com.hr
www.croatia.embassy.gov.au

Embassy of India
Boskoviceva 7a
10000 Zagreb
t +385 (0)1 487 3239
f +385 (0)1 4817 907
embassy.india@zg.htnet.hr
www.indianembassy.hr

Consulate General of Ireland
Miramarska 23
10000 Zagreb
t +385 (0)1 6674 455
f +385 (0)1 2413 901

New Zealand Consulate Zagreb
Vlaska ulica 50A
10000 Zagreb
t +385 (0)1 461 2060
nzealandconsulate@email.t-com.hr

Embassy of the United States of America
Thomasa Jeffersona 2
10010 Zagreb
t +385 (0)1 6612 200
f +385 (0)1 6612 373
www.usembassy.hr

Removal Companies

Removal Group
46–48 Mere Green Road
Sutton Coldfield
Birmingham B75 5BT
t 0870 240 7432
sales@removalgroup.com
www.removalgroup.com

Burke Brothers Moving Group
Fox's Lane
Wolverhampton
West Midlands WV1 1PA
t (01902) 714 555
f (01902) 427 837
sales@burkebros.co.uk
www.burkebros.com

R46
Unit 16, Wedgwood Road
Bicester
Oxfordshire OX26 4UL
t 0800 234 646
info@r46.eu
www.r46.eu

PSS International Movers
1–3 Pegasus Road
Croydon
Surrey CR9 4PS
t (020) 8686 7733
sales@p-s-s.co.uk
www.pssremovals.com

Credo Movers
Koranska 1c, Zagreb
t +385 (0)1 6171 449
f +385 (0)1 6152 743
credo1@zg.htnet.hr
www.credo-movers.hr

Estate Agents

Dream Property Croatia
Andrea Marston
5–6 High Street, Windsor
Berkshire SL4 1LD
t (0)1753 831 182
f (0)1753 853 188
uk@dreamcroatia.com
www.dreamcroatia.com
Highly knowledgeable about all aspects of the Croatian property market, with permanent English-speaking offices in Dublin, Dubrovnik, Split and Pula.

A Place in Croatia
Carol Southgate
Prolaz Joze Duisina 2
21216 Kaštel Novi
Dalmatia
t +385 (0)21 246 290
www.aplacindalmatia.com
British-owned estate agency specialising in Dalmatia, with properties all over Croatia.

Croatian Property Services

Peter Ellis
Farini 1
HR-52463 Visnjan
Istria
t +385 (0)99 6938 856/9
f +385 (0)52 449 440
info@croatiapropertyservices.com
www.croatiapropertyservices.com
A great resource for up-to-date information on the legal and financial implications of buying a property in Croatia as well as an estate agency specialising in Istria.

Croatia Select
André Wilding
The Office, Syderstone Business Park
Mill Lane, Syderstone
King's Lynn
Norfolk PE31 8RX
t (0)1485 529 458
f (0)1485 529 458
service@croatiaselect.co.uk
www.croatiaselect.co.uk
Experts on property across inland Croatia as well as project management and renovations.

Property In Croatia
Sandra Jakšić
t +385 (0)21 630 461
sandra@property-in-croatia.com
www.property-in-croatia.com
Specialises in property on the island of Brač, with superb local knowledge.

Dussmann Homes
Andreas Dussmann
t +385 (0)52 842 227
andreas@dussmannhomes.com
www.dussmannhomes.com
Developer of off-plan traditional-style villas in central Istria.

Milenka Real Estate
Ljiljana Poklepović
Brižak b.b. 21405
Milna ot. Brač
t +385 (0)21 636 221
f +385 (0)21 636 428
ljiljana@milenkarealestate.com
www.milenkarealestate.com

Hvar Property Services
Paul Bradbury
info@croatianhouse.com
www.croatianhouse.com

Accommodation

Istra Život
Glavani 4
HR-52207 Barban
t +385 (0)52 522 920
f +385 (0)52 522 921
www.istra-zivot.com

Apartments Little Vinišće
Bumbaci 2
21226 Vinišće
Trogir
t +385 (0)21 796 547
mail@littlevinisce.com
www.littlevinisce.com

Hvar and Split
t +44 7748 933256 or t +385 (0)917 243 639
www.hvarandsplit.com

Online Resources

- **www.visit-croatia.co.uk**: Information, useful links and enlightening message boards on a whole variety of Croatia-related subjects.

- **www.buyassociation.co.uk**: Articles and podcasts offering advice on buying property in Croatia.

- **www.adriatica.net**: A one-stop shop for arranging a trip to Croatia including private accommodation and car hire. Lots of travel information.

Croatian Vocabulary

See also **Settling In**, 'Learning and Speaking the Language, pp.142–4.

Pronunciation

Although occasional parades of consonants strike fear, Croatian is not quite as terrifying as it looks. Every letter is pronounced, and most are spoken as English except for those explained below. As a rule of thumb, the stress falls on the first syllable, and never on the last.

C is pronounced as 'ts' as in 'cats', **č** is pronounced as 'ch' as in 'church' and **ć** is softer, like the 'ch' of 'cheese'.

Ð/đ is spoken as the 'j' of 'jam'.

G is always hard, as in 'get'.

J is spoken as 'y' as in 'yacht' and looks a tongue-twister when combined with other consonants but is straightforward: **nj** is said as 'ny' as in 'canyon', like the Spanish ñ; **lj** as the 'li' of 'million'.

Rs are rolled luxuriantly on the tongue and function as a vowel when placed between two consonants such as in 'Hrvatska' (Croatia).

Š is pronounced as the 'sh' of 'sheet'; **Ž** is pronounced as the 's' of 'leisure'.

Vowel sounds are short: **a** as in 'cat'; **e** as in 'met'; **i** as in the 'ee' of 'feet'; **o** as in 'dog'; and **u** as in 'oo' of 'hoot'.

Useful Vocabulary

Greetings and Courtesies

hello	*dobar dan* (literally 'good day')/*zdravo*
goodbye	*doviđenja*
hi/bye!	*bog!*
good morning	*dobro jutro*
good evening	*dobra večer*
goodnight	*laku noć*
please	*molim* (also used as 'You're welcome')
thank you (very much/for your help)	*hvala (lijepo/na pomoći)*

how are you? (formal)	*kako ste?*
(informal)	*kako si?*
fine, thanks	*dobro, hvala*
I am from England/Scotland/Wales/	*ja sam iz Engleske/Škotske/*
Ireland/ USA/Canada	*Velsa/Irske/Amerike/Kanade*
pleased to meet you	*drago mi je*
sorry (apology)	*pardon/oprostite*
excuse me	*oprostite*
I am lost (m/f)	*izgubio/izgubila sam se*

Basic Words and Phrases

yes/no/maybe	*da/ne/možda*
do you speak English?	*govorite li engleski?*
I (don't) understand	*(ne) razumijem*
I don't speak Croatian	*ne govorim hrvatski*
can I have...	*mogu li dobiti...*
do you have...	*imate li...*
how much is it?	*koliko košta?*
that's cheap/too expensive	*to je jeftino/preskupo*
keep the change!	*zadržite sitan novac!*
do you take credit cards?	*primate li kreditne kartice?*
large	*veliko*
small	*malo*
hot	*toplo*
cold	*hladno*
why?	*zašto?*
when?	*kada?*
where?/where is?	*gdje?/gdje je?*
where can I park the car?	*gdje mogu parkirati auto?*

Days, Months and Time

Monday	*ponedjeljak*
Tuesday	*utorak*
Wednesday	*srijeda*
Thursday	*četvrtak*
Friday	*petak*
Saturday	*subota*
Sunday	*nedjelja*
what day is it today?	*koli je danas dan?*
January	*siječanj*
February	*veljača*
March	*ožujak*
April	*travanj*
May	*svibanj*

June	*lipanj*
July	*srpanj*
August	*kolovoz*
September	*rujan*
October	*listopad*
November	*studeni*
December	*prosinac*

what time is it?	*koliko je sati?*
early/late	*rano/kasno*
in the morning	*ujutro*
in the afternoon	*popodne*
day/week/month	*dan/tjedan/mjesec*
today/yesterday/tomorrow	*danas/jučer/sutra*

Numbers

1	*jedan*
2	*dva*
3	*tri*
4	*četiri*
5	*pet*
6	*šest*
7	*sedam*
8	*osam*
9	*devet*
10	*deset*
11	*jedanaest*
12	*dvanaest*
13	*trinaest*
14	*četrnaest*
15	*petnaest*
16	*šesnaest*
17	*sedamnaest*
18	*osamnaest*
19	*devetnaest*
20	*dvadeset*
21	*dvadeset i jedan*
22	*dvadeset i dva*
30	*trideset*
40	*četrdeset*
50	*petdeset*
100	*sto*
101	*sto i jedan*
200	*dvjesto*
500	*petsto*
1,000	*tisuća*

Medical

I am feeling ill (m/f)	*Osjećam se bolesnim/bolesnom*
ache/pain	*bol*
I've a headache/earache/stomach ache	*Boli me glava/uho/želudac*
toothache	*zubobolja*
diarrhoea	*proljev*
doctor	*liječnik/doktor*
dentist	*zubar*
hospital	*bolnica*
pharmacy	*ljekarna*

Around Town

open	*otvoreno*
closed	*zatvoreno*
entrance	*ulaz*
exit	*izlaz*
toilet	*zahodi/ WC (pronounced 'vay-tsay')*
ladies	*ženski*
gents	*muški*
bank	*banka*
bureau de change	*mjenjačnica*
to change	*promijeni*
police/police station	*policija/policijska stanica*
embassy	*ambasada/veleposlanstro*
post office	*pošta*
airport	*zračna luka/aerodrom*
(main) railway/bus station	*(glavni) željeznički/autobusni kolodvor*
(ferry) port	*(trajektna) luka*
market	*tržnica*
tourist office	*turistički ured/turistički informativni centar*
museum	*muzej*
gallery	*galerija*
cinema	*kino*
church/cathedral	*crkva/katedrala*
monastery	*samostan*
old town	*stari grad*
street	*ulica*
square	*trg*
beach	*plaža*
how far is it?	*koliko je daleko?*
far	*daleko*
near	*blizu*
left	*lijevo*
right	*desno*
straight on	*ravno*

Dictionary of Useful and Technical Terms

adresa	address
advokat	lawyer
agent u posredovanju pri kupnji	
i prodaji nekretnina	letting agent
agent za rad sa nekretninama	estate agent
antički	antique
anulirati	to cancel
aparati	appliances
apartmani	apartment
arhitekta	architect
auto	car
autobus	public bus
autobusni kolodvor	bus station
autocesta	motorway
autokamp	campsite
banjom	bath
banka	bank
bankomat	ATM
bankovni račun	bank account
bazen	swimming pool
benzinska stanica	petrol station
biblioteka	library
blagovaonica	dining room
blakon	balcony
bojler	boiler
bolnica	hospital
bravar	locksmith
brdo	hill
brzi	fast train
buk	waterfall
bura	seasonal coastal wind
burza	stock exchange
casco	fully comprehensive insurance
cementa	cement
centar	centre
cesta	road
četvorni metar	square metre
cigle	bricks
cijena	price
cijeniti	to estimate
cijevi	pipes
ćilim	carpet

cjenjkanje	bargain
cjenovnik	pricelist
crijep	roof tile
crkva	church
d.d.	stock company
daljinski	remote
dekorater	decorator
dekorirati	decorate
depozitni	deposit
diskont	discount
djubre	rubbish
dobro	good
dolina	valley
dolje	downstairs
dom	house
donji grad	lower town
dostupan	available
dozvola	permission
draga	bay
drvo	wood
drvodjelac	carpenter
drzavljanin	citizenship
dućan	shop
dugoročni	long-term
dvor	courtyard
električar	electrician
električna brojila	electricity meter
električna grijalica	electric heater
engleski	English
evikcija	eviction
faktura	invoice
farmacija	pharmacy
fasada	façade
FINA	Croatian Financial Agency
fortica	fortress
francuskim ležajem	double bed
gableci	mid-morning snack
gaj	grove
garaža	garage
gat	quay
glavna ulica	main street
glavni trg	main square
godina	year

gore	upstairs
gornji grad	upper town
gospodarska komora	chamber of commerce
grad	town
graditelj	builder
gradnji	building
gradonačelnik	mayor
gradska vijećnica	town hall
gradu	city
granica	boundary
greben	cliff
grijač ulja	oil heater
grijač za vodu	water heater
grijalo koje se uroni utekućinu	immersion heater
grijanje	heating
hladno	cold
hrana	food
Hrvatska udruga za zastitu potrosaca (HUZP)	Croatian Association for Consumer Affairs
Hrvatske Željeznice	Croatian Railways
Hrvatski zavod za zdravstveno osiguranje (HZZO)	Croatian Institute for Health Insurance
identifikacijska isprava	identity document
informacije	information
inventarna	inventory
irske	Ireland
isplata	payment
ispravu	document
izlaz	exit
iznajmiti	to rent
Izvadak iz matice umrlih	death certificate
Jadran	Adriatic Sea
jahta	yacht
jastuk	pillow
javnibilježnik	notary
jedinstveni matični broj građana (JMBG)	Croatian national identity number
jeftino	cheap
jesen	autumn
jezero	lake
kabina	cabin
kaldrma	pavement
kamata	interest
kamen	stone

kamenac	limescale
kampiranje	camping
kancelarija	office
kaštel	castle
kat	floor
katastarski ured	land registry office
kavana	café
keramilki	ceramic tile
klimatizacija	air conditioning
ključ	key
knjižara	bookshop
kokoš	chickens
konoba	inn
korporacija	corporation
koš	barn
kratkoročan	short term
kredit na nepokretnu imovinu	mortgage
krov	roof
kubični metar	cubic metre
kuća	house
kuhinja	kitchen
kupaona	bathroom
kvaka	door handle
lavabo	sink
liječnik	physician
lijep	pretty
livada	lawn
ljeto	summer
lokalan	local
lućka kapetanija	harbourmaster's office
luka	port
malo	small
mansarda	attic
marenda	mid-morning snack
maslinici	olive grove
Maticni Ured	Croatian Registry of Vital Statistics
menadžer projekta	project manager
merdevine	ladder
mesnica	butcher
mikrovalna	microwave
miran	quiet
mjesec	month
mjesto	location
modernizacija	modernisation
moler	painter

more	sea
most	bridge
nadničar	handyman
nadstrešnica	penthouse
nadzor	survey
najmiti	lease
najviši kat	top floor
naknaditi	to restore
namještaj	furniture
naseljiv	habitable
nastavak	instalments
neboder	skyscraper
nedopusten	illegal
nekretnina	property
nezauzet	unoccupied
noćenje i doručak	bed and breakfast
novac	money
obala	shore
obilje	luxury
obnoviti	to refurbish
održavanje	maintenance
ognjište	fireplace
ograda	fence
okvir od prozora	window frame
općina	municipality
opreaviti	to repair
opremljen	equipped
opskrba električnom energijom	electricity supply
osiguranje	insurance
osiguranje protiv trecega	third party insurance
osnova škola	primary school
otok	island
pać	oven
palača	palace
parkiralište	car park
PDV	Croatian tax equivalent to VAT
pekarna	bakery
perilica rublja	washing machine
perivoj	park
planina	mountain
plaža	beach
plaža kamenita	stony beach
plaža pješčana	sandy beach
plaža šljunčana	pebbly beach

plina	gas
plinsko kuhalo	gas cooker
podne	noon
podrum	basement
pogled na more	sea view
pokućstvo	furnishings
policija	police
policijska stanica	police station
poljana	field
poljoprivredna	farm
poluotok	peninsula
polupansion	half-board
porez na imovinu	property tax
posjednik	landlord
pošta	post office
poštanska marka	stamp
povijesni	historic
pozajmiti	loan
praonica	launderette
pravo na pristup	right of access
predgradje	suburb
predsoblje	hallway
prenosiv	negotiable
prestanak ugovora	termination of a contract
prikolica	caravan
pristojba za licencu	licence fee
prizemlje	ground floor
prodaja	sale
prodati	to sell
proljeće	spring
promet	traffic
propisi o iznajmljivanju	rent regulations
prozor	window
put	road
putanja	lane
putnički vlak	passenger train
računovođa	accountant
račun	bill or receipt
radijator	radiator
referenca	reference
reklamna cijena	bargain
rekonstruisati	to reconstruct
rent-a-car	car rental
restoran	restaurant
rezervaciju	reservation
rezervoar pitke vode	water storage tank

rijeka	river
riva	seafront
rodni list	birth certificate
roletna	shutters
rublje	bed linen
ručak	lunch
ruševina	ruins
samoposluga	supermarket
samostojeca kuca	detached house
sanitarni tank	septic tank
sat	hour
selco	village
selidbena kola	removal van
seljak	rustic
seoce	hamlet
sezona	season
skupo	expensive
slavina	tap
smještaj	accommodation
snabdjeti	grocery
soba	room
spavaća soba	bedroom
spojene dvije obiteljske kuće	semi-detached
staklo	glass
stanar	tenant
stanje konstrukcije	condition
star	old
stari grad	old town
staza	path
stovarište	timber yard
stran	foreign
strop	ceiling
stručna sprema	qualification
struktura	structure
stube	stairs
sudnica	courthouse
šuma	forest
susjed	neighbour
sveučilište	university
svijetlo	light
tapeta	wallpaper
tečaj	exchange rate
tekuće cijene	quotation
telekartu	phonecard
televizor	TV set

terasa	terrace
tjedan	week
toalet	toilet
toplo	hot
tradicijska	traditional
trajekt	ferry
trajektna luka	ferry terminal
tramvaj	tram
trg	square
trijem	porch
tržnica	market
turist	tourist
turisticke atrakcije	tourist attractions
turisticki ured	tourist office
tuš	shower
tušem	shower
učešće	down payment
ugovor o najmu	lease contract
ugovor o radu	employment contract
ugovoriti	contract
ulaz	entrance
ulica	street
upravljanje projektom	project management
ured za graditeljstvo i prostorno uredenje	planning office
uređen	furnished
utišati	quiet
uvala	bay
veleposlanstvo	embassy
veličina	size
Velike Britanije	Great Britain
veliko	large
vez	mooring
vikend	weekend
vikendica	holiday home
vinarija	wine cellar
vinarstvo rajon	wine region
vinograd	vineyard
visoka škola	secondary school
vjenčani list	marriage certificate
vlak	train
vlaznost	humidity
voda	water
vodoinstalater	plumber
vozačka dozvola	driving licence
vrata	door

vrijednost svojstva	property value
vrt	garden
vrtlar	gardener
zajutrak	breakfast
zakonito boraviti	resident
zaliha	storage
zaljev	gulf
žarulja	light bulb
zatvoreno	closed
zdenac	well
zemlja	land
zid	wall
zidar	bricklayer
zima	winter
zračna luka	airport

Croatian Holidays and Festivals

Public Holidays

1 January	New Year's Day
6 January	Epiphany
March or April	Easter Sunday and Easter Monday
1 May	Labour Day
June	Corpus Christi
22 June	Anti-Fascist Resistance Day
25 June	Statehood Day
5 August	Victory Day and National Thanksgiving Day
15 August	Assumption
8 October	Independence Day
1 November	All Saints' Day
25–26 December	Christmas

Feast Days and Festivals

3 February	Feast of St Blaise, Dubrovnik
Sunday before Shrove Tuesday	Carnival Procession, Rijeka
Shrove Tuesday	Carnival Procession, Split
Good Friday	Procession of the Religious Brotherhoods, Korčula
23 April	St George's Day
7 May	Feast of St Domnius, Split
8 May	Birthday of Cardinal Stepinac, Krašić
25 July	Feast of St James; Kumpanjija Sword Dance, Korčula
27 July	St Christopher's Day, Crossbow Tournament, Rab

Croatia – Naturally

Naturism has been popular along the Adriatic ever since the early years of the 19th century, but King Edward VIII is credited with putting Croatia on the map as a naturist destination. During his short reign as king he spent the summer of 1936 on the island of Rab with his soon-to-be wife Wallis Simpson, and was permitted by the local authorities to swim nude in Kandarola Bay. The idea grew into the concept of commercial naturist resorts, and the first naturist camps opened in Istria and Dalmatia during the 1960s. Today there are more than 20 naturist resorts in Croatia, ranging from beaches and campsites to hotels and apartment complexes.

All along the Croatian coast you will see beaches marked with an FKK symbol. This stands for *Freikörperkultur* ('Free Body Culture' in German) and means that naturism is permitted. The website **www.cronatur.com** lists FKK beaches in Croatia along with a guide of resorts. It also offers some advice on naturist etiquette if you do use an FKK beach:

- Don't risk causing offence by stripping off in non-nudist areas. If you are unsure which is which, as a rough guide the further you walk from the point of access, the more acceptable nudity is likely to be.

- Be careful about taking photographs. Photographs and videos should only be taken with the permission of those in the shot.

- It is important to leave sites as clean as or cleaner than you found them for the next person. Pick up cigarette butts from the ground. No one likes skinny-dipping in an ashtray.

- Respect the privacy and space of others. Don't gawk or stare; it's rude.

- Use your own towel when sitting on benches, chairs, pool furniture and other furniture and don't sit on anyone else's towel or blanket.

29 July	Feast of St Theodore, Moreška Sword Dance, Korčula
5 August	Feast of Our Lady of the Snows
15 August	Feast of the Assumption
16 August	Feast of St Rock; Moštra Sword Dance at Postrana and the Kumpanjija Sword Dance in Korčula
27–29 August	Feast of St Pelagius, Novigrad
8 September	Mala Gospa (Birth of the Virgin)
8 October	Feast of St Simeon, Zadar
1 November	Svi Sveti (All Saints' Day)
11 November	Martinje (Feast of St Martin)
6 December	Sveti Nikola (Feast of St Nicholas)
25 December	Božić (Christmas)

Cultural Festivals and Events

May	Accordian Festival, Roč
	Festival of One Minute Films, Požega
July	Krk Festival
	Split Jazz Festival
	Klapa Festival, Omiš
	Sajam Naïve (Naïve Art Fair), Koprivnica
	Osorske Večeri, Cres (International Chamber Music Festival)
	International Folklore Festival, Zagreb
July–August	Dubrovačke Ljetne Igre (Dubrovnik Summer Festival)
August	Sinjska Alka, Sinj
	Valkana Beach Festival, Pula
	Trka na Prstenac (Tilting at the Ring), Barban
	Croatian Film Festival, Pula
	International Film Festival, Motovun
September	Grape Harvest Festival, Zagorje
September–October	Varaždin Festival of Baroque Music

Further Reading

Julienne Eden Busic, *Lovers and Madmen: A True Story of Passion, Politics and Air Piracy*. Fascinating story of four Croats and an American woman who hijacked a plane in America in 1976 to publicise the Croatian fight for independence.

Slavenka Drakulić, *As If I Was Not There*. A deeply cutting novel by one of Croatia's most well-regarded novelists about a Bosnian woman detained in a Serbian internment camp.

Misha Glenny, *The Fall of Yugoslavia*. A former BBC central Europe correspondent describes the conflict of the 1990s from a front-line perspective.

Ivo Goldstein and Nikolina Jovanovic, *Croatia: A History*. Good, albeit brief overview of the history of the country by a professor at the University of Zagreb, who is at his best when writing about the 20th century.

Brian Hall, *The Impossible Country*. Part history lesson, part humorous travelogue, the book describes Hall's journey through a disintegrating Yugoslavia during the summer of 1991.

Robin Harris, *Dubrovnik: A History*. A highly readable history of this most fascinating of cities.

Clea Koff, *The Bone Woman: A Forensic Anthropologist's Search for Truth in the Mass Graves of Rwanda, Bosnia, Croatia, and Kosovo*. Harrowing and personal account by a forensic anthropologist who worked on missions with the UN War Crimes Tribunal.

Miroslav Krleža, *The Return of Philip Latinowicz*. One of Croatia's most famous works of literature, which follows a tragic romance set in rural Slavonia at the end of the First World War.

Michael McConville, *A Small War in the Balkans*. A detailed observational account of the British commando campaigns in Yugoslavia during the Second World War.

John MacPhee, *The Silent Cry: One Man's Fight for Croatia in Bosnia*. Not an objective account but an absorbing story that vividly demonstrates the human carnage and mental scars left by the Balkan conflicts.

Stipe Mesić, *The Demise of Yugoslavia: A Political Memoir*. Written by Croatia's current president, who was also the last president of an ailing Yugoslavia and the first prime minister of a nascent Croatia.

Arrigo Petacco, *A Tragedy Revealed: The Story of Italians from Istria, Dalmatia and Venezia Giulia, 1943–1956*. A newly researched account of a tragic period of Croatian history by one of Italy's most respected journalists.

Marcus Tanner, *Croatia: A Nation Forged in War*. The most up-to-date and readable history of Croatia, written by a journalist from the *Independent*.

Dubravka Ugrešić, *Culture of Lies*. A collection of essays exploring the dark side of Croatian society during the 1990s by a Croatian author who spent much of the decade in self-imposed exile.

Rebecca West, *Black Lamb and Grey Falcon*. Considered one of the classics of travel literature, the book is a colourful and opinionated account of West's journey through Yugoslavia in the 1930s.

Jasna Capo Zmeqac, *Strangers Either Way: The Lives of Croatian Refugees in Their New Home*. A slightly dry look at the forgotten story of 'ethnic Croats' forced to leave their homes in Serbia to establish a new life in Croatia.

Climate Charts

Average Daily Temperature in Zagreb (°C)

Jan	Feb	Mar	April	May	June	July	Aug	Sept	Oct	Nov	Dec
0	1	7	13	17	16	23	21	17	10	6	1

Average Number of Rainy Days per Month in Zagreb

Jan	Feb	Mar	April	May	June	July	Aug	Sept	Oct	Nov	Dec
7	6	10	13	11	14	8	11	10	9	12	9

Average Daily Temperature in Dubrovnik (°C)

Jan	Feb	Mar	April	May	June	July	Aug	Sept	Oct	Nov	Dec
12	13	14	17	21	25	29	28	25	21	17	14

Average Number of Rainy Days per Month in Dubrovnik

Jan	Feb	Mar	April	May	June	July	Aug	Sept	Oct	Nov	Dec
13	13	11	10	10	6	4	3	7	11	16	15

Appendix

Checklist – Do-it-yourself Inspection
of Property 212

10

Checklist – Do-it-yourself inspection of property

TASK	✔
Title	
Check that the property corresponds with its description in the title	
Number of rooms	
Plot size	
Plot	
Identify the physical boundaries of the plot	
Is there any dispute with anyone over these boundaries?	
Are there any obvious foreign elements on your plot such as pipes, cables, drainage ditches, water tanks, etc.?	
Are there any signs of anyone else having rights over the property? Footpaths, access ways, cartridges from hunting, etc.?	
Garden/Terrace	
Are any plants, ornaments etc. on site not being sold with the property?	
Walls – stand back from property and inspect from outside	
Any signs of subsidence?	
Walls vertical?	
Any obvious cracks in walls?	
Are walls well pointed?	
Any obvious damp patches?	
Any new repairs to walls or re-pointing?	
Roof – inspect from outside property	
Does roof sag?	
Are there missing/slipped tiles?	
Do all faces of roof join squarely?	
Lead present and in good order?	

Checklist – Do-it-yourself inspection of property

TASK	✔
Guttering and Downpipes – inspect from outside property	
All present?	
Securely attached?	
Fall of guttering constant?	
Any obvious leaks?	
Any recent repairs?	
Grass or vegetation growing in gutters?	
Enter Property	
Does it smell of damp?	
Does it smell 'musty'?	
Does it smell of dry rot?	
Any other strange smells?	
Doors	
Signs of rot?	
Close properly – without catching?	
Provide proper seal?	
Locks work?	
Windows	
Signs of rot?	
Close properly – without catching?	
Provide proper seal?	
Locks work?	
Excessive condensation?	
Have they been painted and maintained?	

Checklist – Do-it-yourself inspection of property

TASK	✔
Floor	
Can you see it all?	
Does it appear in good condition?	
Any sign of cracked or rotten boards?	
Does it bow in the middle?	
Do the floorboards bounce?	
Under Floor	
Can you get access under the floor?	
If so, is it ventilated?	
Is there any sign of rot?	
How close are joists?	
Are joist ends in good condition where they go into walls?	
What is maximum unsupported length of joist run?	
Is there any sign of damp or standing water?	
Roof Void	
Is it accessible?	
Is there sign of water entry?	
Can you see daylight through the roof?	
Is there an underlining between the tiles and the void?	
Is there any sign of rot in timbers?	
Horizontal distance between roof timbers?	
Size of roof timbers (section)	
Maximum unsupported length of roof timbers	
Is roof insulated – if so, what depth and type of insulation?	

Checklist – Do-it-yourself inspection of property

TASK	✔
Woodwork	
Any sign of rot?	
Any sign of wood-boring insects?	
Is it dry?	
Interior Walls	
Any significant cracks?	
Any obvious damp problems?	
Any sign of recent repair/redecoration?	
Electricity	
Check electricity meter:	
How old is it?	
What is its rated capacity?	
Check all visible wiring:	
What type is it?	
Does it appear in good physical condition?	
Check all sockets:	
Is there power to socket?	
Does socket tester show good earth and show 'OK'?	
Are there enough sockets?	
Lighting:	
Do all lights work?	
Which light fittings are included in sale?	
Cold Water – Where does the water come from?	
The mains?	
A rural water scheme?	

Checklist – Do-it-yourself inspection of property

TASK	✔
A well?	
Do all hot and cold taps work?	
Is flow adequate?	
Do taps drip?	
Is there a security cut off on all taps between mains and tap?	
Do they seem in good condition?	
Is hot water 'on'? If so, does it work at all taps, showers etc?	
What type of hot water system is fitted?	
Age?	
Gas	
Is the property fitted with city (piped) gas? If so:	
Age of meter	
Does installation appear in good order?	
Is there any smell of gas?	
Is the property fitted with bottled gas? If so:	
Where are bottles stored?	
Is it ventilated to outside of premises?	
Central Heating	
Is the property fitted with central heating? If so:	
Is it 'on'?	
Will it turn on?	
What type is it?	
Is there heat at all radiators/outlets?	
Do any thermostats appear to work?	
Are there any signs of leaks?	

Checklist – Do-it-yourself inspection of property

TASK	✔
Fireplaces	
Is the property fitted with any solid fuel heaters? If so:	
Any sign of blow-back from chimneys?	
Do chimneys (outside) show stains from leakage?	
Do chimneys seem in good order?	
Phone	
Does it work?	
Number?	
Satellite TV	
Does it work?	
Is it included in the sale?	
Drainage	
What type of drainage does property have?	
If septic tank, how old?	
Who maintains it?	
When was it last maintained?	
Any smell of drainage problems in bathrooms and toilets?	
Does water drain away rapidly from all sinks, showers and toilets?	
Is there any inspection access through which you can see drainage taking place?	
Is there any sign of plant ingress to drains?	
Do drains appear to be in good condition and well pointed?	
Kitchen	
Do all cupboard open/close properly?	
Any signs of rot?	

Checklist – Do-it-yourself inspection of property

TASK	✔
Tiling secure and in good order?	
Enough plugs?	
What appliances are included in sale?	
Do they work?	
Age of appliances included?	
Bathroom	
Security and condition of tiling?	
Ventilation?	
Appliances	
What appliances generally are included in sale?	
What is not included in sale?	
Furniture	
What furniture is included in sale?	
What is NOT included in sale?	
Repairs/Improvements/Additions	
What repairs have been carried out in last 2 years?	
What improvements have been carried out in last 2 years/10 years?	
What additions have been made to the property in last 2 years/10 years?	
Do they have builders receipts/guarantees?	
Do any additions or alterations comply with the building regulations?	
Defects	
Is seller aware of any defects in the property?	

NOTES

Index

Discover the true spirit
of Croatia

ZAGREB
SPLIT
DUBROVNIK
ZADAR
PULA

Choose Croatia Airlines for your flights to and within Croatia.

NEW in the summer timetable:
London Gatwick - Zagreb 3 times a week

For information on special offers visit our website
or call 0870 4100 310.

CROATIA AIRLINES

www.croatiaairlines.com

A REGIONAL STAR ALLIANCE MEMBER

More Than a Comfortable Flight

CROATIA – *A GOOD PLACE TO INVEST*

Since breaking free from Jugoslavia in the early nineties, Croatia has worked hard to rebuild the tourist industry that it was famous for in the seventies and eighties. Under the slogan 'The Mediterranean as it used to be', it has moved steadily ahead.

Following concerns by their tourist authorities, who had seen for themselves the effects of overdevelopment of the Spanish coastline, the country moved to protect its amazing coastline and put restrictions on development directly on the coast and even certain restrictions on developments up to 1km back. They also realised that if they were to have sustainable tourism, they would need to consider the best use of what they had to offer. The outcome of this has been to move towards higher net worth tourism, attracting a wealthier type of tourist and working at this.

Places like the Italianate Istria were ideal. The Northern part has a wonderful hinterland, redolent of Tuscany or Umbria, with fascinating hilltop towns, like Grosnjan and Motovun with jazz and film festivals. The vineyards and olive groves surrounding traditional stone houses were many people's dream location, especially when it was such an accessible region.

Ryanair fly all year round into Trieste, just across the border in Italy and have flights in to Pula, in Istria, during the summer. Globespan have been flying there, too, from Durham/Teesside and Edinburgh, whilst Thomson fly there from regional airports like Bristol and Manchester. Even Venice is only a couple of hours away, by car or hydrofoil and both Easyjet and Ryanair fly there, including flights from places like Liverpool.

The infrastructure has been steadily improving, as new roads have been built, designed by Britain's Ove Arup, and ADSL and GSM wireless internet access were introduced. The new marina at Novigrad complemented the existing ones at Vrsar and Umag and hosts Istria's first five star hotel. Three new golf courses have already got permission and sites for others, at places like Tar, are also planned.

In the wake of this, property prices have been increasing steadily. Stone houses with pools are particularly popular, as not only do they have good capital growth potential, there is a huge demand for them for holiday rentals. Owners rent out through websites like **www.ownersdirect.co.uk** Prices of this sort of property have been increasing by up to 30%pa, although until this year they were starting to slow up at the upper end, as there was a shortage of wealthier buyers. Happily, this has also changed, as serious investors with funds in excess of Eur500,000 have started to buy and stone houses of all sizes are increasing steadily in value.

Finally, Istria's great strength is position, always critical. Most of Europe drives there, as it is the nearest point on the Mediterranean.

When the eco lobbying really kicks in and long distance flights to places like Turkey, Florida, the Cape Verde Islands and more exotic locations become prohibitively expensive, leading to falls in property values, Croatia will still be holding up.

Peter Ellis
Visnjan Sales Office
Croatia Property Services
A trading name of Peter Ellis Grupa d.o.o.
SELLING IN THE NEW TUSCANY!
Tel: +385 (0)981 82 62 40   +385 (0)99 69 38 856   +385 (0)99 69 38 859
Fax:+385 (0)52 44 94 40
http://www.croatiapropertyservices.com   http://croatiaproperty.proboards16.com

The most famous and respected Real Estate company in CROATIA

Established in the community.
The agency specialises in Sale and Rental of villas and cottages throughout the Croatian Coastline.

Join the locals, join Dalmatian Villas.
Let us make the land of a 1000 islands be your dream home.

English, Italian, Russian speaking.
We await your call. +44 (0)1536 790909

www.dalmatianvillas.co.uk

Dobar Dan from Dalmatian Villas, perhaps the most famous and respected Croatian Real Estate and holiday letting company in the country. Featuring in national newspapers and magazines giving their professional opinions on the peculiar yet wonderfully attractive property market in Croatia.

Established in the communities and hearts of the coastal and island people of Croatia. Known from the impressive towns of Split and Dubrovnik down to the tiniest fishing village on the smallest island.

Our staff are full English, Italian and Russian speaking and have been trained professionally in the total property/holiday business. We have offices in Split, Makarska, Hvar, England, Romania and are opening in Dubrovnik and Zadar.

We can provide last minute holiday accommodation, great special offers on that villa with a swimming pool or the farmer's cottage set amongst the olive groves and grapevines above the Adriatic.

We pride ourselves on our professionalism and can supply to our property buying clients full legal package with local solicitor/notary, architects, surveyors, builders, the complete team.

Our letting department offers a full service and we are constantly finding new and interesting properties for those seeking to rent accommodation of distinction. Stone villas with swimming pools, fisherman's lodges, shepherd's simple abodes, apartments on the Riviera or stylish town houses.

YOUR DREAM CAN COME TRUE

In short, we are part of Croatia and it's environment, from the sea, the olives, the wine, the crisp air, the inspiring mountains, the charm, to the history, now add Dalmatian Villas as a thoroughly Croatian product.

Join them…

Let us make the land of a 1000 islands be your dream home.

English, Italian, Russian speaking.
We await your call. **+44 (0)1536 790909**
Please send your confirmation to **KREMPEL@UKONLINE.CO.UK**

Tingle d.o.o.

Established in 2000 Tingle d.o.o. consists of a vibrant team of experienced, reliable and inspired English/Croatian nationals who offer an efficient service to those who wish to acquire property in the beautiful country of Croatia.

Prompt responses ensure that your enquiry is dealt with in a knowledgeable and professional manner without delay. High calibre project management provides peace of mind at all stages and a speedy conclusion of all works to the highest quality.

Client satisfaction is our main priority. Every effort is made to adhere to the client's requests with constant supervision of all work to completion. Our consultancy service is available to suit your needs and we are always at hand to ensure this is achieved.

We specialise in full renovation projects, custom designed villas, sourcing land plots for development & general property sales.

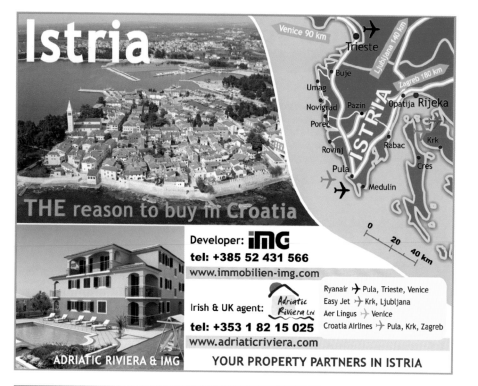

Cadogan Guides

WORKING AND LIVING

THE SUNDAY TIMES
WORKING AND LIVING
FRANCE
Monica Larner
CADOGANguides

THE SUNDAY TIMES
WORKING AND LIVING
PORTUGAL
Steven Hilton
CADOGANguides

THE SUNDAY TIMES
WORKING AND LIVING
ITALY
Kate Carlisle
CADOGANguides

THE SUNDAY TIMES
WORKING AND LIVING
SPAIN
Nancy Harmon
CADOGANguides

THE SUNDAY TIMES
WORKING AND LIVING
USA
Jonathan Williams, Robyn Flemming and Heather Sudlow
CADOGANguides

THE SUNDAY TIMES
WORKING AND LIVING
AUSTRALIA
Jacqueline Swartz
CADOGANguides

THE SUNDAY TIMES
WORKING AND LIVING
NEW ZEALAND
CADOGANguides

THE SUNDAY TIMES
WORKING AND LIVING
CANADA
Patrick Twomey
CADOGANguides

CADOGANguides
well travelled **well read**

'Excellently written, bursting with character'
Holiday Which

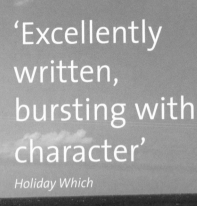

'Impressively comprehensive'
Wanderlust Magazine

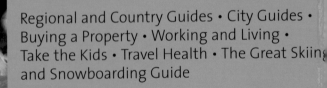

Regional and Country Guides · City Guides · Buying a Property · Working and Living · Take the Kids · Travel Health · The Great Skiing and Snowboarding Guide